Challenging Repairs to Interesting Clocks

by
Edwin U. Sowers III, MSME, CMC

Acknowledgments

Thank you to Steven G. Conover, editor of *Clockmakers Newsletter*, for allowing us to reprint articles by Ed Sowers previously published in his *Clockmakers Newsletter* and for providing the digital files of this work.

Thank you to Amy Dunn, marketing director and editor of the *Horological Times*, for allowing us to reprint articles by Ed Sowers previously published in the *Horological Times* and for also providing digital files. The *Horological Times* is the journal of the American Watchmakers-Clockmakers Institute.

Challenging Repairs to Interesting Clocks
© 2012 by the National Association of Watch & Clock Collectors, Inc.
ISBN No. 978-0-09823584-6-7

All rights reserved. No part of this publication may be stored in a retrieval system, reproduced, or transmitted in any form by any means, electronic, mechanical, photocopying, recording, or otherwise, without written permission from the publisher.

Printed in the United States of America
The National Association of Watch and Clock Collectors, Inc.
Editor: Diana M. DeLucca
Associate Editors: Freda Conner, Hugh Dougherty, Amy L. Klinedinst

Requests to use material from this work should be directed to:
The National Association of Watch and Clock Collectors, Inc.
514 Poplar Street, Columbia, PA 17512

Founded in 1943, the National Association of Watch and Clock Collectors, Inc. (NAWCC) is a nonprofit member organization whose purpose is to encourage and stimulate interest in the art and science of horology for the benefit of NAWCC members and the public.

See the last page of this book for more information about the NAWCC and a reproducible membership application.

All images in this publication are courtesy of the author unless otherwise noted.

Introduction

This reference book presents 32 articles, initially distributed among three horological publications. They were written by Edwin U. Sowers III (d. 2012), who was a retired research and development project manager, with an M.S. degree in mechanical engineering. He was a member of the NAWCC and the AWCI and was a Certified Master Clockmaker (CMC). Ed had a repair business for many years. He reported that each clock coming into his shop went out working correctly; none were rejected. This practice is noteworthy, because taking on everything leads one into many challenging, interesting, and varied situations.

The repairs described in these articles were somewhat more complex than many repairs; they presented interesting challenges that required sometimes uncommon approaches to resolve the particular problem. Notes and pictures were taken during initial analyses and subsequent repair work, resulting in clearly definable methods and techniques used in each repair situation. The results presented in the articles here describe what did work—successful resolutions to difficult clock repair problems. It is hoped that this material will be helpful to others who encounter similar problems.

The articles in this collection were published by the National Association of Watch and Clock Collectors *Watch & Clock Bulletin*, the American Watchmakers Clockmakers Institute *Horological Times*, and the *Clockmakers Newsletter*. The author thanked each of the editors for their help and cooperation and for the excellent presentation of the articles.

Editor's Note

This compilation of articles was created at the request of Ed Sowers, who thought that clock repairers would benefit from his careful documentation of the challenges he encountered in his workshop. We agreed with Ed that his work warranted gathering into a single publication. Ed died suddenly in April 2012, soon after submitting a notebook of this work and his introductory comments. We very much regret that he was unable to enjoy seeing this final project to completion.

The articles listed in the Table of Contents on the facing page were publshed in the *Watch & Clock Bulletin* (WCB), *Clockmakers Newletter* (CN), or the *Horological Times* (HT). The initials following the name of the article indicate where the article was originally published. The publication month and year is stated within each article.

The articles are grouped into three sections: the first section includes repairs to specific clock models, the second section includes general repairs not associated with specific models, and the third section includes dial and case repairs.

Table of Contents

Atmos Timekeeping Adjustment (CN) 7
Removal and Replacement of Atmos Balance Suspension Wire (CN) 10
   Appendix: Installing the Regulator Clamp and Wire Locking Screw
   on an Atmos Suspension Spring 14
The Atmos Clock Winding System (CN) 16
New Life for a Banjo Clock (WCB) 19
A Troubled Barr Clock (WCB) 23
Fabrication and Replacement of Brocot Escapement Pallets (CN) 30
Movement Carrier (CN) 35
The Jacob Guthart J-Hook (CN) 36
The Herschede Two-Weight, Five-Tube Movement (HT) 38
Restoration of a New Haven No. 1 Office Clock: The Deadbeat Pallets (CN) 42
Restoration of a New Haven No. 1 Office Clock: Pendulum Repair (CN) 52
Restoration of a New Haven No. 1 Office Clock: Center Arbor Repair (CN) 56
The Ingenious Poole Clock (WCB) 58
The Fascinating "Terry's Patent" Calendar Clock: How It Works (WCB) 64

Using the Bushing Machine (CN) 70
Repair of a Cone Cup Screw (CN) 72
Cuckoo Music Movement Repair (CN) 75
Fabrication of a Cuckoo Clock Chain Wheel Locking Spring (CN) 83
Rebuilding Deadbeat Escapement Pallets (CN) 86
   Appendix A: Rebuilding Deadbeat Escapement Pallets (CN) 89
Closing a Deadbeat Pallet (CN) 90
Adjusting Drop with a Recoil Escapement (CN) 93
Multiple Repairs to a Mainspring Barrel (WCB) 94
Maintaining Power (HT) 100
Hour Wheel Tooth Repair (CN) 103
Creating a Six-Tooth Segment for a Tall Case Hour Wheel (HT) 106
Ratchet Teeth on a Tallcase Date Wheel: A Novel Repair Technique (WCB) 109

A New Face: Successfully Installing a Paper Dial (HT) 112
Practical Repair and Restoration: Clock Case Repair (WCB) 116
A Case Study—Reproduction of the Missing Rosette (WCB) 119
Clock Case Veneer Restoration (WCB) 123
Horological Helps (CN) 130

ATMOS TIMEKEEPING ADJUSTMENT
(Refer to Jaeger-LeCoultre Repair Notes)
Edwin U. Sowers III, MSME, CMC

This article originally appeared in the November 2000 Clockmakers Newsletter *and is reprinted here with permission.*

The following presents a procedure for adjusting the timekeeping accuracy of Atmos clocks. A reference which defines the Atmos components used to correct timekeeping, and the magnitude of correction realized through use of appropriate components, is the Jaeger-LeCoultre Repair Notes Calibre No. 528 Atmos VI, specifically Figure 10. The Repair Notes are available from most suppliers who handle Atmos repair parts, including Merritt's Antiques, Inc. (1-800-345-4101).

The procedure is directly applicable to Models 528 and 519; it is expected the basic approach is applicable to most models.

1. To check timekeeping accuracy, first set the regulator index lever, on top of the clock, to the midpoint. Turn the balance 3/4 revolution from forward position (impulse roller front) and release. This will initiate a 1-1/2 revolution balance rotation.

2. Determine the actual time for the minute hand to advance 15 minutes on the dial, using an accurate stopwatch, which displays minutes, seconds, and 1/100 seconds. Start the stopwatch immediately upon the minute hand moving towards and *stopping* at a screw location in the dial, at one of the quarter hour positions. When the minute hand *stops* at the next quarter hour screw location, immediately stop the watch. Note that the minute hand moves in steps.

3. Record under paragraph 8 (original column) the actual stopwatch time in minutes and seconds, rounding off the 1/100 sec. reading to the nearest second.

Calculate the error between the 15 minute hand rotation and the actual time defined by the stopwatch. If the watch time exceeds 15 minutes, as by one second, the clock is slow by 1 second. Record the error in seconds (+ for fast and - for slow).

4. If the error is less than 1 second/15 minutes, proceed to Step 12. If more than 1 second/15 minutes, correction by changing the thickness of the regulating weights, and/or the studs which are located beneath the balance, and are defined by Figure 10 of the Repair Notes, will be necessary. To facilitate access to the studs and weights, remove the base. Be sure to remove and save the balance locking pin and the locking spring beneath it, which are located in the locking lever lifting collar on top of the base. Lift out the pin and carefully turn over the removed base and catch the small coil spring.

The Atmos clock.

Place a piece of drafting tape on the front of the balance, in line with the impulse roller. Do not allow the balance to rotate more than 3/4 revolution from the front while changing weights or studs. Treat the balance with care.

The regulating weights are secured by the studs, with the *same* set of weights and studs mounted on the two opposing sides beneath the balance. Timekeeping is *speeded* up by *decreasing* thickness.

5. The correction in timekeeping per mm of thickness change for weights and studs is as follows: large changes are made with weights, small with studs.
- **Regulating weights: 7 sec/15 min. per 1 mm.**
- **Studs: 2 sec/15 min. per 1 mm.**

The available thicknesses of timekeeping weights and studs are:
- **Regulating weights: 1, 1.5, and 2 mm.**
  (Part No. 3521)
- **Studs: 6 to 11 mm. in .5 mm. increments**
  (Part No. 3522)

Regulating weights and studs are normally available from suppliers who handle Atmos repair parts, including Merritt's Antiques, Inc. They may be ordered by part number along with a definition of the desired thicknesses.

6. As an example of a simple correction; should a 3.0 sec/15 min. *slowing* in timekeeping be required, this can be accomplished by *increasing* the thickness of both studs by 1.5 mm. (1.5 mm. x 2 sec/mm. = 3 sec). If the existing studs are 7 mm. they should both be replaced by 8.5 mm. studs.

7. Needed corrections may well require changes in regulating weights and studs combined; large changes accomplished with regulating weights and small changes with studs, as noted above. First define the thicknesses for each of the existing weights and studs. (Stud thickness may be stamped on the top of the stud.) Then establish the total sec./15 min. correction required. Calculate the changes in thicknesses of weights and studs that will yield the required time keeping change, adding up the changes in sec./15 min. resulting from each component change. All changes must be made equally to both sides.

Again, an example. Consider the need to *speed up* timekeeping by 10 sec./15 min. Referring to paragraph 5, this could be accomplished with the following thickness *decreases* (assuming starting with the defined weights and studs):

Replace a 2 mm. weight both sides with 1 mm.
   1 mm. x 7 sec./mm. = 7 sec.
Replace a 10 mm. stud both sides with 8.5 mm.
   1.5 mm. x 2 sec./mm. = 3 sec.

Total correction: +10 sec./15 min.

8. To implement a correction, first remove and record in the following table the number and thicknesses of the original weights and studs. **Must be the same both sides.** Calculate and record the revised weights and studs that add up to the desired correction, per paragraph 7, and enter the new set in the following:
The above table should now represent the original weights and studs, the original watch time and error, and the new weights and studs intended to correct timekeeping to within 1 sec./15 min.

	Original		New	
	No.	Size	No.	Size
Weights	___	___	___	___
	___	___	___	___
Studs	1	___	1	___
Watch Time	___		___	
Error (+ −)	___		___	

9. Install the newly defined weights and studs. (Install studs with counterbore toward the balance).

10. Conduct a timekeeping test in accordance with steps 1 and 2 to establish the new timekeeping rate. It is recommended that the test be performed 2 or 3 times to ensure a repeatable stopwatch reading. Record the new results above. Ensure the error is now within 1 sec./15 min. If satisfactory proceed to paragraph 12.

11. If the prior test results are not satisfactory, review correction calculations and the stopwatch test. Revise studs or weights if required, and retest, recording data as before. Initial data is the same as the prior new. Tabulating initial and new data in adjacent columns is helpful in clarifying the effects of thickness changes.

	Initial		New	
	No.	Size	No.	Size
Weights	___	___	___	___
	___	___	___	___
Studs	1	___	1	___
Watch Time	___		___	
Error (+ −)	___		___	

12. To ensure adequate accuracy to permit final adjustment with the index on top of the clock, conduct a one hour test to establish that the error is *less* than 4 sec./60 minutes. Record results.

Watch time _____
Error _____

13. When the error is less than 4 sec./hr., final adjustment can be accomplished with the index on top of the clock (Repair Notes, Fig. 10). At this point timekeeping is evaluated in terms of sec./*day*. An error of 4 sec./hr. translates to 96 seconds per 24 hour day. Each division on the upper bridge represents an adjustment of 10 seconds per day. An adjustment of plus or minus 50 seconds per 24 hours can be achieved by moving the index from the center to one or the other end of the scale.

14. If necessary, further adjustment can be realized by resetting the index with respect to the regulator setting sleeve; (it is actually rotation of the regulator setting sleeve that modifies timekeeping). To achieve additional speeding up of timekeeping after the index has already been moved fully to the right, place a punch vertically in the notch in the sleeve closest to the right hand cutout in the index plate. Move the index to the left end of the scale while preventing the sleeve from turning by means of the punch. The sleeve can now be further rotated counterclockwise to increase timekeeping rate by moving the index to the right. Added reduction of timekeeping rate requires a reversed procedure.

The regulator setting sleeve should not be rotated in either direction more than the equivalent of 15 divisions from the original setting of paragraph 1, with a maximum timekeeping correction of 150 sec./24 hrs.

15. Continue to test for 24 hr. periods and adjust as necessary to achieve the desired accuracy. When this is accomplished, again lock the sleeve with a punch, and set the index to the midpoint of the scale.

16. Install the balance locking spring, followed by the locking pin (rounded end up) in the locking lever lifting collar of the base. Replace the base.

17. Further minor adjustments of the index over a period of time will probably be required to finalize timekeeping adjustment.

REMOVAL AND REPLACEMENT OF ATMOS BALANCE SUSPENSION WIRE

Edwin U. Sowers III, MSME, CMC
Steven G. Conover, Editor, *Clockmakers Newsletter*

This article originally appeared in the October 2007 Clockmakers Newsletter. *The Appendix section originally appeared in the November 2007* Clockmakers Newsletter. *Both are reprinted here with permission.*

A Note on the Illustrations
CN Figure numbers are bolded, such as: **Fig. 1.** References to illustrations in the Jaeger-LeCoultre "Repair Notes, Caliber No. 528, Atmos VI" are in this form: Fig. 11, Ref. 1. (The complete references are printed at the end of this article.) The "Repair Notes" are available from parts suppliers.

Fig. 1. Model 519 Atmos clock.

Proper servicing of the Atmos Clock requires serious attention to details in many areas. A procedure is here presented that addresses the servicing of the balance assembly, including building a new suspension wire assembly, installing the wire assembly into the balance tube, and poising the balance assembly.

In some cases an Atmos clock can be serviced with no major involvement with the balance assembly. However, when testing or observation indicates that the balance must be disassembled and repaired, it is hoped that this procedure will be helpful.

This procedure is intended to be compatible with the Jaeger-LeCoultre "Repair Notes, Caliber No. 528, Atmos VI" listed as Ref. 1 at the end of this article. Refer to the "Repair Notes" for part numbers, part locations, and Jaeger-LeCoultre illustrations.

The procedure applies to models 519, as shown in **Fig. 1,** and Models 526, 528, and others, with possibly some variances. Where specifications and procedures for other models deviate from what is here presented, they govern.

Disassembly of the Balance

Note: All tweezers, clamps, and pliers referred to must be smooth-jawed to prevent damage to the wire.

1. Remove the movement from the base plate 3530 (4 or 6 screws beneath the plate). Be sure to retain two .098" diameter pins and the small compression spring located in the balance locking device.

2. Loosen the regulator pipe screw 3553 and the wire pipe screw 3555.

3. Rest the balance 3539 on a 4" diameter x 1/2" thick piece of foam. Carefully work out the suspension wire pin 3518 from the wire pipe with smooth jawed pliers.

4. Lift up the movement to separate it from the balance and stem. (Stop collar 3524 above lower bridge 3499 must pass through the hole in the lower bridge.)

5. Remove the impulse roller assembly 3508 by loosening screw 3552.

6. Place clamp XI Fig. 11, Ref. 1, or equivalent, **Fig. 2,** on the larger diameter of stop collar 3524 and secure in a vise. Loosen cylindrical nut 3526 beneath the balance, with special wrench VI Fig. 11, Ref. 1, or equivalent, **Fig. 3,** and remove the nut. Remove the balance.

7. Loosen wire locking screw 3561, with the stop collar still held by the clamp. Remove the clamp.

8. Hold the balance stem 22 at 45°, with the lower end raised. Fully loosen and gently pull out on the wire locking screw to which the wire is attached. Rotate the wire back and forth to work out the wire with attached regulator clamp 3510. Do not allow the regulator clamp to slide off the upper end of the wire.

9. If you desire to replace the wire only, and use the existing regulator clamp and wire locking screw, see Appendix procedure to fabricate a suspension wire assembly 3517. The wire alone is presently available from Timesavers, Part No. 22696, Ref. 2. If you intend to reuse the regulator clamp and wire locking screw, pull the regulator clamp off the end of the wire and save it, and remove the wire locking screw using spreading pliers described by the Appendix, and save. Do not lose the small brass tube inside the regulator clamp.

10. Jaeger-LeCoultre stocks as 3517 a complete suspension wire assembly, including the wire and both the regulator clamp and the wire locking screw (not the wire alone). You must contact Jaeger-LeCoultre (Ref. 3) for purchasing information.

Note: The following steps are based on using the 3517 suspension wire assembly available from Jaeger-LeCoultre or an *identical assembly* prepared per the Appendix.

Preparation for Assembly

11. Set timekeeping regulator index, Fig. 10, Ref. 1, to zero and check clearance 29, Fig. 8, Ref. 1. (One can make a brass feeler gauge to check for the specified dimension.) If not within 1.65 to 1.75mm, slip (forced rotation) regulator setting sleeve 3513, Fig. 10, Ref. 1, to correct. To increase, insert a 1/32 diameter steel wire into the notch on top of the setting sleeve on the right side, towards the front. Push the lever to the left, remove the wire, and return to center. This will force the setting sleeve to slip counterclockwise with respect to the regulator index, which will increase the clearance and speed up timekeeping. Repeat if necessary. To decrease clearance, reverse the process.

This clearance allows for adequate vertical movement of the regulator pipe 3512 and the regulator clamp attached to it, for timekeeping adjustment. (The vertical movement of the jaws of the regulator clamp changes the effective length of the suspension wire and changes the balance oscillation frequency.)

Fig. 2 *A homemade wooden clamp holds the stop collar so the balance can be loosened.*

Fig. 3 *Homemade wrench for loosening the cylindrical nut on the balance.*

Assembly of the Balance

12. To begin reassembly of the balance, first move the large end of the regulator clamp to 3/8" from the end of the wire. *Make sure the regulator remains where it is positioned; it must not readily slide about on the wire.* Turn the bottom of the stem up and grasp the wire locking screw 3561. Holding the stem at 45°, feed the wire assembly down through the stem, rotating the locking screw 45° back and forth to prevent it catching within the tube.

13. With the stem held vertically, bottom up, secure the stop collar in clamp XI, Fig. 11, Ref. 1, or equivalent, **Fig. 2,** place in vise and tighten. Carefully *thread the wire locking screw into the bottom of the balance stem and tighten.*

14. Secure the balance to the wire locking screw with the cylindrical nut, with the stop collar still held in the clamp. **Fig. 3** shows a custom made tool for this purpose. Before final tightening, turn the balance as necessary so two spokes supporting the balance ring are parallel to the flat surface of the wire. To check, stand up the assembly with stem vertical and spokes crosswise in front of you; wire should fall over the back of the tube, on the opposite side from you. This positioning of the balance will later provide a reference for the orientation of the flat surface of the wire.

15. Replace the impulse roller and slightly tighten the screw 3552; *do not stretch roller mounting spring, 3504.*

Poising the Balance

16. To prepare for balance poising, move the regulator clamp down from the end of the suspension wire and secure the upper end of the wire in a locking clamp (as a modified fishing fly tying vise shown by **Fig. 4**) with the balance and stem freely suspended. Position the balance over a table top, close to its surface, so the balance will drop only a short distance should the wire slip from the

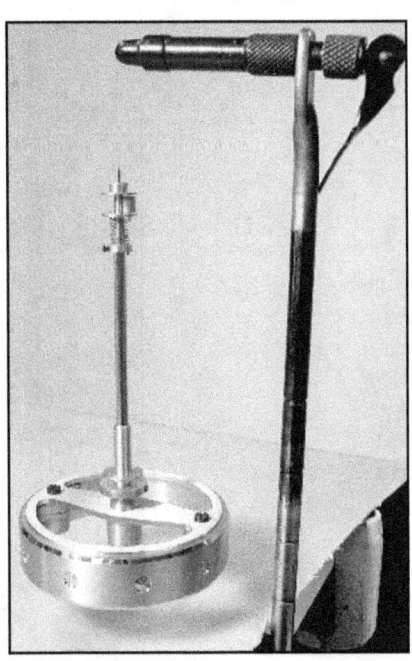

A fly tying vise holds the suspension wire for poising the balance.

Challenging Repairs to Interesting Clocks · 11

clamp. Push the regulator clamp down the wire so the smaller diameter only fits down into the top of the roller assembly. *Be sure the regulator clamp does not slide down into the tube where it will not be recoverable.* (Contact a fishing equipment supplier for a fly tying vise; you may want to modify it so the clamp is perpendicular to the mounting bar, and also to increase the length of the bar.)

17. To poise the balance, rotate the balance one revolution and allow it to rotate back and forth. *Ensure that the regulator clamp remains centered within the top of the roller assembly.* If it does not, the tube is probably bent.

Fig. 5 shows a gap on the left side of the top of the roller assembly. This indicates that the stem is bent to the left. To bend it to the right, install the poising tool IX, Fig. 11, Ref. 1, or equivalent, on the right side, as shown by **Fig. 6**. Place the lower leg of the tool on the stem immediately above the increased tube diameter. By turning the thumb screw clockwise the attached pad will push in on the tube, bowing it slightly, thus pushing the stem top to the right.

Fig. 7. *Feeding the suspension wire (right arrow) through the horizontal movement, towards the hypodermic needle (left arrow).*

Do not overtighten. Gradually work up to the bending pressure. You may have to move location of the poising tool a few times until the stem is straightened.

Installation of Balance Unit into Movement

18. Have available a 4" diameter x 1/2" thick piece of foam rubber.

19. Place a 20 x 1-1/2 hypodermic needle into top of wire pipe. Hold in place with a small piece of Rodico.

20. Cut off wire to 2" above top of impulse roller assembly.

21. Position top of regulator clamp 0.30" above top of roller assembly.

22. *Lay movement on side* on a 10-12" high box to place movement at eye level, with rear plate forward. Place 1-1/2" block under top of movement to level it. *Ensure considerable light on the end of the needle.*

23. Rotate needle so beveled edge is up.

24. Move the balance assembly, with projecting wire, through the movement towards the top of the movement and carefully fit end of wire into needle, **Figs. 7 and 8.** Move wire forward through needle until regulator clamp is close to needle.

25. Pull out needle. Gently pull on wire and move top of regulator clamp into regulator pipe 3512. **Warning!**

Fig. 5

The gap (shown by the arrow) to the left of the regulator clamp indicates the tube is bent to the left.

Fig. 6

The poising tool is shown bending the tube to the right to poise the balance assembly.

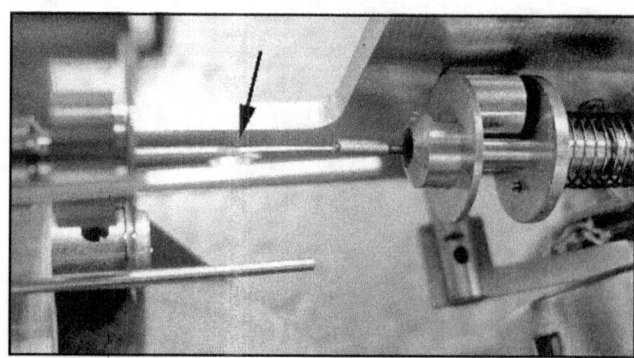

Fig. 8

Suspension wire entered into needle (at arrow).

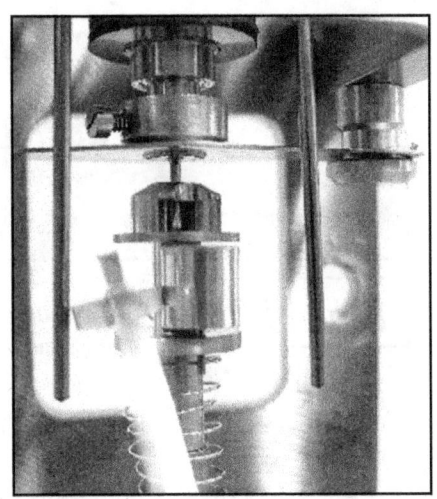

Fig. 9.

Top of the regulator clamp in regulator pipe; bottom located in top of roller assembly.

This is a sensitive step, due to the need to fit the *regulator clamp* into the regulator pipe at the same time that the upper diameter of the *stop collar* must be fitted into the hole in the lower bridge. Keep your eyes on both locations!

26. Pull on the wire and advance it until large diameter of stop collar is up against bottom of lower bridge. Be sure regulator clamp remains in both the regulator pipe and the roller assembly, otherwise there is a good possibility of kinking the wire.

27. Holding onto balance, and *making sure regulator clamp stays within both regulator pipe and top of roller assembly,* **Fig. 9,** carefully stand movement and balance upright on table, with balance resting on the 4" diameter foam.

28. Ensure that the flat of the suspension wire is parallel to the front plate. To assist in this, in Step 14 the flat of the wire was oriented parallel to the two "spokes" of the balance, so that presently positioning the "spokes" parallel to the front plate should properly orient the flat of the wire.

29. Lift up the movement by placing two tongue depressors under each leg. Lift up each leg separately, only enough to place tongue depressors in position. This provides access to the regulator clamp between the regulator pipe and the top of the roller assembly, **Fig. 9.** Insert a tweezers into this space and adjust the position of the lower end of the large diameter to the 0.8-1.0 mm dimension of 35, Fig. 8, Ref. 1.

Tighten the regulator pipe screw 3553. Remove the tongue depressors.

30. Make sure the 4" diameter x 1/2" foam is pressing the larger diameter of the stop collar up against the bottom of the lower bridge. With a clamp, pull up on the wire. Insert the brass pin *between* the wire pipe screw 3555 and the wire; push down firmly.

31. Lift up the movement and set it down on the table without the foam. Check the clearance between the stop collar and the lower bridge. Upper and lower clearance should be nearly equal with no interference. If there is not enough clearance below, *lightly* tap with a hammer on the brass pin; this will drop down the wire. When clearance is satisfactory, tighten the wire pipe screw 3555.

32. With the balance hanging free, not rotating, and the suspension wire parallel to the front plate, loosen screw 3552 and rotate roller mounting collar 3507 so the roller directly faces the front of the movement. Secure screw. Do not pull down on roller spring; collar must hang free.

33. Reassemble the base of the movement and ensure satisfactory operation of the balance locking mechanism. Be sure to replace the two .098" diameter pins and one small compression spring into the balance locking device, with the spring located between the two pins.

34. To finalize beat adjustment, first place movement on solid table and level the base. As a result of the prior preliminary beat adjustment of step 32, the roller should be facing nearly forward when at rest. Rotate the balance 3/4 revolution in either direction and release. The roller must stop at the same location on both sides. If the roller stops further forward on the right side, loosen screw 3552 and rotate roller collar counterclockwise, then secure the screw. Repeat as necessary, with a similar approach on the left side, until roller rotation is the same on both sides. Do not pull down on the collar containing the 3552 screw; it must hang free with no tension on spring. When assembly of the full clock is completed and it is in operation, the beat should again be checked.

Up to this point, we have covered the removal of a complete suspension wire unit from an Atmos clock and the installation of a new wire unit. That discussion assumed the regulator clamp and wire locking screw were already in place on the wire. We conclude with an Appendix describing how to install these parts on a wire purchased from a parts supplier. ***See "Repair Notes," Ref. 1, for part names and numbers, part locations, and illustrations.***

APPENDIX
Installing the Regulator Clamp and Wire Locking Screw on an Atmos Suspension Spring

1. The suspension wire must be installed into the regulator clamp so the smaller diameter, with jaws, points towards the wire locking screw.

2. The regulator clamp incorporates within it a small brass tube which functions to center the wire within the gripping jaws of the clamp. **Fig. 10** shows the clamp with the tube pulled out and the wire passing through both tube and clamp. Note that the tapered end of the brass tube points toward the jaws.

3. There are two ways to feed the wire into the clamp; into the back of the larger diameter, or into a small hole on the side of the jaws. The former must be accomplished before installing the wire locking screw, the latter either before or after

4. To feed into the back, first insert the tube into the regulator clamp, push it in until snug, start the wire into the tube **Fig. 11** and push front until it stops at the jaws. Then grasp the wire with a tweezers *.020" -.030" from the clamp.* Carefully work the wire forward past the jaws; *be careful not to buckle the wire.* When it is through the jaws, pull the wire through from the jaw end.

5. The second approach is to feed the wire through the small hole in the side of the jaws. First *remove the brass tube* by inserting a small watch cutting broach, of 0.004-0.005" tip thickness, into the back of the regulator clamp and pull out the tube. Do not lose it.

6. Now feed the wire into the small hole at approximately 30° **Fig. 12**. Gently work it through and out the back. Pull out from the rear. Put the brass tube onto the wire, tapered end first, and fix it snugly into the large end of the regulator clamp. Pull the wire out of the jaws parallel to the clamp center and slide the wire to the center while pulling. Feeding the wire into the small hole in the tapered end of the brass tube may be difficult; this may suggest using the rear entry approach.

7. Ensure that there is enough friction so the regulator clamp won't slide about on the wire by itself. Replace it if not satisfactory.

8. To install the wire into the wire locking screw 3561, first place a piece of index card around the threaded section of the screw to protect the threads.

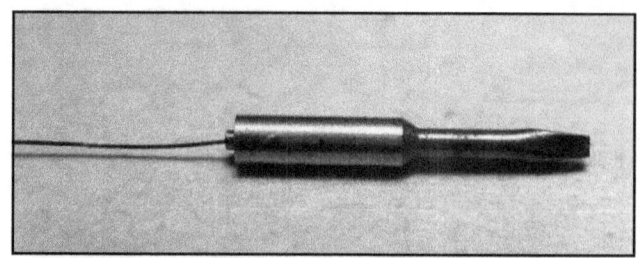

Fig. 11 *The suspension wire has been fed into the back of the regulator clamp. The end of the small brass tube is just visible at the left.*

9. Secure the screw vertically in a drill press vise with the jaws up.

10. Hold the jaws of the wire locking screw open with a special spreading pliers which may be made by modifying an end cutting pliers. An example is shown by **Fig. 13**. The lower portions of the two cutting edges are fitted into the sides of the locking screw jaws and are used to pry them open. The upper portion was ground away on a grinding wheel to provide visual access to the locking screw jaws.

11. With *small end* of the regulating clamp *pointed towards the locking screw,* carefully place the suspension wire down into the jaws, slightly opened by the spreading pliers, and *center the wire in the jaws.* Hold the wire in position and gently release the jaws.

12. A wire securely clamped in the jaws of the wire locking screw is shown by **Fig. 14**.

13. Be sure the wire is centered in the jaws.

14. You may have to open the jaws slightly and shift the wire to center. (Careful! you may lose, bend, or break the wire.)

15. The suspension wire here created, and similar to the Jaeger-LeCoultre 3715 wire assembly, is ready for installation into the stem of the balance assembly. It includes the wire, the regulating clamp with brass tube, and the wire locking screw. To again restate an important requirement: make sure the regulator clamp is *tight enough* so it cannot slide down the wire into the stem, where it would be extremely difficult to recover without completely removing the wire from the tube.

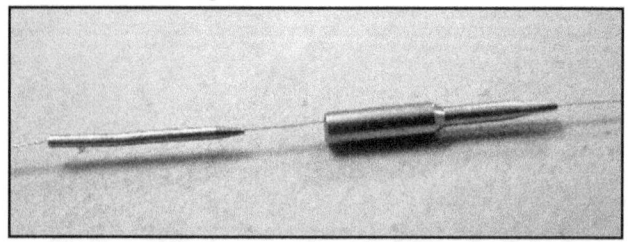

Fig. 10 *The small brass tube is shown on the left, then the wire, and the regulator clamp on the right.*

Fig. 12 *The wire is fed into the hole in the side of the regulator clamp jaws. The small brass tube has been removed.*

Fig. 13 *Specially modified spreading pliers shown gripping the jaws of the wire locking screw.*

Fig. 14 *The wire is secured in the wire locking screw.*

References

1. Jaeger-LeCoultre, "Repair Notes, Caliber No. 528, Atmos VI" Available from Merritt's Antiques, Part No. B-180. 1-800-345-4101, and Timesavers Part No. 15640.
2. Timesavers, Box 12700, Scottsdale, AZ 85267. 1-800-552-1520.
3. Jaeger-LeCoultre. After Sale Service, 111 Eighth Ave., Suite 500, New York, NY 10011. 1-800-552-4230.
4. "The Atmos Winding System," Edwin U. Sowers III, MSME, CMC, in this book.
5. "Atmos TimekeepingAdjustment," Edwin U. Sowers III, MSME, CMC, in this book.
6. "Inspection and Repair of Atmos Clocks," Edwin U. Sowers III, MSME, CMC, in this book.

Acknowledgments

The author has written a series of Atmos articles dealing with repairing, a description of the self-winding process, and the adjustment of timekeeping: References 4, 5, 6.

The author's thanks and acknowledgments are extended to the editor for assisting in development and testing of this procedure and to Mr. Jeff Hamilton for the valuable information he dispensed at the June 2007 AWCI class on Atmos repairing.

Tools

Special tools for repairing Atmos clocks are shown by Fig. 11, Ref. 1 (Jaeger-LeCoultre "Repair Notes"). A set of similar tools is available from Timesavers, Part No. 23781, Ref. 2. Tools that can be individually fabricated are shown throughout the procedure.

Supplies

- 20 x 1-1/2 hypodermic needles; from family doctor.
- 4 *flat* tongue depressors; medical supply store or family doctor.
- 1/2" thick foam rubber, 6" wide; fabric or hobby store.
- Stock of three suspension wires. Timesavers, Part No. 22696. 1-800-552-1520.
- Rodico. Timesavers, Part No. 14330.

THE ATMOS CLOCK WINDING SYSTEM
Edwin U. Sowers III, MSME, CMC

This article originally appeared in the December 2002 Clockmakers Newsletter *and is reprinted here with permission.*

Fig. 1 Atmos clock.

The Jaeger-LeCoultre Atmos Clock, shown by Figure 1, has been referred to as a perpetual motion clock. Laws of physics demonstrate that this is not really possible. However, the Atmos clock does not require manual winding. So, how is it wound? It is wound by a bellows. As is commonly understood, the pressure within a bellows increases with an increase in temperature, thus expanding the bellows; the reverse occurring with a temperature decrease. It is this phenomenon that makes the Atmos clock possible.

This article defines the components and phenomena involved in the Atmos winding process. It applies directly to the Models 519, 526, and 528; the same basic approach applies to other models. A helpful source of component definition is presented by the Jaeger-LeCoultre Calibre 528 Repair Notes. (Ref. 1).

A bellows is contained within the round housing attached to the rear of the movement, shown by Figure 2. It expands and contracts as a consequence of changes in temperature. The acting face of the bellows expands inward toward the movement with increased temperature, and retracts outward with decreasing temperature. Through an arrangement of springs, clicks, wheels, and a chain, which can be seen in the close-up of Figure 3, the temperature induced movements of the bellows are creatively used to wind a small mainspring, which in turn drives the clock. The mainspring barrel is shown attached to the left side of the great wheel. To the left of the barrel is the mainspring click wheel, and next to it on the left is the chain wheel. A click is located between the mainspring click wheel and the chain wheel. The chain can be seen attached to the chain wheel, which then passes around a pulley and back toward the bellows.

The rate of expansion and contraction of the bellows is controlled by a heavy coil spring upon which the bellows presses. The spring is positioned within the center section of the bellows, as depicted by Figure 4, a schematic representation of the Atmos winding system. The movement of the bellows contact surface is on the order of 0.025 inches per degree of temperature change. Changes in atmospheric pressure also affect the bellows, but this effect is comparatively small.

This article describes how the Atmos clock harnesses the temperature induced movements of the bellows to wind, and to maintain the wound state, of the Atmos mainspring. The following will be described:

1. The chain wheel/click wheel mechanism
2. Temperature induced action
3. The winding sequence
4. Achieving equilibrium
5. Maintaining equilibrium

1. The Chain Wheel/Click Wheel Mechanism

The schematic drawing, Figure 4, depicts and defines the components which, together, implement winding of the Atmos clock mainspring. A key component of the winding system is the chain wheel/click wheel assembly. It couples a chain, acted upon by the bellows, to the mainspring. It is necessary to understand the interactions between the chain wheel and the click wheel to comprehend the winding phenomena.

The chain, which moves inward and outward through action of the bellows, is attached to the chain wheel. The click wheel is coupled to the mainspring, it being fixed to the mainspring arbor. The chain wheel is mounted on the mainspring arbor, but is not attached to it. Click C1 is the component which connects the chain wheel to the click wheel, and through this connection, the chain to the mainspring.

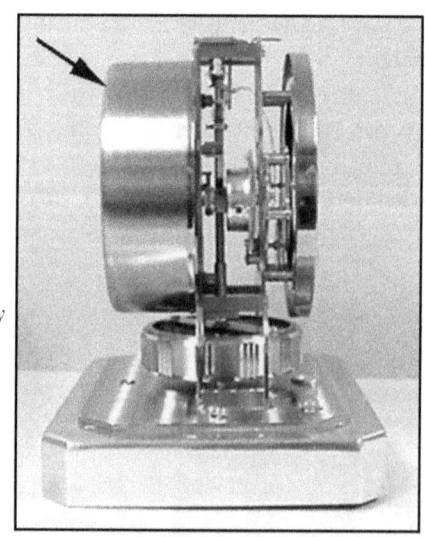

Fig. 2. Side view of the clock. The bellows housing is indicated by the arrow.

16 • Challenging Repairs to Interesting Clocks

Fig. 3. A close-up view of the Atmos winding system.

2. Temperature Induced Action

Now, consider the series of events which occur when temperature increases, then decreases. First, observe the 52 mm winding spring shown by Figure 4. This crucial component is located inside the bellows control spring. It is compressed between the rear plate of the movement and the bellows contact surface. It is this spring which, when it moves outward, supplies the force to pull the chain outward.

When *temperature increases,* the bellows will expand inward towards the movement rear plate. Depending upon the relative positions of the outer end of the winding spring and the bellows contact surface, the bellows will push in upon the winding spring. Upon the outer end of the winding spring is positioned the spring guide to which the *chain is attached;* it is this spring guide which is contacted by the bellows when it is pushing in on the winding spring.

Since the bellows, when it expands inward, always exerts a greater force than the resisting force of the winding spring, the bellows will compress the winding spring and move it inward. Click C2 holds the click wheel and mainspring, preventing the mainspring from unwinding. The chain tension spring acts to pull on the chain, keeping it taut, and rotating the chain wheel clockwise, moving click C1 clockwise about the click wheel. There is no winding of the mainspring when the bellows moves inward. It must be noted that, compared to the winding spring, the chain tension spring is very weak. It is effective only when chain tension is overcome by the bellows pushing in on the winding spring, when the chain would otherwise slacken.

When *temperature decreases,* the bellows contracts and is pushed back by the control spring. The bellows contact surface moves away from the movement. The compressed winding spring is then permitted by the bellows to move outward, pulling on the chain. Now if the chain pulling

When the chain is pulled to the left, the chain wheel is rotated in a counterclockwise direction (as depicted by the drawing). The mainspring acts to turn the click wheel in a clockwise direction. C1 is connected to the chain wheel. When the chain wheel rotates counterclockwise, it latches, through C1, onto the click wheel and drives it counterclockwise. This then, through the main spring arbor (attached to the click wheel), winds the mainspring. This winding, as will be discussed later, can only occur when the counterclockwise chain wheel torque, generated by the chain, exceeds the clockwise torque imposed on the click wheel by the mainspring.

There is a second click, C2, which is attached to the movement frame. It permits the click wheel to rotate in a *counterclockwise direction only,* preventing release of the mainspring.

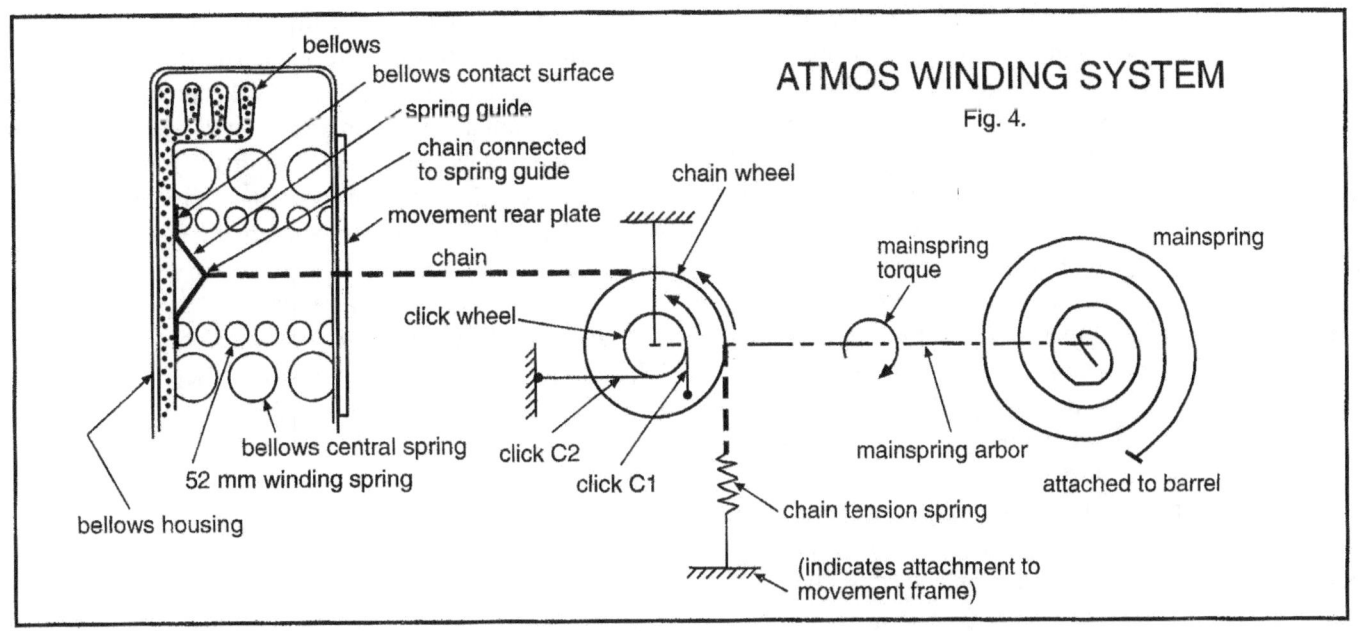

the chain wheel creates a greater counterclockwise torque on the click wheel (through click C1) than the clockwise torque imposed by the mainspring, the pulling chain will cause the chain wheel and click wheel to rotate in a counterclockwise direction and will wind the mainspring. The winding spring will pull out on the chain and wind the mainspring to the limit allowed by the bellows contact surface, or until the counterclockwise torque of the chain wheel is matched by the torque imposed by the mainspring, as will be discussed later.

3. The Winding Sequence

Summarizing from above, the sequence of events that occur when starting out with an unwound, or partially wound mainspring, is as follows. As temperature increases and decreases, the bellows moves forward and back, pushing in upon the winding spring then moving back out again. When the winding spring is pushed in, the chain tension spring rotates the chain wheel and C1 clockwise about the click wheel; *no winding occurs.* C2 holds the click wheel and the mainspring. As the bellows moves out, the winding spring pulls on the chain, causing counterclockwise rotation of the chain wheel and, through C1, the click wheel, the result being *winding* of the mainspring. *Winding occurs only* as the bellows retracts and moves outward.

4. Achieving Equilibrium

The above sequence will continue with temperature increases and decreases to the point where, as the bellows moves back and allows the winding spring to expand outward, the counterclockwise chain wheel torque can no longer overcome the clockwise mainspring torque exerted upon the click wheel. The torque created by the mainspring has increased to the point where it is then in balance with the torque generated by the winding spring.

When the mainspring is only partially wound, the torque generated by the winding spring is much greater than that created by the mainspring. The winding spring and chain will then simply follow the movements of the bellows, with the winding spring remaining in contact with the bellows under normal operating conditions. However, as equilibrium is approached, the spring characteristics of the winding spring come into play. Hooke's law states that the force exerted by a spring is proportional to its compression, in linear dimensions, (as lbs. per inch of deflection). When the winding spring is pushed in by the bellows to a specific position, the force with which it can pull on the chain when the bellows moves out is a certain value. Now, as the bellows moves out, two things occur simultaneously. (1) The mainspring is *wound,* increasing its *clockwise torque,* and (2) the winding spring moves outward, *decreasing* its compression and consequently the chain force and the counterclockwise torque imposed upon the click wheel. A point is reached where the decreasing winding spring torque and the increasing mainspring torque become equal, and are in balance. Equilibrium has then been established, and there is then no more movement of either spring; winding stops.

5. Maintaining Equilibrium

Now if the bellows moves out, losing contact with the winding spring (since torque equilibrium exists) and again pushes in to the *same position* relative to the back plate of the movement, with the mainspring remaining in the same wound state, there will be no further winding. The prior defined balance remains in effect. However, when a greater temperature is encountered than before, the bellows will move in further than before. The winding spring will be compressed further (closer to the rear plate) and can now pull on the chain with a greater force than that at the prior equilibrium position. As the bellows moves out, the winding spring will follow, and since now pulling harder on the chain, will further wind the mainspring until another equilibrium condition is reached, with the mainspring now at a slightly higher torque, and the winding spring not expanded outward as far as before, and exerting a greater force on the chain.

The second occurrence which changes the equilibrium state is the unwinding of the mainspring. As the mainspring unwinds, still held by C2, the clockwise torque imposed upon the click wheel is reduced. Where it had been in balance with the chain wheel torque (imposed by the winding spring), it is now less. When permitted by the bellows, the winding spring can now expand, pulling on the chain, causing the chain wheel and click wheel to rotate counterclockwise, winding the mainspring. As the winding spring moves outward and the mainspring winds, a new equilibrium state will be achieved.

It must be noted that the changes which occur once equilibrium is established are small. The teeth upon which C1 and C2 latch are very fine. A small change in temperature and a small amount of mainspring unwinding can lead to a one tooth click movement. The maintaining of equilibrium is a continuing, small increment process, except when responding to large temperature changes.

Reference

1. Jaeger-LeCoultre Repair Notes. Calibre #528, Atmos VI. Available from Merritt's Antiques, 1860 Weavertown Road, Douglassville, PA 19518-0277.

New Life for a Banjo Clock

by Edwin U. Sowers III (PA)

Finally, a solution to a long-standing problem . . . a banjo clock without a movement.

In 1978 I bought a Mason & Sullivan banjo clock kit. The round top and moldings were furnished, but the remainder was flat lumber—Honduras mahogany, that had to be shaped and assembled. Figure 1 shows the outcome of my efforts. Figure 2 is the movement, which originally worked. If you look closely at the lower right barrel teeth, you may have a premonition of what's coming.

A number of years ago, the failure of a prior tooth replacement jolted the movement, leading to four lost teeth in the barrel, two lost teeth in the No. 2 wheel, and a bent No. 2 arbor (Figure 3).

Since that time, I have been looking for a replacement or a mode of repair. I have not been able to replace the movement. To repair it, I looked for a barrel. I searched through boxes of barrels but found none with the same tooth spacing (defined by pitch, or module). Many Hermle barrels were close, but not the same.

I had come to the end of the line, and then I had a eureka moment! Could I match a Hermle barrel and No. 2 arbor into the movement? The module of the barrel great wheel and the No. 2 pinion would of course match. How about, then, removing the original No. 2 wheel and putting it onto the Hermle No. 2 arbor—compatible modules from the barrel up through the No. 2 pinion—then compatible from the No. 2 wheel through the rest of the movement.

Figure 1, right. The Mason & Sullivan banjo clock with no movement.

Figure 2, below. The original movement.
Figure 3, below right. The two problems.

What suitable Hermle barrel and No. 2 arbor could be found? I expected it would be necessary to modify the No. 2 pivots along with replacing the wheel. Moving the barrel and No. 2 arbor might also be necessary.

I started checking Hermle movements. Finally, looking closely at a 351-020 strike train, the barrel and No. 2 wheel were close to the same size as the banjo components. I checked the spacing between the barrel and No. 2 arbors, the Hermle vs. the original (Figure 4). To my surprise, and delight—they were the same. Not only close, the same. In addition, the Hermle No. 2 arbor could indeed be adapted so the arbor with the original wheel would match up to the

This article originally appeared in the October 2009 NAWCC Bulletin.

mating movement components. The No. 2 wheel being from the original movement and the Hermle arbor being placed in the original pivot holes; the No. 2 arbor, with replacement wheel, had to match up perfectly to the center arbor.

Looking now at the barrel; the diameters and tooth counts of the Hermle barrel and No. 2 wheel pair differed slightly from the original components; however, the prior measurements taken from both movements indicated that the Hermle barrel arbor could be located in the original pivot holes. (The smaller diameter of the Hermle barrel was balanced by a larger pinion diameter.) Differing tooth counts, of 1 and 2 teeth, can possibly affect run time, but that was expected to be minimal and acceptable.

The No. 2 wheel and arbor were dealt with first. The wheels of both arbors were driven off. To do this in each case, the end of the shoulder onto which the wheel was pressed, the outer end of which was mildly riveted, was turned down flush to the face of the wheel. The wheel of each arbor was placed onto a heavy opened vise, pinion down, and the arbor was driven off using a brass punch. The inside diameter (I. D.) of the original banjo movement wheel was lightly cleaned up with a broach. Then the Hermle wheel mounting shoulder was turned down for a light interference fit with the original wheel I. D. The wheel was driven on, into the end of the pinion. The arbor was placed in the lathe and the wheel adjusted slightly to ensure it was perpendicular to the arbor. Since the Hermle arbor was longer than the original, the pivots were moved in with my Unimat 3 lathe, sizing the diameters to the movement pivot holes.

Figure 4, right. Barrel to No. 2 arbor comparison—original and Hermle movements.

The arbor was held upward in a clamp, flux applied, and small pieces of Tix solder laid around the shoulder/wheel interface as shown in Figure 5. An alcohol lamp was brought up under the wheel and the solder was melted until it flowed down into the interface. As soon as it flowed, the heat was removed and water was applied to cool it, to minimize the chance of softening the brass wheel. The rear side of the wheel was checked to ensure the solder had flowed down through the interface. The finished No. 2 wheel and arbor are shown in Figures 6 and 7. (In Figure 7, the flow-through solder can be seen.)

Looking now at the barrel. The Hermle barrel was to be mounted on the original banjo arbor. The required action here was to bush both ends of the barrel to adapt to the smaller diameters of the banjo arbor. Both brass bushings were made with a shoulder to help secure

Figure 5, left. Original No. 2 wheel on Hermle No. 2 arbor, with three small pieces of Tix solder in place for heating. **Figure 6, center.** Wheel after heating with alcohol lamp. **Figure 7, right.** Wheel from pinion side with flow-through solder visible.

Figure 8, left. Barrel bushings soldered in place.

Figure 9, right. Completed Hermle barrel on original movement arbor.

them to the barrel. The bushings were secured with Tix solder, with the shoulder on the outside with the great wheel end, and inside with the end cap (Figure 8). The completed barrel is shown in Figure 9.

The movement was then reassembled (Figure 10). All arbors were checked for shake, and the full train was spun to ensure free turning. So far so good! It was set up on a test stand, put in beat, and….success!

With the reconstituted movement in place, the banjo clock, brought back to life, and running for more than eight days, is shown in Figure 11.

Figure 10. Hermle barrel and Hermle No. 2 arbor, with original wheel, installed into original movement.

Comment

This solution is not appropriate for a museum-quality timepiece, when maintaining original construction is crucial. But for some other clocks, where mainspring fracture or unhooking occurs and causes tooth damage to the barrel wheel and the No. 2 pinion, this is an approach that may indeed restore the clock to a functioning state.

Figure 11. The banjo clock—with a new lease on life.

Challenging Repairs to Interesting Clocks • 21

The Barr clock, and its predecessor, the Poole clock, are unique and fascinating timekeepers. I have a Poole clock. Mine works and works well. So when I was contacted concerning a Barr clock that did not work, along with a request for help, I was doomed. The clock, once working, was to be displayed by a museum in the area where they were made.

What makes the Barr and Poole clocks so different is that the pendulum drives the movement. That's a switch. So what keeps the pendulum going? What is called a gravity arm falls and gives it a boost, or impulse, when the amplitude decreases. It falls? Then what gets it back up so that it can fall again when needed? That's where the second essential component comes in—the armature arm. This armature arm is driven down vigorously by an electromagnet, latches onto the gravity arm, and bounces back up, taking the gravity arm with it. Now that is different!

When I received the clock, I sat down and watched it try to work. Not much luck. I have had the pleasure of teaching an up-and-coming clockmaker, my brother Chris, and concluded it would be good experience for us to work together on this. He agreed, and we proceeded. It was an interesting experience to analyze the problem together: to first define what various functions should occur, and if indeed the functions were occurring properly, to then determine how to correct where required, to correct, and to evaluate results.

I am unaware of an extensive reservoir of troubleshooting and repair information on Barr and Poole clocks. It is hoped that a recounting of our experience and findings may be of interest and benefit to those who find these novel timekeepers fascinating.

Figures 1 and 2 show the Barr clock. The movement is essentially the same as that of my Melrose Model No. 20 Poole clock. I published an article describing the mechanism and operation of the Poole clock in the October 2000 NAWCC Bulletin.[1] A condensed summary of the detailed description is included on the following page to provide some insight into how these unusual clocks work and to make the troubleshooting more readily understood.

A Troubled Barr Clock

by Edwin U. Sowers III, MSME, CMC (PA)

Figure 1, left. Front view of Barr clock. The movement is similar to a Poole clock. **Figure 2, right.** Rear view of Barr clock, with battery drawer visible.

This article originally appeared in the August 2007 NAWCC Bulletin.

Poole and Barr Clocks
How They Work

The gravity arm (Figure 3), which pivots on the right, drops down with the attached impulse roller. The roller falls onto the right side of the impulse pin (below the roller), which is attached to the pendulum crutch. The dropping roller pushes the pin, the crutch, and the pendulum to the left, thus giving the pendulum its needed boost.

The armature (Figure 4) rotates about a pivot point at the center of an iron armature bar, with the lower tip of the downward projecting armature arm rotating down and away from the lower end of the gravity arm. This allows the latch on the armature arm (Figure 5) to hook onto the knife edge on the gravity arm to lift it back up. Armature arm motion is referred to as down or up because latching under the knife edge is a prime consideration.

What triggers this process and what determines when the pendulum amplitude has decreased so that it needs an impulse to rejuvenate it? The sensing device is the Hipp Toggle (Figure 6), which is attached to the pendulum crutch. The toggle pivots at a point above its center so its free position is vertical. The tip of the toggle rubs along the toothed surface of a notched pad.

With a sufficiently large pendulum amplitude the toggle will drop off of both ends. As the amplitude decreases, however, the case will occur where, with the toggle moving to the right, it will stop before getting to the edge; the tip of the toggle will be tilted to the left and lodged in one of the notches. When the pendulum and crutch start to swing back to the left, the toggle will rotate clockwise, lift up on the notched pad and trip the latch (Figure 5), moving it to the left of the knife edge, thus releasing the gravity arm.

Following the impulse, the gravity arm must be reset to its upward position. This is done by the armature arm with the help of an electromagnet. As the gravity arm falls to the bottom of its drop, the fingers of an electrical switch (Figure 7), attached to the arm, close onto the switch contact posts attached to the front plate of the movement. This closes the circuit to activate a battery-powered magnet (Figure 8), which drives down the armature arm to latch onto the gravity arm and then bounces upward, with the attached gravity arm, to the reset position. As the gravity arm bounces upward, the switch contacts are opened, and the electromagnet is deactivated. All components are now in position ready for the next impulse cycle.

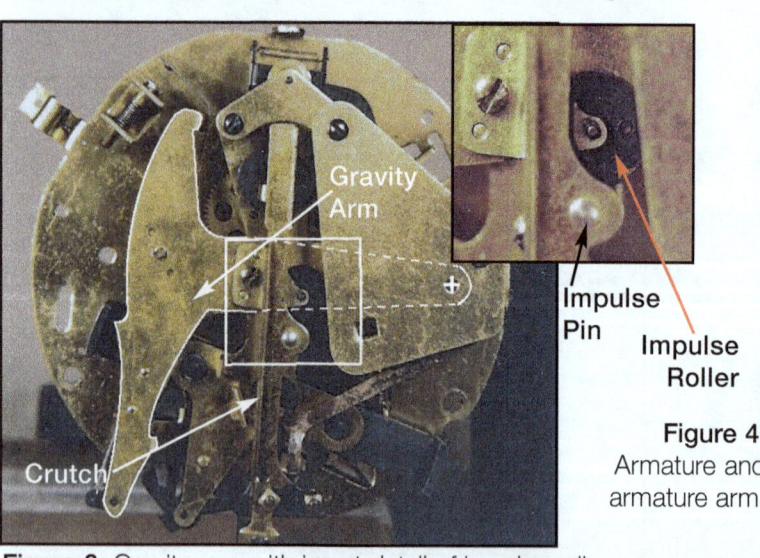

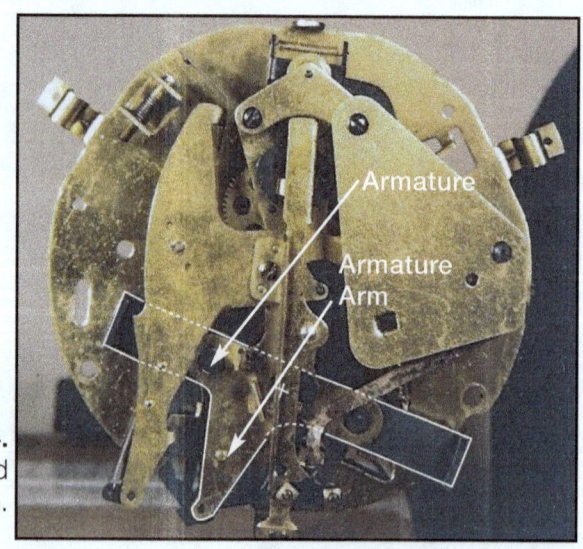

Figure 3. Gravity arm with insert detail of impulse roller.

Figure 4. Armature and armature arm.

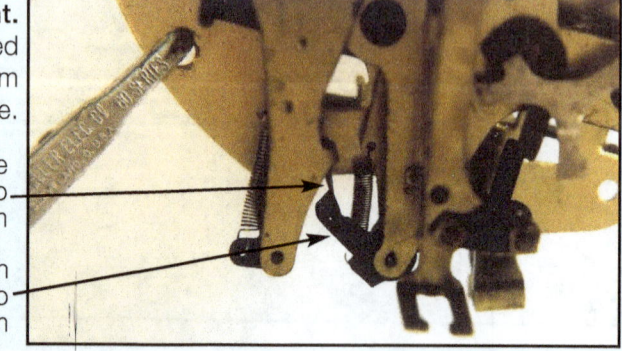

Figure 5, right. Latch hooked onto gravity arm knife edge.

Figure 6, right. The Hipp Toggle, which detects reduced pendulum amplitude.

Figure 7, left. Switch fingers attached to gravity arm, dropped onto switch posts.

Figure 8, right. Electromagnet and related components.

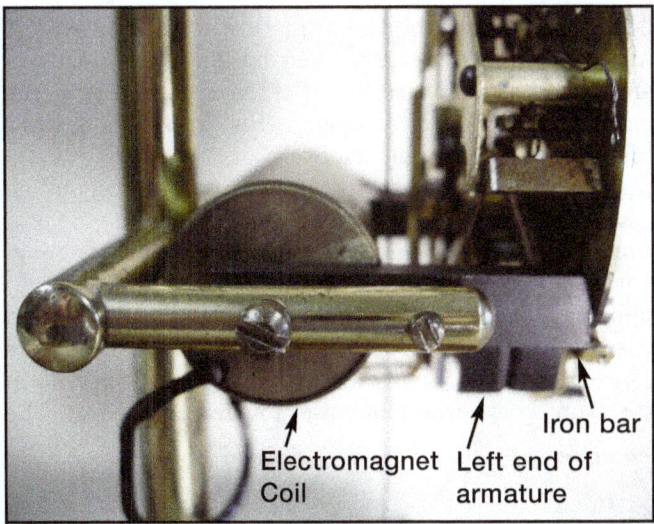

Sitting and watching what the Barr clock in its non-functioning state was attempting to do, I observed the following.

Armature Arm Concerns

The first observation was that the armature arm action was sluggish. To function properly, it had to consistently drive down hard and latch to the gravity arm and bounce back up vigorously, taking the gravity arm up with it. Due to some sluggishness, it did not do that successfully.

A number of factors were examined. The armature arm is driven down hard by the electromagnet when a switch is closed by the falling gravity arm. Things that could affect the magnetic force were checked.

Wiring Check. The condition of the wiring from the batteries, through the switch to the electromagnet, was examined. Both the positive and negative wires in the area of connection to the batteries (Figure 9) were frayed. The positive wire had only one strand left. Both wires in that location were replaced with stranded insulated wire.

Switch Check. It was observed that the electromagnet circuit closed satisfactorily when the gravity arm, with attached contact fingers (Figure 7), dropped onto the switch posts. Reliability is enhanced by the redundancy of two switches acting in parallel.

Coil Check. The resistance of the electromagnet coil (Figure 8) was checked with an ohmmeter to ensure there were no internal shorts. To measure the resistance, the batteries were removed and leads were coupled to the positive and negative wires in the battery housing in the base of the clock. The gravity arm was dropped to close the electrical contacts and complete the circuit; check the circuit drawing (Figure 10). Resistance was 26 Ω, the same as that of my functioning Poole clock, and was considered satisfactory.

Increasing Armature Arm Driving Force. There are iron bars on each side of the Barr movement; they extend from the electromagnet forward to the ends of the armature (Figure 8). They transmit a magnetic force to the armature, pushing down on the right side (from the front) and up on the shown left side. The imposed force is increased when the gap between the

Figure 9. Battery drawer, where wire was replaced.

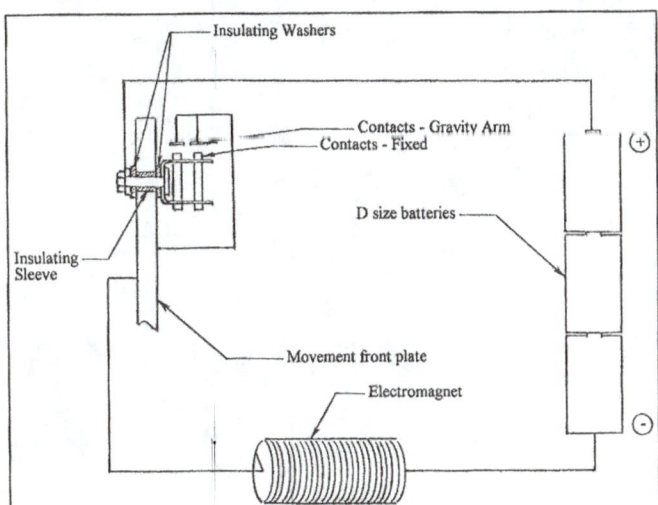

Figure 10. The electrical circuit.

bar and the end of the armature is decreased. To increase the downward force on the right side to enhance the downward thrust of the armature arm, the gaps were reduced by moving the iron bars inward toward the ends of the armature.

The bar on the left was shifted first. To accomplish this, the side screw toward the front (Figure 8) was removed, and the larger screw at the center of the magnet coil was loosened. The screw through the front plate that secured the bar (Figure 11) was removed and the bar allowed to drop, still held by the screw at the center of the coil. Using a small round fine, the hole in the front plate was elongated toward the center. The

Figure 11, above. Screw securing iron bar to front plate. Hole in plate was elongated to shift bar to right.
Figure 12, below. Hipp Toggle mounting.

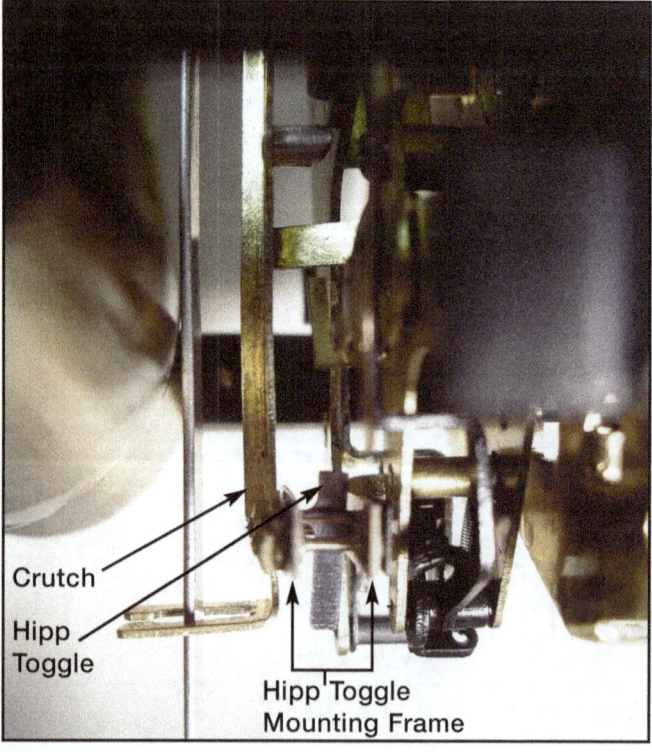

iron bar was moved back into position. The forward side screw was installed but not tightened. The front screw was inserted and while pushing inward on the bar, tightened. Clearance was checked and determined to be approximately .008". All loosened screws were tightened, the forward side screw not excessively. The same improvement was made to the right side to achieve an .008" clearance there also. There was noticeable improvement, but the armature arm action was still marginal.

In retrospect, it is considered that this should be done as a last resort since this leads to a variance from the original successful design. Although suitable operation was achieved through the series of steps taken, it is possible that it could have been done without this step.

Mechanical Concerns

A number of mechanical problems were observed and dealt with.

Crutch Interference. It was noted that the crutch (Figure 3) rubbed against the rear of the movement and reduced pendulum amplitude. The crutch was bent back slightly, away from the movement, to resolve the problem.

Hipp Toggle Adjustment. The Hipp Toggle (Figure 6), which detects the decreased pendulum amplitude, did not function reliably in tripping and causing the gravity arm to drop. The frame incorporating the toggle and attached to the crutch (Figure 12) hung down toward the front, forward of the crutch. It was thus too far below the fixed notched pad (Figure 6) above it for satisfactory contact with the pad. With considerable difficulty, the frame left side was bent upward sufficiently to provide adequate contact. The left vertical piece was grasped with a needle nose pliers and twisted counterclockwise. It was difficult because the crutch, to which it was attached, was quite rigid.

Gravity Arm Concerns

The dropping of the gravity arm, with the intended impulse to the pendulum, was observed for some time. A number of problems were detected.

Unsatisfactory Roller Dropping. The impulse roller attached to the gravity arm (Figure 3) is intended to impinge on an impulse pin on the pendulum crutch to provide a leftward (from the rear) impulse to the pendulum. The roller did not drop far enough to accomplish this satisfactorily. Resolution of this problem is addressed in the next section.

Pendulum Amplitude. As a check of the effectiveness of the impulse to the pendulum, the amplitude of the pendulum swing immediately following the impulse was monitored. The amplitude of the swing was measured at the bottom tip of the pendulum rod. The Barr amplitude was indeed somewhat less than that of my Poole clock and is related to the above problem.

Barr: 1 1/16"
Poole: 1 1/8"

Interrelationships Between Gravity and Armature Arms

The satisfactory dropping of the armature arm with an adequate impulse to the pendulum by the roller and the following upward rebounding to the reset position caused by the armature arm are intertwined. An understanding of the involved phenomena is necessary to optimize the actions that occur. (A review of the prior article would be helpful.)

Three Requirements: The following requirements must be satisfied for optimum dropping and rebounding of the gravity arm:

1. The gravity arm must fall far enough to provide adequate side thrust to the crutch impulse pin.
2. The armature arm must latch to the gravity arm at the bottom of the gravity arm fall.
3. The armature arm must bounce up, and the switch contact open <u>immediately</u>, after being driven full down by the electromagnet and latched to the gravity arm.

One must consider the means that limit the downward movement of the gravity arm and the armature arm. The gravity arm downward movement is limited by the electrical switch contact points (Figure 7). The armature arm is limited by the right-hand end of the leaf spring in front of the front plate (Figure 13). Tab "e" attached to the armature, projects through the plate and also initiates the upward bounce.

Another fact to keep in mind is that the gravity arm falls by itself when released because of its weight and with the help of a downward pulling spring located between the plates. The armature does nothing to assist in its drop. The armature arm does nothing until the gravity arm drops to the point where the switch contacts close and the armature arm is instantly and vigorously driven down by the magnet. As mentioned before, it is driven down until it hits the leaf spring and then is instantly bounced upward. So latching must occur in the instant before the armature arm is bounced upward. Note: The armature arm is driven down only by the magnet. The armature arm, along with the attached gravity arm, are then bounced upward, immediately breaking electrical contact and magnetic action. The armature arm is returned upward to its reset position by two coil springs in front of the forward plate (Figure 13).

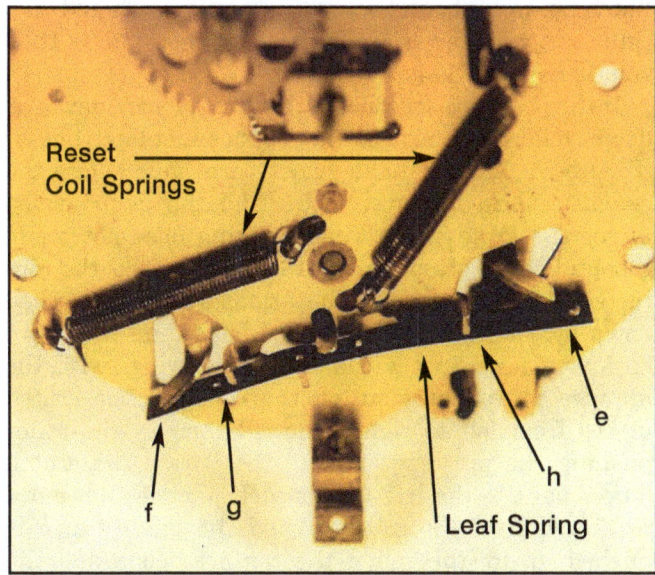

Figure 13, above. Leaf spring attached to front plate. Provides upward bounce to armature arm and establishes reset position. **Figure 14, below.** Switch posts with adjusting screw driver slots.

Electrical Switch Considerations

As earlier noted, the downward movement of the gravity arm is limited by the fingers of the electrical switch, attached to the gravity arm, falling onto the fixed contact posts. The contact posts are attached to the mounting frame by adjustment threads (Figure 14). The vertical position of the tops of the posts may be moved up or down by means of screwdriver slots on the bottom of each. By turning counterclockwise the posts are moved down, allowing for more downward travel of the gravity arm.

If the posts are set too high, the drop of the gravity arm and of the attached impulse roller is reduced. This causes the impulse, applied by the dropping roller to the crutch pin and to the pendulum, to be reduced. Pendulum swing amplitude is reduced, so the number of cycles before tripping by the toggle is reduced.

Latching and rebound occurs, so operation should continue but with fewer oscillations between pulses then should be achievable.

If the posts are set too low, the gravity arm may drop down so far that the armature arm cannot latch onto it (Figure 5). Note that the gravity arm falls before the armature arm is driven down and the latch moved under the knife edge. When latching does not occur, rebound of the gravity arm cannot take place; the contacts remain closed and the armature arm is locked down by the magnetic force. The pendulum will move back and forth (not a complete free swing) with the impulse pin pushing up on the roller as the crutch moves from left to right, followed then by the roller pushing the pin down and to the left as the crutch moves back to the left. (The crutch pin does not move to the right of the roller.) When the gravity arm is pushed up by the roller, the contact opens and the armature arm lifts. When the gravity arm moves down, the contact closes and the armature arm is driven down. So the pendulum continues to move back and forth with both the armature arm and the gravity arm rising and falling, with no latching or resetting of the gravity arm. This is a small, dysfunctional, pendulum movement, apparently maintained by a small input of energy from the armature arm. Indeed, pendulum movement may altogether stop.

Summarizing

Posts too high:
1. Impulse roller drop too little.
2. Impulse to pendulum inadequate.
3. Normal operation, but cycles per impulse too small.

Posts too low:
1. Armature arm cannot latch onto gravity arm and lift it to reset position.
2. Pendulum may move back and forth to left of impulse roller only (from rear), with upward and downward movement of the gravity and armature arms, but with no reset and no normal pendulum swing.

Going back now to the three requirements for optimum dropping and rebounding of the gravity arm, it becomes apparent that all three of these requirements are indeed tied together with adjustment of the switch posts.

Switch Adjustment

Adjustment of the position of the switch posts was a crucial step in optimizing performance, requiring some experimentation. It was found that a workable approach was to first elevate the posts to approximately .070" to .080" above the top of the mounting bracket. In this position continuing operation should be realized, but the number of oscillations between impulses would not yet be maximized. The posts were both then adjusted downward, with oscillations between pulses increasing as expected. When a point was reached where operation became erratic, adjustment was discontinued and the posts moved up slightly.

Elevation of Reset Position

Although the above described adjustment yielded satisfactory operation, it proved to be sensitive. A slight adjustment up or down from the best position led to unsatisfactory operation. Continued reliable operation could not be expected. It was concluded that an extended drop of the armature arm would enhance the

Figure 15, above. Test: paper shim inserted beneath tab to drop left end of leaf spring to permit more clockwise rotation of armature.

Figure 16, above. Permanent brass shim for depressing left end of leaf spring.

Figure 17, above. Shim secured under tab with epoxy.

ability of the latch on the bottom of the arm to move under the gravity arm knife edge (Figure 5) and also that it could improve the rebound; both improvements would increase the adjustment range.

It was expected that placing a shim beneath the left-hand positioning tab (Figure 13 "g") would increase the drop. This shim would depress the left-hand end of the leaf spring. With the end of the spring depressed, the stop pad "f," attached to the armature, would rotate further counterclockwise before stopping in the reset state, raising the position of the armature arm.

It appeared possible that raising the reset position of the armature arm would allow a greater clockwise rotation (from the front) and acceleration of the armature when energized, before stop tab "e" impinged on the right side of the leaf spring. The higher impact velocity could then depress the spring further and allow the latch on the bottom of the armature arm to more easily move under and catch onto the gravity arm knife edge. It also was expected that the higher impact velocity would enhance the rebound.

The concept of raising the reset position was discussed with Steven Conover, editor of *Clockmakers Newsletter*,[2] who has published articles concerning operation and servicing of Poole clocks. He indicated that he had tried something similar in shimming the armature with a Poole movement of a somewhat different configuration. His positive results (August 1998, p. 6)[2] were encouraging.

To test the present concept, two thicknesses of .009"-thick card stock were inserted between the positioning tab and the leaf spring (Figure 15). Latching and rebound were indeed enhanced, with good continuing operation.

A small brass L-shaped 020"-thick tab was made (Figure 16). It was slipped under the positioning tab (Figure 17) and secured with epoxy against the tab. Stable continuing operation was realized, with reliable latching over a significantly extended adjustment range and with a noticeably enhanced rebound.

Success! Pendulum swings of 26 per impulse were realized. Stable operation was indeed achieved, with adequate pendulum swings between impulses; in addition, a great amount of understanding was gained concerning troubleshooting and adjustment of the movement.

Summary

The steps taken with the presently described Barr clock did restore it to a satisfactory operating state. It must be noted that all Poole and Barr clocks may not have the same problems and may not require the same corrective action. However, the troubleshooting approach used, and some of the specific actions taken, could indeed be effectively directed to other Barr and Poole clocks.

References

1. Sowers III, Edwin U. "The Ingenious Poole Clock." *NAWCC Bulletin* (October 2000): pp. 611-616.
2. Conover, Steven. *Clockmakers Newsletter* (July 1998): pp. 1, 7, 8 and (August 1998): pp. 1, 6, 7, and 8.

Acknowledgments

I thank my brother, Christopher Sowers, Lebanon, PA, for his insightful assistance in helping to identify and resolve the problems with the Barr Clock, which led to its ultimate satisfactory operation.

I also thank George York, Auburn, NY, who provided the Barr Clock and allowed us to engage in the most enlightening task of restoring it to its operating status. It will be displayed in the Old Brutus Historical Society Museum of Weedsport, NY—close to its birthplace.

Addendum

George York reports that prior to forwarding the Barr Clock to me, he disassembled the movement and cleaned it ultrasonically, using L&R No. 677 Waterless Cleaner, followed by a rinse in L&R No. 3 Watch Rinsing Solution. A cleaning solution that does not loosen lacquer, as is the case with L&R No. 677, should indeed be used. It is a good idea to eliminate the possibility of producing loose flakes of lacquer that could lodge in sensitive components.

It was suggested that I point out in this article Poole and Barr clocks must not be oiled. I did include a significant discussion on this subject in Reference 1 and concur with this suggestion. Oil viscosity changes with temperature and can affect timekeeping accuracy; also, the forces encountered in these movements are so small that lubrication is not necessary. To clinch the matter, a manufacturer's label in my Poole clock clearly states: "Important—Never Oil this Clock."

Steven Conover, in his July 1998 *Clockmakers Newsletter*,[2] describes in detail a procedure for disassembling and cleaning a Poole clock, which would be equally applicable to a Barr clock.

The subject of raising the reset position of the armature arm to enhance latching and rebound has been discussed by the present article. There is another significant benefit that can be realized: eliminating interference between the bottom of the impulse roller and the impulse pin. I have elsewhere observed this interference where the gravity arm and the armature arm are in the reset position and the pendulum is swinging normally, but the impulse roller is suspended a bit too low. This interference, of course, reduces the pendulum swings per impulse.

FABRICATION AND REPLACEMENT OF BROCOT ESCAPEMENT PALLETS

Edwin U. Sowers III, CMC

This article originally appeared in the April and May 2005 Clockmakers Newsletter*s and is reprinted here with permission.*

Figure 1 shows an outstanding Tiffany clock that was meticulously cleaned and polished by its owner. The clock housed a French movement with an internal Brocot escapement. I received the clock for cleaning, repairing, and oiling.

There was but one significant problem; the Brocot pallets were worn. A descriptive drawing of a Brocot escapement is shown by Figure 2. The Brocot pallets are essentially a half cylinder. The escape wheel tooth (on the right) contacts, and applies a force to the convex impulse surface, as the pallet rotates upward from the position shown. Applied force to the pallet continues until the escape wheel moves forward and the tooth arrives at the cut off rear section of the half cylinder. At this point, the tooth is released from the pallet. By this time, the pallet to the left will have moved down, the escape wheel will have moved forward (clockwise) and a tooth on the left will contact the pallet in front of it. Through continual impact of the escape wheel teeth upon the pallets, wear of the pallets can ultimately occur. The wear encountered in this case, at the tooth contact surface, is shown by Figure 3.

Fig. 1. An elegant Tiffany clock—with a problem!

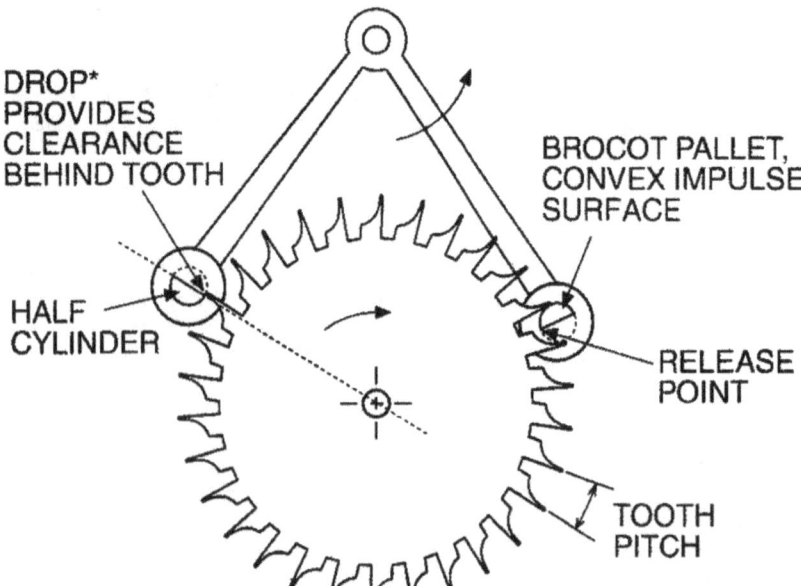

Fig. 2. A typical Brocot escapement.

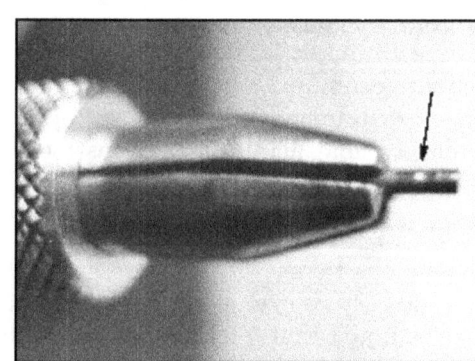

Fig. 3. Pallet wear caused by tooth contact.

My assortment of pallets did not include any that were small enough to use as replacements. Fabrication of replacements was necessary. This article will describe the action taken, accomplished through the following steps:
- Fabrication of Two Pallets
- Inserting and Adjusting the Pallets
- Securing the Pallets • Addendum—Lessons Learned

Fabrication of Two Pallets

The original pallets were driven out from the rear of the pallet arms with a small punch. The body diameter of the pallets was 0.055", reduced to a 0.026" half cylinder thickness in the impulse area. Considering that the original pallets had functioned satisfactorily, it was decided to duplicate them. Laurie Penman, in his book *Practical Clock Escapements* (Ref. 1), defines in detail procedures for calculating the critical dimensions.

I fortunately had some hardened pivot wire of 0.055" diameter and tempered it with a propane torch sufficiently for filing to create the thinned-down half cylinder section. (The availability of tempered stock of a suitable size would, of course, eliminate the tempering step). It was realized that the very small pallets would be hard to hold and to accurately reduce to an 0.026" thickness by hand filing and stoning, if done individually. It was concluded that this could be better done by filing two at a time from one piece of stock, with the two mounting ends towards the outside, and the filed half cylinder section in the center, end-to-end.

The pivot wire was secured for filing by mounting one end of the wire in the chuck of my Unimat 3 lathe and the other in the tailstock chuck, as shown by Figure 4. The width of the center filed section was greater than that required for the length of two pallets. This made it pos-

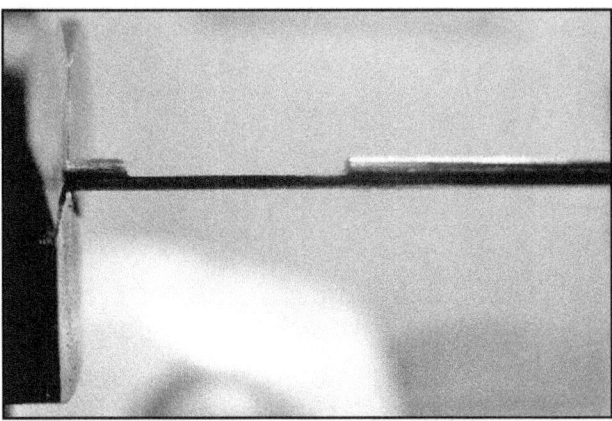

Fig. 5. Half cylinder section finished.

sible to more readily check for constant thickness with a micrometer. Filing was accomplished with a long, narrow coarse file, followed by a fine #4 cut file.

Thinning to 0.026" was accomplished with a 600-grit 1/4 x 1/8 x 6" hard aluminum oxide polishing stone, (see Ref. 2), which was repeatedly dipped in kerosene to keep it clean and effectively cutting. The thinned pivot wire, from which to create the two pallets, is shown by Figure 5.

The next step was to reharden the tempered pallet stock. To prevent scaling when heating to cherry red, the stock was dipped in boric acid, Figure 6. It was heated adequately to melt the boric acid, then dipped into it again while hot. This formed a coating to prevent oxidation. The pivot wire was heated to cherry red and immediately quenched, to make it glass hard. Indeed, there was no scale formation.

Fig. 4. Pivot wire held in lathe for filing.

Fig. 6. Boric acid coating prior to hardening.

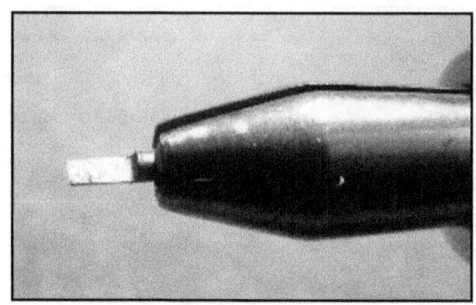

Fig. 7. A completed pallet.

The wire was cut in half with a Dremel cut-off wheel. The half cylinder section of each was cut back to a length of 0.10" and the total length to approximately 0.23" using the Dremel cut-off wheel. The pallet was placed into the lathe chuck to stone a slight chamfer on the shank end with the cutoff wheel. The pallet (not yet cleaned) is shown by Figure 7.

Inserting and Adjusting the Pallets

The next step was to insert the pallets into the pallet arms. It was discovered that the diameter of the pallet body, which had been earlier checked and determined to be the same as the originals, did not indeed fit into the holes. The original pallets may actually have been installed during manufacturing with a tight fit. The holes were broached to fit the pallets. While broaching yielded satisfactory results, it is not ideal since the hole could be cocked and it will be somewhat tapered, both of which can lead to positioning problems. It would have been better to earlier stone the ends of the pallets to fit the holes; this preferred approach will be addressed later under Addendum - Lessons Learned.

The pallets inserted into the pallet arms are shown by Figure 8. Rotational orientation of the flat portion of the pallets relative to the escape wheel is critical. Rotation of the pallets is frequently required to obtain the desired drop. Drop is the relatively small forward movement of an escape wheel tooth from drop off (or release) by a pallet to when the wheel and tooth are stopped by a tooth on the other side of the escape wheel when it contacts the pallet in front of it. This forward motion after drop-off provides the necessary clearance between a released tooth and the back of the pallet from which it was released.

The ideal rotational orientation of the flat side of the pallet is such that the flat side is essentially parallel to a line from this flat surface, Figure 2, to the center of the escape wheel (this with the pallet in contact with a tooth, not raised above it). The escape wheel rotation in the Figure is clockwise. The present escape wheel, as considered in the following, was also clockwise. The fabricated pallets were inserted into the pallet arms with the convex surfaces towards the left, and rotated slightly clockwise from the ideal. The pallet unit was mounted between plates along with the clockwise rotating escape wheel, and the drop checked. As was anticipated, it was too great due to premature release. *To reduce drop,* the pallets were rotated slightly *counterclockwise* from the starting position. This moved the release point forward, (Figure 2). Through a number of steps; removing the pallets, slightly rotating them, replacing the pallets, and testing, the pallets were rotated *counterclockwise* sufficiently to achieve a satisfactory drop. The objective was to reduce the drop as much as possible while still insuring that both pallets, following the release of a tooth, could move down behind that tooth without touching it, and also that the drop from both pallets was essentially the same.

There are other criteria that must be satisfied for correct escape operation, including the spacing between the escape wheel arbor and the pallet arbor, and the width between the two pallets fixed into their pallet arms. In the present case, no such adjustments were necessary. A fully detailed discussion of Brocot escapement operation and adjustment is presented by Laurie Penman, Ref. 1.

Securing the Pallets

Following satisfactory positioning of the pallets, they were secured with shellac. The shellac was prepared by mixing flake shellac, obtained from Nancy Fratti, Ref. 3, with denatured alcohol. The flakes were placed in a small bottle, the alcohol poured in, and stirred, then allowed to mix overnight. The mixture was made fairly thick. The holes in which the pallets were positioned included countersinks front and back, to form a reservoir for the shellac surrounding the pallets. Using a cleaned oiler, the shellac was flowed into both the front and rear reservoirs. This completed the process. The pallets in place in the movement, and a front view of that movement, are shown by Figures 9 and 10.

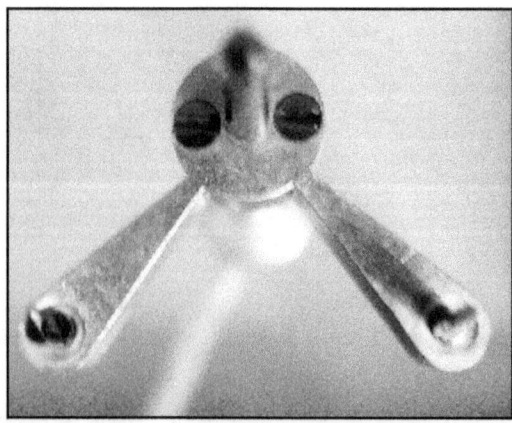

Fig. 8. Pallets installed in pallet assembly arms.

Addendum - Lessons Learned

A major objective in the procedure previously described was to form two pallets simultaneously from one piece of stock, to eliminate the difficulty of handling two small pieces while accurately hand filing and stoning them. The undesirable phase of the procedure was the broaching of the pallet holes in the pallet arms to achieve a satisfactory fit. While micrometer measurements indicated that the replacement pallets were of the same diameter as the originals, they could not be installed.

An approach, which allows for preliminary sizing of the pallet end diameters, and doing this prior to hardening, would be preferable; a revised procedure is here presented. Except for the addition of this step, and the elimination of pallet arm broaching, the prior described procedure remains basically the same.

Figure 11 on the next page presents more suitable dimensions for a piece of stock to use in fabricating the pallets.

Starting again, in the present case with the .055" pivot wire, *temper* it and cut off a 1" length. The 3/16" long body diameters on each end may be reduced in diameter as required to fit into the two pallet holes. A small notch should be made 3/16" from each end, to define the inner edge of the pallet ends. Make the notch *on the side of the pivot wire to be filed.*

Identify each pallet end and the hole into which it will be fitted. Chamfer slightly both ends. By testing, fitting the piece (including the center section) into a lathe and carefully filing or stoning, fit the pallet ends to their respective holes.

The final finish must be smooth; the fit must be snug, but such as to permit later careful turning with a pliers. Keep in mind that the finished pallets will be glass hard and fragile. The pallets will be secured by the shellac. Do not taper the ends; ensure a constant diameter along the length. Be careful *not to mar the surface of the pallet impulse section.*

Now with the pallet ends fitted to the hole in the pallet arm for each, the original procedure may be followed. The pallet ends may be mounted between the lathe chuck and the tail stock chuck as before, and the center half cylinder section filed and stoned to the required thickness.

Fig. 9. Pallet in movement.

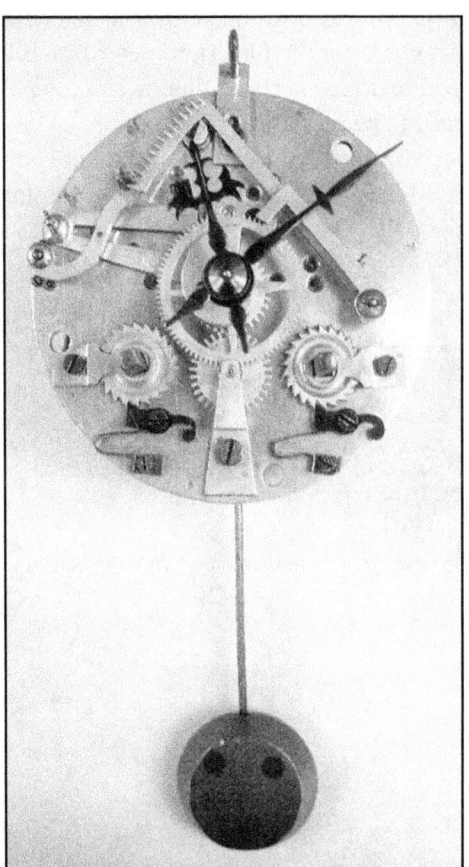

Fig. 10. The French movement.

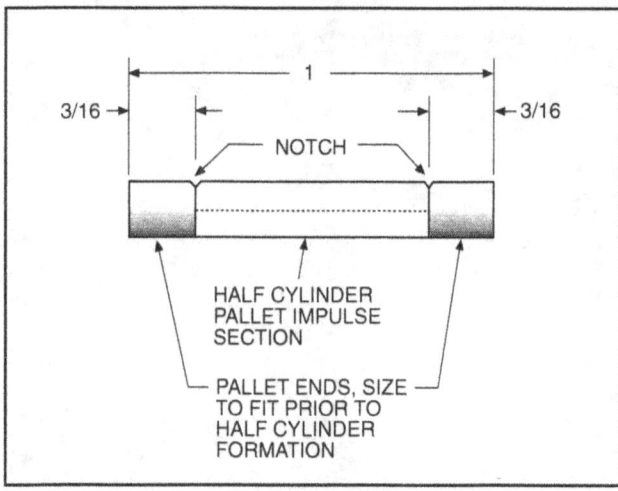

Fig. 11. Preferred length dimensions for pallet fabrication stock. (Not drawn to scale, dimensions are in inches)

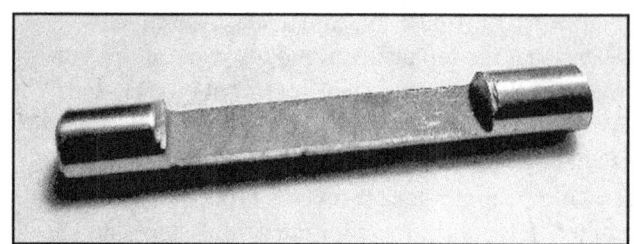

Fig. 13. The completed "test piece" was a success.

To prove that a piece of stock of Figure 11 dimensions could be satisfactorily mounted in a lathe and the half cylinder filed, a test piece was prepared per the drawing and subjected to the filing procedure. Figure 12 shows the piece mounted in the lathe with filing in progress. Note that a cutting tool was positioned towards the headstock to serve as a guide for the file. This was extremely helpful in obtaining a flat filed surface. Figure 13 shows the end result, judged to be quite satisfactory.

When arriving at the stage where rotational adjustment of the pallets takes place, it should now be possible to do this with the pallets in place, using a flat nosed, smooth jawed pliers.

Warning: Laurie Penman, Ref. 1, prescribes a body diameter equal to the escape wheel tooth tip pitch minus the drop. Exceeding this dimension can lead to major problems in attempting to adjust the escapement. It is usually better to be slightly undersized than oversized.

References

1. Laurie Penman, *Practical Clock Escapements*, Clockworks Press, Int., Inc., Shingle Springs, CA 95682. 1998, pp. 130-147.

2. Part #05093802. MSC Industrial Supplies. Tel. 800-645-7270; e-mail: mscdirect.com.

3. Nancy Fratti, P. O. Box 400, Canastota, NY 13032. Tel. 315-684-9977.

From the Author
The Tiffany clock on which I reported in this article was received in immaculate condition. The owner, David Bachman of Lebanon, Pa., is indeed to be complimented.

Fig. 12. The test piece is filed in the lathe. Note that a lathe tool bit is used as a filing guide. It would be very difficult to file evenly without some type of guide.

MOVEMENT CARRIER
Edwin U. Sowers III, CMC, Lebanon PA

I use the movement carrier shown in the photo to transport tall case and grandmother clock movements. The carrier is deep enough to accommodate the lower projecting portion of tall case dials, and it protects the crutch, which frequently extends below the seatboard. I use 2 1/2" clamps to secure the seatboard to the carrier.

The carrier can readily be fabricated from the following materials:
  2 pieces of wood 2 x 3 x 5-1/2
  2 pieces of wood 1 x 4-1/2 x 14
  #8 coated sinker or common nails

Depending on the size of movements encountered, carriers of different lengths can be made.

This repair tip originally appeared in the June 2000 Clockmakers Newsletter *and is reprinted here with permission.*

THE JACOB GUTHART J-HOOK
Edwin U. Sowers III, CMC

Jacob Guthart, of Lebanon, Pennsylvania, used an unusual method, employing what has been referred to as a "J-hook" to initiate and stop the strike sequence of his tall case clocks. The concept, which is probably of Swiss origin,[1] eliminated the conventional warning cycle.

In addition to clockmaking, Guthart, (1779-1867) was an active politician, serving as Lebanon's first Chief Burgess, a Justice of the Peace, County Treasurer, and State Representative from 1814 to 1817.[2]

Figures 1 and 2 show a Guthart clock and dial. Figure 3 shows a movement with the dial removed.

The J-hook, a uniquely modified rack hook, is shown by Figures 4 and 5. As shown by Figure 4, an arm attached to the rack hook extends downward from the rack hook arm at approximately 60° from the arm. At the lower extremity is a pin extending outward. This serves as a stop pin. At the conclusion of striking, it is lifted *upward* so that it is impinged upon by a long gathering pallet tail. This stops the strike train.

During striking, while the rack hook passes over the typical rack teeth, as shown by Figure 4, the stop pin is not lifted high enough to interfere with the pallet tail.

The means by which the rack hook is lifted at the conclusion of striking is shown by Figure 5. The left end of the rack incorporates an elevated tooth which raises the rack hook higher than when passing over the preceding teeth. It is this elevated tooth which causes the stop pin to be raised into the path of the pallet arm, thus stopping the strike train. There is a notch in the rack hook which rests upon the elevated tooth in the stopped condition.

Fig. 1

Fig. 2

Figures 1 and 2 courtesy of S. Perlmutter.

This article originally appeared in the September 2000 Clockmakers Newsletter *and is reprinted here with permission.*

Fig. 3

Fig. 4

Fig. 5

Description of the Strike Sequence

After striking, the strike train remains at rest, with the gathering pallet tail locked against the stop pin, as shown by Figure 5. To initiate striking, the strike lifting pin acts upon the lifting lever to raise the rack hook. This releases the rack. It also raises the stop pin, so the tail is not yet released. When the lifting lever drops off of the lifting pin, the rack hook drops. The stop pin also drops, releasing the tail. Striking commences, without the occurrence of a warning cycle.

Striking proceeds, with the rack hook not lifted high enough to place the stop pin in the path of the pallet tail. Striking continues until the gathering pallet causes the hook to ride up onto the extended tooth. This action lifts the hook and stop pin; the gathering pallet arm contacts the stop pin and stops the striking sequence.

The J-Hook concept does away with the need for both a warning lever and a warning pin. It also eliminates the need for timing the orientation of a warning pin relative to the gathering pallet at the stop position. Ingenious!

References

1. Edward LaFond, clock restorer, Mechanicsburg, Pa.

2. Hon. E. Benjamin Bierman, Ph.D. "Lebanon County in Our State Legislature." Lebanon County Historical Society, Vol. II, No.13, 1904, p. 373.

The Herschede Two-Weight, Five-Tube Movement

Edwin U. Sowers III, CMC, MSME

This article originally appeared in the June 2001 Horological Times *and is reprinted here with permission.*

The Herschede Hall Clock Company produced a variety of tubular chime movements. The most interesting of these is the two-weight, five-tube movement. I have encountered the normal two-weight movement, as well as one that is motor driven. The latter movement is essentially the same as the former, but is driven by two motors, one for time, and a second to drive the chime/strike mechanism.

Figure 1 shows the silvered brass dial which was used with movements furnished to various clock manufacturers. Figure 2 shows the movement with the chime/strike drum, hammer pulling levers, and five tubes. The movement which accomplishes the timekeeping, chime, and strike functions, performs these three functions with but two gear trains. The time train performs the timekeeping function; the second train deals with both the chime and the strike functions.

To simplify the discussion, the second gear train will be referred to as the chime train. The chime train drives the chime/strike drum, which incorporate pins on the periphery that act upon hammer levers. The hammer levers, in a conventional manner, pull on strings connected to hammers that impact upon five chime tubes to generate the Westminster chime sequence, then strike the hour. The fascinating feature of the movement is the concepts involved in accomplishing the chime and strike functions by shifting the chime/strike drum through three lateral positions during three full revolutions of the drum.

In the first position (to the right), the four quarter-hour chime sequences are accomplished within two revolutions of the drum. After chiming the fourth quarter (completing two revolutions), the drum shifts to the left. This disengages the chime pins from the chime hammer levers, and positions a row of strike pins to engage the strike hammer lever. Striking proceeds through the correct number of strikes, at which time the drum shifts again to the left, disengaging the strike pins from the strike hammer lever. The drum, however, continues to rotate to completion of a full revolution. The drum has now rotated a total of three full revolutions. It is subsequently reset to the first position (to the right) as the minute hand approaches the first quarter position.

Figure 3 shows the mechanism which controls chiming. The upper lever, pivoted to the left, and with a vertical extension, is the locking lever. Below that is a detent arm which pivots to the left on a screw attached to the front plate;

Figure 1.

there are two detent notches on the right-hand end. Below the detent arm, and also pivoted to the left, is the warning lever. Suspended from the warning lever is the lifting lever. The lifting lever lifts the warning lever by means of the pin which can be seen immediately to the left of the tail of the second hand.

The action which takes place in the course of an hour, plus the manner by which automatic chime correction is achieved, is presented by the following:

First Quarter

At the first quarter, a lifting cam on the minute hand arbor, with 4 pins acting as lifting lobes, raises the lifting

Figure 2.

Figure 3.

lever. This raises the warning lever, the detent arm, and the locking lever. Warning occurs. The locking lever is latched in a raised position by a pin on the lever which engages the *lower right notch* of the detent. When the lifting lever is released by the lifting cam, the warning lever drops, the drum commences rotation and chiming begins. The locking lever is held in an elevated position by the detent. The detent latching also determines the lateral position of the vertical arm of the locking lever; the lower notch positions the vertical lever arm to the left of that for the upper notch. As shown by Figure 4, the tip of the arm incorporates a hook.

The locking lever hook is acted upon by stop pins critically positioned about the drum. There are three pins; the first two (chime stop pins) lead to stopping of the drum the upper notch. As shown by Figure 4, the tip of the arm incorporates a hook.

The locking lever hook is acted upon by stop pins critically positioned about the drum. There are three pins; the first two (chime stop pins) lead to stopping of the drum at the end of the first, second and third quarter chiming, the third (strike stop pin) to stopping at the end of striking. The position of the first two pins is as shown by Figures 3 and 4; above and to the left of the locking lever hook. When the locking lever is engaged by the lower notch of the detent arm, the locking lever arm is shifted to the left, in line with the shown stop pin.

The drum, which has commenced rotation, continues until nearing completion of the first quarter chime. At this point the first stop pin on the drum catches the locking lever hook, lifting and rotating the locking lever counterclockwise. The detent disengages and drops. The locking lever is lifted further by the pin and rotates until the hook moves sufficiently to the left to disengage on the right side from the pin. The locking lever then falls to the position shown by Figures 3 and 4, and stops the drum, coincident with completion of the first quarter chime.

Figure 4.

Challenging Repairs to Interesting Clocks · 39

Second Quarter

A similar sequence occurs at the second quarter, where the drum is stopped by a second chime stop pin, after completion of the second quarter chiming sequence. This pin is located in the same lateral position as the first.

Third Quarter

The same occurs at the third quarter, with stopping effected by the first chime stop pin, which had caused stopping at the end of the first quarter. There are five, 4-note tunes generated by one revolution of the drum. The first quarter plays one, the second two. The melody played at the third quarter is comprised of the last two tunes (of five) from the first full revolution, plus a repeat of the first tune at the start of the second revolution. Thus the first chime stop pin is in the correct position for stopping the third quarter chime sequence.

Fourth Quarter

At the fourth quarter, the lifting lever is *lifted less* than for the prior quarters, due to a pin on the lifting cam placed at a smaller distance from the arbor center. This pin will subsequently be referred to as the short cam lobe. The action is the same as for the prior quarters, except that the detent latches the locking lever pin in the *upper notch*, since the locking lever is not lifted high enough to engage the pin in the lower notch (refer to Figure 3). This places the vertical arm of the locking lever to the *right* of the position for the prior three quarters. In this position the locking lever *bypasses* the *second chime stop pin*. The drum continues to rotate to completion of the fourth quarter (or hour) chime. At this point the drum has completed two full revolutions and proceeds into the strike mode. Note that in normal operation it is possible to proceed into the strike mode *only* when the second chime stop pin is bypassed by the locking lever; this occurs only when the locking lever is latched into the upper detent notch.

Striking

At the end of two full chiming revolutions, the drum is shifted to the left through action of a fixed spiral grooved flat cam at the left of the drum, as shown by Figure 5. A cam pin on the left end of the drum follows the cam groove for the two revolutions during chiming, then drops off onto the depressed surface of a moveable segment behind and towards the center of the flat cam. A spring on the right, shown in Figure 4, causes the drum to shift to the left.

The drum continues to rotate, with a row of striking pins now contacting the strike hammer lever, and causing striking. The pins are shown in Figure 3, on the right end of the drum. (The chime pins have been shifted out of contact with the chime hammer levers.) Striking continues until the cam pin encounters a discontinuity which allows the pin to shift to a second and lower level, moving the drum further to the left. This disengages the strike pins from the strike hammer lever and stops striking. The location of this discontinuity is established by gearing which connects to the hour hand tube, as shown by Figure 6. The drum continues to rotate, *with no striking*, to completion of one revolution. The 12 striking pins are positioned around the drum such that a 12-strike requires the full one revolution. Upon completion of the striking revolution, a third pin (the strike stop pin) on the drum acts upon the locking lever to stop the drum. The strike stop pin is located on the drum in such a position that it is bypassed by the locking lever except when the drum is in the third (left) position. The drum has now completed three full revolutions during the chiming of the four quarters and striking of the hour.

Drum Reset

It remains to reset the drum to the right hand position. This is accomplished by a pin on a gear coupled to a gear on the minute hand arbor. The gear with the pin rotates once per revolution of the minute wheel. As the minute hand approaches the first quarter position, the pin acts upon a reset lever which pushes against the left end of the drum arbor, moving it to the right. The reset lever can be seen in Figure 6. The pin wheel is marginally visible at the bottom of the reset lever. The drum is held to the right by the cam pin on the left side of the drum which is positioned against the flat cam. The cam pin is pivoted and spring loaded such that it springs out to the beginning of the flat cam when the drum is shifted to the right. The drum is thus reset to the right, to permit actuation of the chime hammers, prior to initiation of the first quarter chime.

Automatic Chime Correction

An error between chiming and the minute hand position can occur typically where the chime sequence lags behind that which is correct for the position of the minute hand.

Correction will occur at the first hour reached by the minute hand. The short lifting cam lobe will cause the locking lever to latch onto the upper detent arm notch. The locking lever arm and hook will then be positioned to its right-hand position. Regardless of what quarter is being struck both chime stop pins will be bypassed by the locking arm hook, so the drum will not stop at the end of any quarter. The drum will proceed into the strike mode, will strike the hour defined by the hour hand, will shift fully to the left into the end-of-strike position, and will be stopped by the strike stop pin. Reset of the drum to the right will take place as the minute hand approaches the first quarter; correction will then be completed.

Should the error be reversed, where the hand lags the chime sequence, correction will also occur when the minute hand reaches the hour position. The sequence of events in some causes is more complex. This error, however, is not highly probable.

Figure 5.

Figure 6.

RESTORATION OF A NEW HAVEN NO. 1 OFFICE CLOCK
THE DEADBEAT PALLETS

Edwin U. Sowers III, CMC

This article originally appeared as a series in the February, March, April, and May 2000 Clockmakers Newsletters *and is reprinted here with permission.*

A New Haven No. 1 Office Clock, shown by Figure 1, was presented to me for restoration. The clock and movement are shown in *New Haven Clocks and Watches* by Tran Duy Ly (Ref. 1). This particular clock is exceptionally attractive, boasting a beautiful black walnut veneer.

The restoration included, most importantly, rebuilding of the deadbeat pallets, which had been converted into a most unlikely recoil configuration. The crutch also had been modified, offering no means for beat adjustment. In addition, the pendulum rod did not resemble, in any way, an original, and was not functional. The center arbor, to which the hands attach, was broken off immediately forward of the front plate.

This article will describe the restoration of the pallets to a deadbeat configuration, as nearly duplicating the original as possible. A replacement for the unsatisfactory crutch is also presented. Another article, in Book 5 of this *Clockmakers Newsletter Workshop Series*, will deal with the restoration of the pendulum and broken center arbor. A glossary is provided at the end of this first article to define terms used in discussing the operation of a deadbeat escapement.

Upon inspection of the movement it was obvious that it was of the expected high quality, except for the unfortunate pallet degradation. It was impossible to establish from observing the pallets that they had originally been of a deadbeat configuration: this was, however, apparent through examination of the escape wheel.

The first course of action in restoring the pallets was to define relevant specifications. Some were determined from the available pallet unit and escape wheel; others were obtained from another movement. To create the deadbeat pallets, segments of hardenable steel were silver soldered to the pallet arms. The pallet tips, or nibs, were then shaped, fitted to the escape wheel, and trimmed as necessary to ensure proper engagement. The nibs were heat treated to obtain a hardened wear surface. The pallet unit was then fitted into the movement and adjusted to achieve correct lock and drop. The steps taken to accomplish these tasks will be described in the following. A properly conFigured crutch was also added as part of the restoration.

Specification Development
Data Acquisition

To assist in the analysis and understanding of the relationship between the pallet unit and the escape wheel, both were mounted on an inspection board as shown by Figure 2. The concept is as presented by Laurie Penman (Ref. 2), but using a piece of hard maple instead of the steel plate he prescribed. Holes were accurately drilled for a tight fit for both the escape wheel arbor and the pallet unit arbor, at the

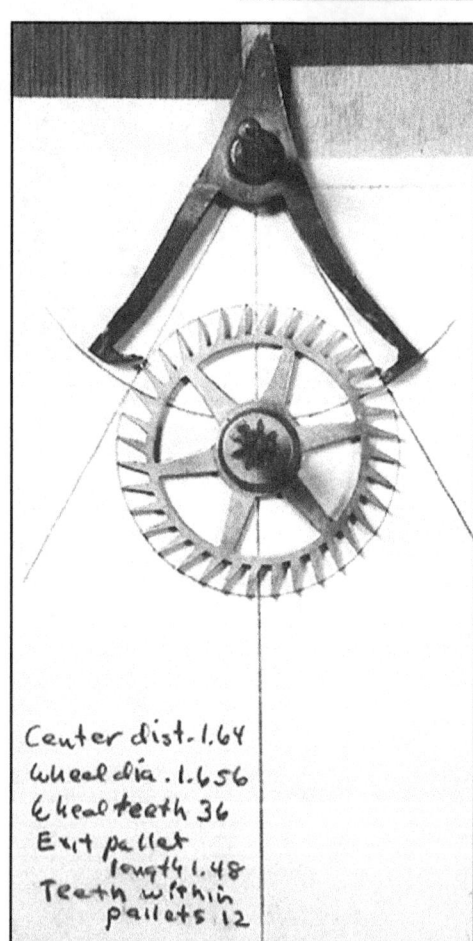

Fig. 1. New Haven No. 1 Office Clock.

Fig. 2. Escape components on inspection board.

spacing established by the movement plates. A slot was cut down from the top to the pallet arbor hole, to enable placement of the pallet arbor into the hole with the crutch attached at the rear. A tapered piece of wood held the pallet unit in place.

Generation of the required specifications is described in the following. A detailed description of the drawing made to define the pallet impulse surfaces is included as a separate section.

1. The spacing between the centers of the pallet arbor and the escape wheel arbor was determined by accurately measuring the distance between the adjacent outer surfaces of the two arbors with a dial calipers, while in the movement. To this was added 1/2 of the micrometer measured diameters of the two arbors. This dimension was determined to be 1.64". Specifications are shown by Figure 2, and by later Figures as they were developed.

2. The diameter of the escape wheel was measured with a dial calipers, and determined to be 1.656".

3. The number of escape wheel teeth was 36. This exceeded the more common 30 to 32 teeth. The large tooth count, the fine teeth, plus incorporation of maintaining power into the time barrel, all confirmed that this was indeed a high quality movement.

4. While the pallet tips, or nibs, were severely modified, it appeared that the outer edge of the exit pallet was original. The distance from the arbor center to the outer edge was 1.48". It was considered highly probable that the outer radius of both pallet nibs had been nominally 1.48".

5. The next question addressed was the number of teeth spanned by the pallets. On an index card beneath the escape wheel of Figure 2, a 1.48" radius was drawn, centered on the pallet arbor center (this was accomplished by placing a snugly fitting pin, with a center point, in the pallet arbor hole.) An escape wheel tooth was moved up to that radius; this is where contact of the entrance tooth with the locking surface of a deadbeat entrance pallet would occur. It was observed that the exit tooth was at a reasonable position for completion of drop-off from the exit pallet. Examining Figure 2, and assuming the radius to indeed be nominally 1.48"with the entrance tooth moved up to the 1.48 radius, the number of teeth spanned by the pallets was 12. This was more than typical, and an even number, (more commonly, odd). While it was considered highly probable that this was correct, confirmation by examination of a similar movement, in original condition, was considered essential. Fortunately, Jack Wyer (Ref. 3) had a clock and movement similar to the one on which I was working. He confirmed that the number of teeth spanned by the pallets was indeed 12. His clock and movement, from which he furnished invaluable data, are shown by *New Haven Clocks and Watches* (Ref. 1, p. 146).

6. Mr. Wyer graciously removed his pallet unit and prepared a tracing for me. Thicknesses shown are greater

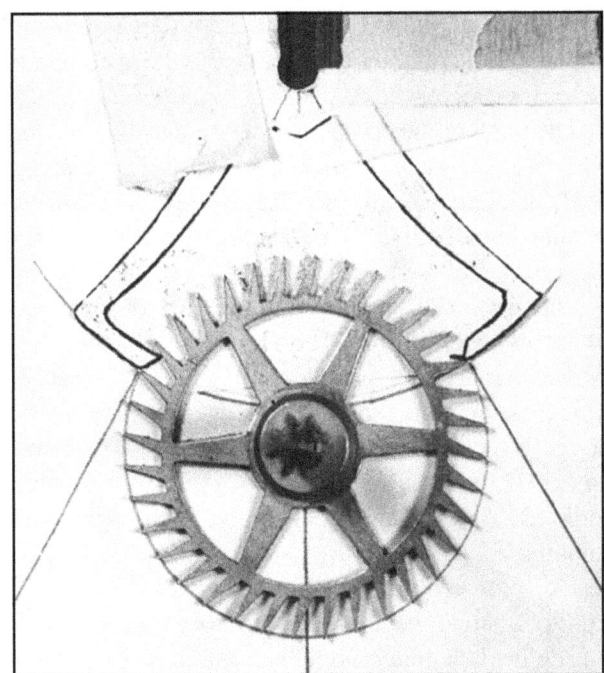

Fig. 3. The tracing of Mr. Wyer's complete pallet unit was added to the inspection board.

Fig. 4. The damaged pallet unit was superimposed upon the Wyer tracing.

than that of the original due to the pencil moving along outside the edge of the pallet unit. The tracing is shown under the escape wheel by Figure 3. It confirms the outer radius of the pallet nibs to be on the order of 1.48". The inner radius was, of course, less by the thickness of the nibs. The tracing also roughly shows the pallet engagement with the escape wheel, and clearly shows the pallets to span 12 teeth.

7. In Figure 4, the pallet unit under consideration is superimposed upon the Wyer tracing. It shows the degree to which the pallet unit was degraded. The correct shape

of the pallet nibs and the pallet arms are shown, which provided a basic reference for reshaping the arms and for the later forming of the pallets.

8. The pitch of the escape wheel, the distance between two teeth, at the same position on each, measured along the outside diameter, was calculated to be .144". This was determined by dividing the circumference, which is ϖ x D, by the number of teeth.

9. The nib thickness is one half the pitch, less the tooth tip thickness and the drop. The deductions are necessary to provide clearance to prevent tooth/pallet interference. The tip thickness and drop were both set at .010". Penman (Ref. 2) suggests a drop of 5% to 10% of pitch (.144) which yields .007" to .014". Actual tooth tip thickness was on the order of .010". The desired pallet nib thickness was then nominally:

$$0.144/2 - .010 - .010 = .052"$$

10. Subtracting the nib thickness from the nib outer radius defined the inner nib radius, which is the exit pallet locking surface, as 1.43".

11. To visualize the factors involved in pallet-nib length, return to Figure 3. The lengths should be aproximately equal. Beyond that, it was not meaningful to define the length relative to the pallet arms. Of significance, instead, was the interaction of the nibs with the escape wheel teeth. With the exit pallet release tip resting on the escape wheel outside diameter, as shown roughly by Figure 3, the entrance pallet must provide the desired lock to the escape wheel entrance tooth, this on the order of .010" to .015". The same locking requirement applied to the exit pallet.

12. The final pallet specification established was the impulse angle. The impulse angle is not the angle of the impulse surface relative to any feature of the pallet unit. It is the angle through which the whole pallet unit rotates about its axis as an escape wheel tooth sweeps across an impulse surface. The impulse angle was defined as 2°, as recommended by (Ref. 4). Where dealing with a 36-tooth escape wheel and with 12 teeth spanned by the pallets, the simpler procedures suggested by Ref. 2 for achieving the desired impulse surface did not appear applicable. The approach presented by Tigner (Ref. 4) was followed. This required the drafting of an enlarged, accurate, drawing of the escape wheel and pallets, primarily where the entrance and exit pallets interacted with escape wheel teeth. One may prefer to read about the simpler procedures given by the noted references, unless faced with the situation I encountered. However, working through the following discussion may clarify some aspects of deadbeat escapements.

Impulse Surface Drawing

Tigner's drawing, reproduced as Figure 5 with the permission of AWI (now called AWCI), provides the means for describing the 10-times size drawing I made to establish the pallet impulse faces and to define a reference for the later filing and stoning to create the actual surfaces. The centers for the pallet unit and the escape wheel were located on a vertical line. The escape wheel diameter, and the known pallet radii aa' and bb' (see ends of radii) were drawn. The entrance tooth was drawn in, resting against the entrance pallet locking surface, radius aa'.

The exit tooth was drawn clockwise from the entrance tooth by the number of teeth spanned by the pallets, plus 1; 12 + 1 = 13. (Note that the Tigner drawing shows the number of spanned teeth as 7—more typical). The escape wheel had 36 teeth, hence the pitch was 360/36 = 10°. The location of the forward tip of the 13th tooth was then 13 x 10 = 130° clockwise from the forward edge of the entrance tooth. At this point the correctness of the pallet outer radius could be checked. Having defined the tooth thickness and drop as .010" each, the pallet radius aa' had to pass by the exit tooth tip .020" from its forward edge (0.200" at 10 x size). If this was not the case, a small correction to aa' and bb' would have been necessary.

Now, on to the impulse angle. A point was defined on the forward surface of the entrance tooth .010" below the tip. This was the knee, the point of intersection of the locking and impulse surfaces, and being so located, provided the desired nominally .010" lock. A line was drawn from it to the pallet center, line LA on the drawing, Figure 5. Following this, a line was drawn 2° below the former, NA on the drawing.

The whole purpose of this drawing was to establish the impulse surface such that as the tip of the tooth starts out at the knee and moves clockwise across the pallet width, it pushes up on the tooth and rotates it 2° by the time the tooth reaches the inner edge of the pallet, the drop-off point. This will be accomplished if the drop-off point of the pallet, on the drawing, falls on the 2° line NA. A line was carefully drawn through the knee and the drop-off point on NA. This, then, defined the impulse surface.

The question may well be asked as to how this developed angle is defined on the pallet unit to permit its formation. This was accomplished through generation of the impulse radius cc' on the drawing. A line from the knee was accurately drawn through, and extended from, the impulse surface. The radius cc', centered on the pallet arbor center, was then drawn tangent to this extended line. The impulse radius was found, in this case, to be .926". Now once the impulse radius cc' was established, both the entrance and exit pallet impulse surfaces could be defined by *it*. By extending a line from the knee of the entrance pallet to the now known radius cc", the impulse surface is defined, as is shown by Figure 5. The exit pallet impulse surface can be defined in like manner.

While the impulse surface was defined on the drawing, it remained to define some physical reference to use as a guide for the hand filing and stoning of the pallet impulse surfaces. To accomplish this, a line drawn from

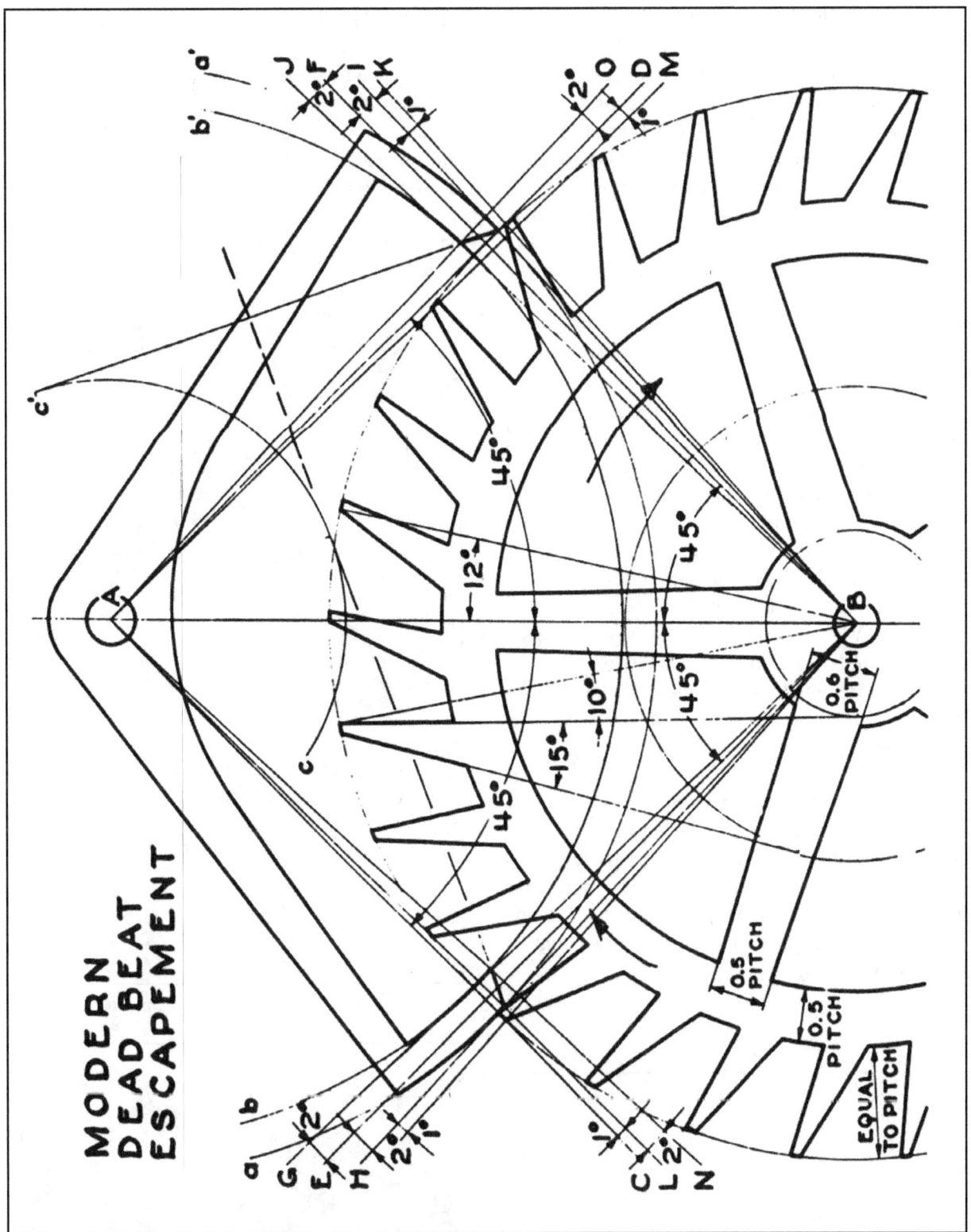

Fig. 5. Deadbeat escapement drawing from James Tigner's chapter "The Graham Dead Beat Escapement" in AWI's book, Questions of and for the Clockmaking Profession. *Used with permission of AWI.*

the entrance pallet knee, then tangent to the impulse radii, can be extended to cross the exit pallet arm, as shown by the dashed line added to Figure 5. The arm can be scribed where the line crosses it. This scribed line, then, becomes the needed physical reference; it was the ultimate objective of this entire exercise. A similar line can be drawn for the exit pallet. The procedure I used to physically accomplish this is described later, where I discuss the actual pallet shaping and positioning of files and stones by directing them towards the scribed lines.

A summary of all of the data developed for restoration of the pallet unit is included in Figure 6.

Challenging Repairs to Interesting Clocks · 45

Pallet Replacement

To confirm that a satisfactory procedure for replacement of the pallets had been envisioned, rough formation of the exit pallet was undertaken first. The results, considered to be successful, are shown by Figure 7. The exit pallet had at that point been taken through the rough filing stage. With a suitable procedure confirmed, the entrance pallet was addressed and photographs taken of the various steps involved.

Figure 7 also shows the entrance pallet arm (not the nib) reshaped to conform to the Wyer tracing. The arm was heated with a BernzOmatic oxygen/propane torch to permit bending. It was concluded that the exit pallet arm was satisfactory.

Proceeding now to the entrance pallet: the end of the pallet was cut off with a Dremel cut-off wheel, Figure 8. It was cut at an angle to provide more contact surface for the silver solder joint than would have been achieved by cutting straight across the arm.

A considerably oversized replacement was cut with a hacksaw from 1/8" hardenable steel plate. The replacement segment was silver soldered to the pallet arm with Silver Braze Solid Wire and Flux, made by Alpha Metals of Altoona PA (Item No. 53500 and available from Ace Hardware Stores). Heating was accomplished with the BernzOmatic oxygen/propane torch. The attached segment is shown by Figure 9.

Initial Pallet Shaping

The arm and nib were hand formed by filing as shown by Figure 10. To ensure satisfactory progress, the pallet unit was periodically inserted into the test board, superimposing it on the Wyer tracing shown by Figure 11. The tip of the nib was intentionally left slightly longer than that shown by the Wyer tracing.

To provide a reference for checking the curvature of the outer and inner radii of the pallet nibs, as filing progressed, a card shown by Figure 12 was prepared and slipped under the pallet unit. The arbor fit tightly into a center hole in the card. Also shown by Figure 12 is the 0.926" impulse radius developed by the earlier described drawing.

As the nib approached the desired configuration and more controlled shaping was in order, a shift was made from filing to stoning with small fine-grit stones.

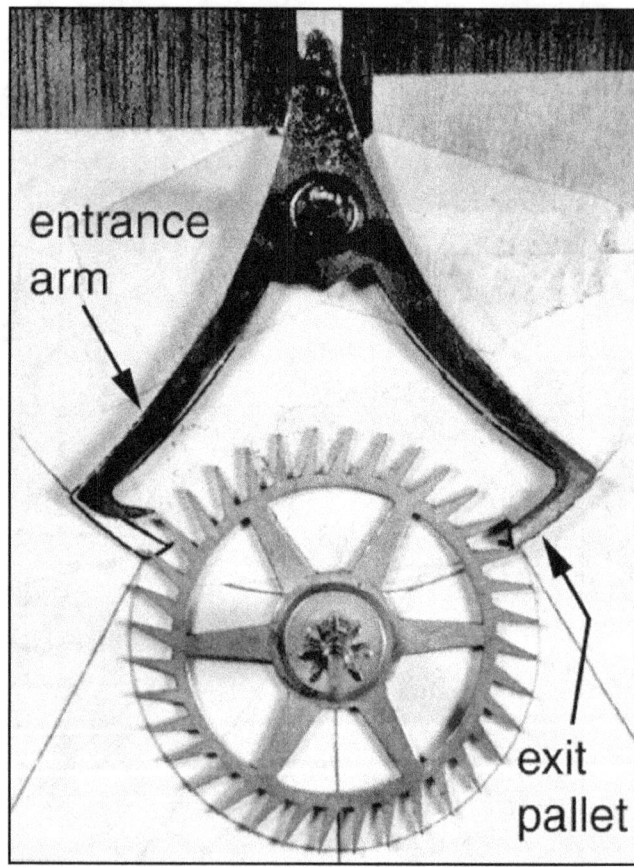

Fig. 7. Initial reworking of the pallet unit.

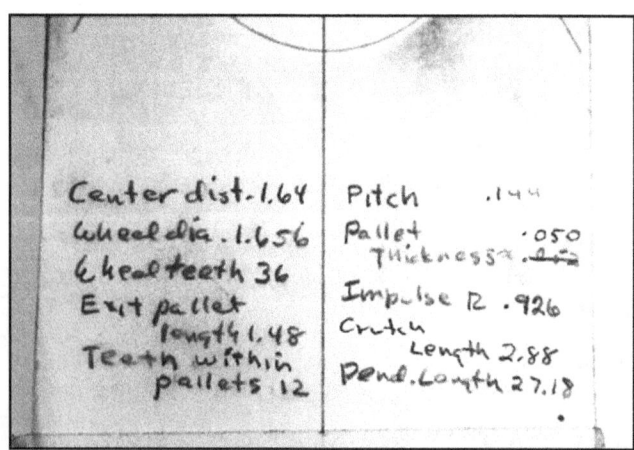

Fig. 6. Escapement data written on the inspection board

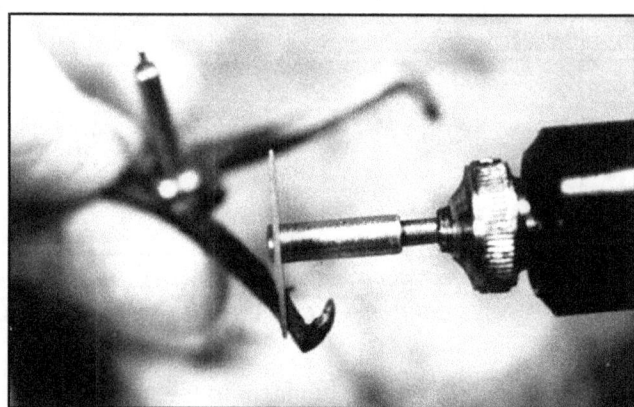

Fig. 8. Cutting off the end of the entrance pallet.

Figure 13 shows the critical intended use of the drawing which established the impulse radius. The nib tips by now approached the final configuration, so shaping of the impulse surfaces could begin. The exit pallet arm was blued. A steel rule was laid against the entrance nib tip and positioned to contact the drawn impulse radius. At the location where the rule edge passed over the exit pallet arm, as shown, a line was scribed. This was the needed reference point required for stoning the entrance pallet impulse surface. To establish the reference for the exit pallet, the rule was placed nearly vertically, with the right hand edge against the tip of the nib and then tangent to the impulse radius. A line was scribed on the pallet arm where the right hand edge of the rule passed over it.

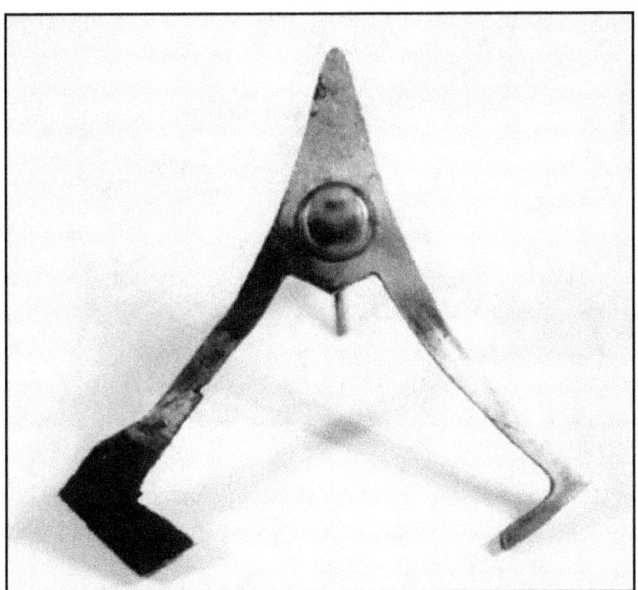

Fig. 9. Oversize replacement entrance pallet after silver soldering.

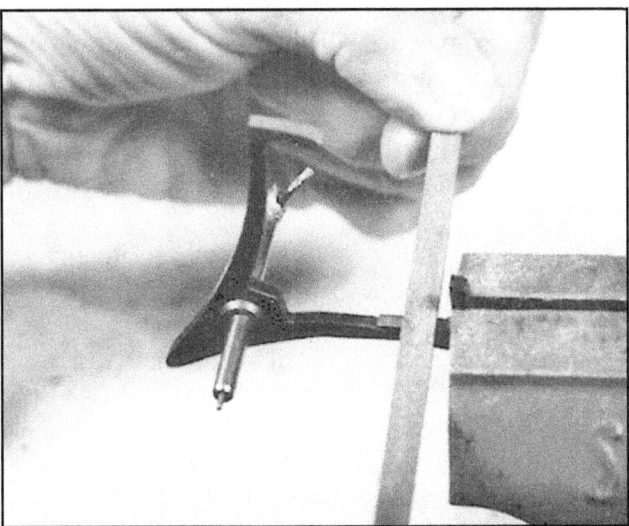

Fig. 10. Forming the entrance arm and nib.

Fig. 11. Checking progress against the Wyer tracing.

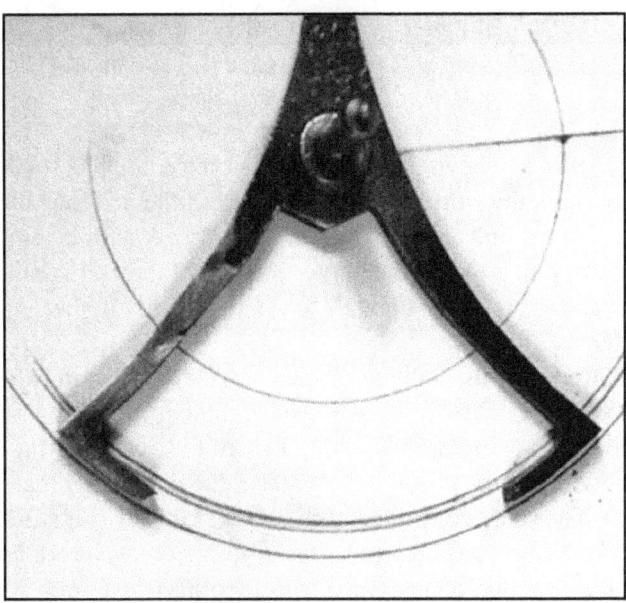

Fig. 12. Pallet radii were drawn on card stock and placed under the pallet unit.

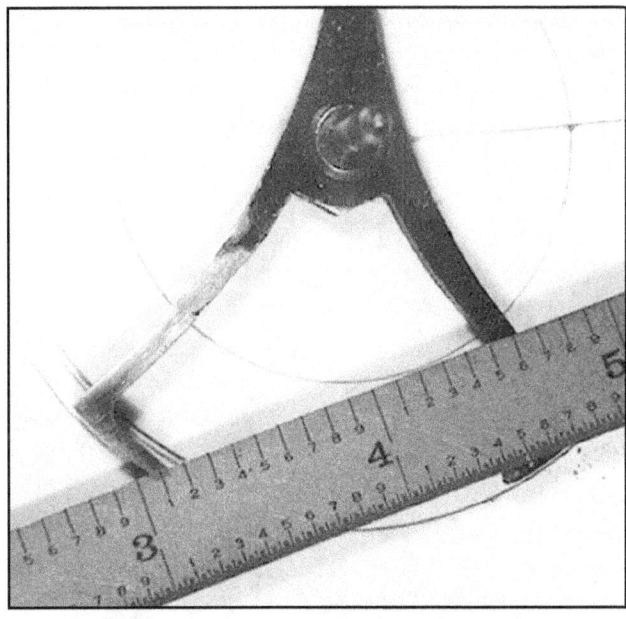

Fig. 13. Using a straightedge to locate the entrance pallet impulse surface (see text).

Challenging Repairs to Interesting Clocks • 47

Fig. 14. Stoning the entrance pallet impulse surface, making use of the reference line (see arrow).

Figure 14 shows stoning of the entrance impulse surface, with the working edge of the stone directed towards the scribed line on the exit arm. The scribed mark is indicated by an arrow in the photo. Stoning of the exit impulse surface is shown by Figure 15, where there is another reference line.

Stoning of the locking surface of the entrance nib is shown by Figure 16. Unfortunately, there is no photograph showing stoning of the locking face of the exit nib, which of course, is the inside surface, the more difficult of the two. The rounded surface of the stone shown by Figure 16 was used on this concave surface. Most stoning was done in the direction of an escape wheel tooth passing over the pallet nibs. Towards the end of stoning all was done in that direction.

Fig. 15. Stoning the exit impulse surface (see arrow).

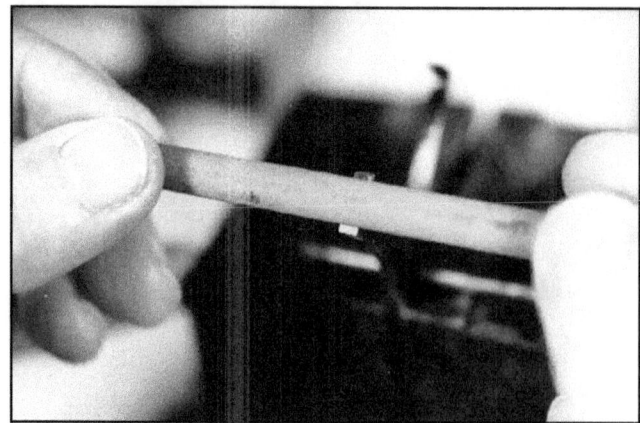

Fig. 16. Stoning the locking surface of the entrance nib.

Extreme care was taken to stone all surfaces parallel to the pallet arbor. Kerosene was applied to the stones to keep them clean and cutting effectively.

Heat Treating

All of the stoning discussed above was accomplished prior to heat treating the pallets. When the nibs neared the desired final shapes, the pallets were heat treated to obtain a hardened wearing surface. Final stoning was left for completion after hardening, leaving adequate material to accommodate any warping that might take place during hardening.

There were a number of considerations relating to heal treating. Hardening of the pallet arms was not necessary; only the nibs, where wear would occur, required hardening. Additionally, it was essential to prevent excessive heating of the silver solder joints where the replacement nibs were attached to the arms. To prevent undue heating of the solder joints, a parallel clamp was placed over the joints to serve as a heat sink, as shown by Figure 17. A BernzOmatic propane/oxygen torch was used, as shown, to heat the nib to a cherry red color. It was then immediately quenched in water. This created a glass hard condition which should yield good wearing characteristics. Since stresses on the nibs would be minimal, there was no need to temper them.

Final Shaping of Nibs

Final stoning of the nibs was done very carefully following hardening, with continued checking by inserting the pallet unit between plates with the escape wheel. A card with more accurate drawings of the inner and outer nib radii was prepared, as shown by Figure 18, and used as a reference. The radii of the locking surfaces, particularly where contact with escape wheel teeth would actually occur, had to be correct to preclude recoil.

The desired nib thickness of 0.052" was achieved through constant checking with a dial calipers.

Achievement of .010" to .015" lock was a critical process. The pallet unit was located between the plates with

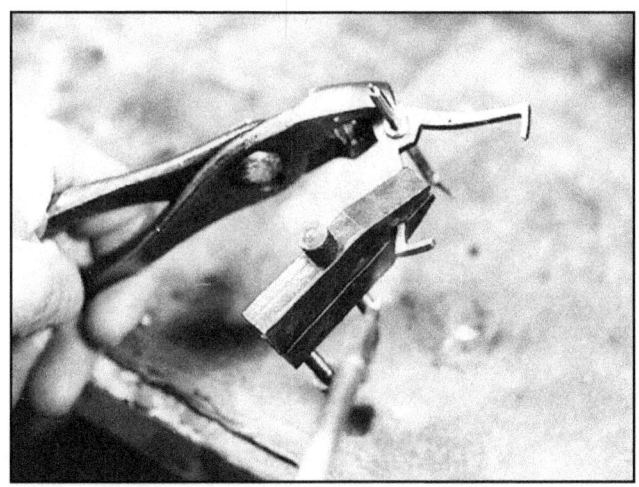

Fig. 17. Hardening the entrance nib.

the escape wheel. The tip of the exit nib was positioned at the diameter of the tooth, and the knee of the entrance pallet checked to ensure it was .010" to .015" inside of an entrance tooth tip. Review Tigner's drawing, Figure 5. Lock of the exit pallet was checked in a similar fashion.

Removal of material from the impulse surface was done with extreme care, with a slight amount of stoning followed by checking against the escape wheel. This was done after stoning the locking faces, to minimize rounding of the locking faces adjacent to the knee. By stoning the impulse surfaces last, any prior rounding during stoning of the locking faces was removed. During all impulse surface stoning, care was exercised to position the stone correctly with respect to the markings on the exit pallet arm. It was also necessary to ensure that the stoned surfaces were parallel to the pallet arbor. All stoning at this point was done in the direction of tooth movement.

Final finishing was accomplished with an Arkansas stone followed by 600 grit 3M Wetordry emery paper (glued to a tongue depressor).

It cannot be overemphasized that at this point all metal removal had be done in *very small increments* and the pallet checked against the escape wheel between plates.

Pallet Adjustment

The final step was to place the pallet unit between plates along with the escape wheel to adjust the pallet/ escape wheel spacing for suitable drop, lock, and entrance of nibs between escape wheel teeth. It is essential to understand how a deadbeat escapement functions and that adjusting to improve one parameter frequently has an adverse effect on another.

Appendix A advances the considerations in achieving suitable drop and lock with a deadbeat escapement by adjusting the pallet/escapement arbor spacing and by removing material. The Tigner chapter (Ref. 4) provides substantial discussion about the operation of deadbeat escapements.

To consider another factor, return to Figure 5. Note that if the exit pallet nib were to rotate clockwise without the escape wheel rotating forward, the nib would run into the rear of the exit tooth, especially with a small drop. The escape wheel moves forward only after release from the entrance pallet locking surface when the pallet knee rises above the tooth tip (lock release). Entrance pallet lock release, then, must occur before the exit pallet gets too close to the rear of the exit tooth. Thickness of the nib is also a factor in achieving adequate clearance with respect to the escape wheel teeth. With the smaller than typical pitch for this escapement, the dimensional tolerances were stringent. It was necessary to stone the nib thicknesses down from the design objective of .052" to .050".

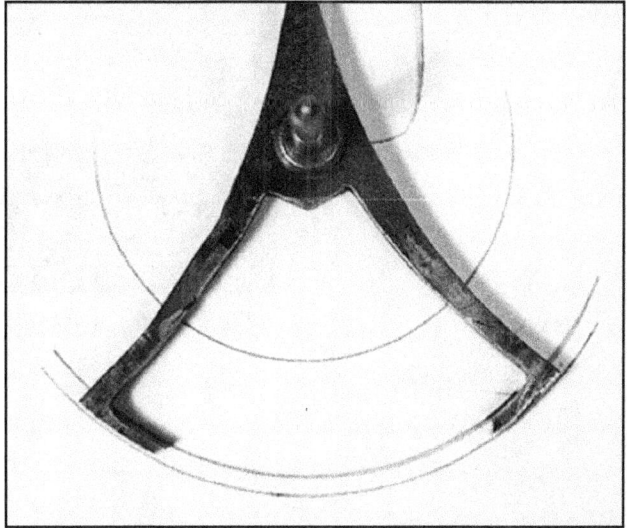

Fig. 18. Radius reference card for final stoning of nibs.

Summary

Figure 19 shows the completed pallet unit with a new crutch added. Note the extremely thin pallet nibs. The restored pallet unit is shown installed in the movement by Figure 20; Figure 21 shows a front view of the assembled movement. Performance of the movement was highly satisfactory.

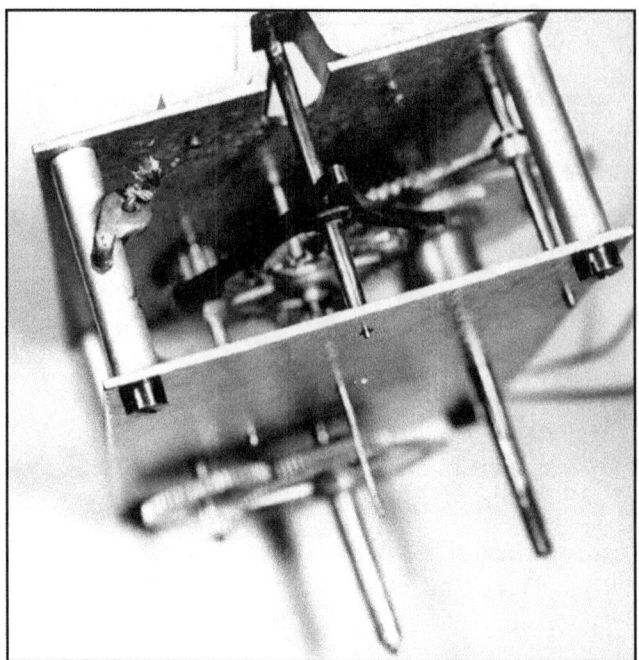

Fig. 20. Restored pallet unit installed in the movement.

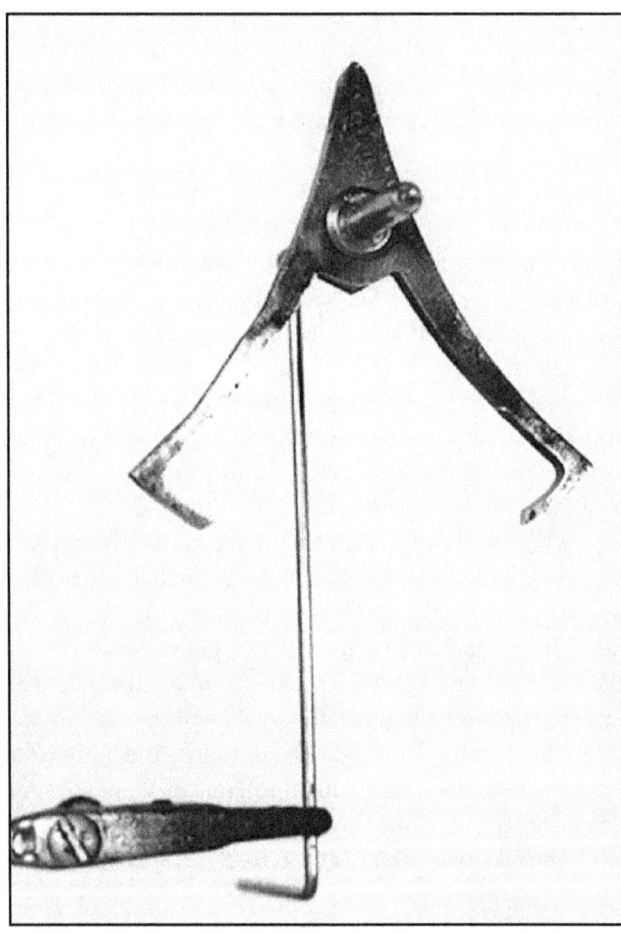

Fig. 19. Completed pallet unit with new crutch wire.

Fig. 21. The assembled New Haven timepiece movement.

Glossary

Entrance Pallet. Of the two pallets, the one which is encountered first by an escape wheel tooth as it moves (clockwise from the front, in this case) into the pallet assembly.

Entrance Tooth. The tooth acting upon an entrance pallet.

Exit Pallet. The second of the two pallets, which an escape wheel tooth encounters as it leaves the pallet assembly.

Exit Tooth. The tooth acting upon an exit pallet.

Nib. Tip of an entrance or exit pallet which incorporates the locking and impulse surfaces.

Locking surface. That surface of a pallet nib upon which an escape wheel tooth initially impinges, stopping rotation of the escape wheel. The pallet, with the tooth pressing upon it, rotates deeper along the tooth, and then moves out again when the pendulum reverses. The unique characteristic of a deadbeat escapement is that as the pallet moves deeper along an escape wheel tooth, the escape wheel does not recoil, or back up, as occurs with a recoil escapement.

Impulse surface. That portion of the pallet nib at the outer tip, which incorporates an angled surface. As the pallet rotates to move outward, the escape wheel tooth changes from contact with the locking surface to contact with the angled tip of the nib. The tooth can now move forward along the angled impulse surface, (the escape wheel now rotating forward), and due to the shape of the nib angle, pushes up on the pallet. This push generates the rotational impulse to the pallet unit which is transmitted to the pendulum and maintains its oscillation.

Knee. The point of intersection where the locking surface meets the impulse surface.

Lock. Usually referred to as the distance on the locking surface between the point of initial impingement of an escape wheel tooth and the knee. That distance must be sufficient so that for all escape wheel teeth, considering irregularities, the tooth must impinge upon the locking surface, not past the knee onto the impulse surface.

Drop. Free movement of an escape wheel tooth from the point where it is released by a pallet tip to the position where it is stopped when another tooth encounters the alternate pallet, and stops rotation of the escape wheel.

Impulse radius. A radius about the pallet arbor center, which when properly established can be used to define a pallet impulse surface. A line from a pallet knee, then tangent to the impulse radius, provides one means for establishing an impulse surface.

Acknowledgment

I wish to commend the owner of this clock. Col. Warren Botz, USAF, Ret., a former pilot with the Flying Tigers, who supported Chiang Kai-shek, General Chenault, and the Chinese Nationalists, for his interest and patience during the extensive restoration period.

References

1. *New Haven Clocks and Watches.* Page 145. case item #548; movement as described for item #549 and shown p. 146. Tran Duy Ly, Arlington Book Co., Inc., Fairfax, VA. 1997.

2. *Practical Clock Escapements.* Laurie Penman. Clockworks Press. Inc., Shingle Springs, CA. 1998. Pages 104 -116.

3. Jack Wyer is a longtime horology enthusiast in Centereach, NY who both collects and restores high quality timepieces. He has been a member of NAWCC since 1977. Mr. Wyer contributes to the quality of Tran Duy Ly's Clock Identification Guides by providing photos of clocks and movements.

4. "The Graham Dead Beat Escapement" by James L. Tigner, CMC. *Questions and Answers of and for the Clockmaking Profession*, Baier, Tigner, and Whiting. American Watchmakers Institute Press, Cincinnati, Ohio. 1981. Pages 169-184.

RESTORATION OF A NEW HAVEN NO. 1 OFFICE CLOCK

PENDULUM REPAIR

Edwin U. Sowers, III, CMC

The restoration of the New Haven No. 1 Office Clock (Figure 1) dealt first with the deadbeat pallets (page xx-xx). Now we proceed to the making of a replacement pendulum. Our final article on this clock covers the repair of the center arbor which was broken forward of the front plate (page xx-xx).

Pendulum Reproduction

As with the earlier pallet restoration, the objective was not just to make something that would work, but to generate a pendulum that was as close as possible to the original.

It proved difficult to find an example of an original pendulum. I was fortunate to locate Jack Wyer, (Ref. 1), whose clock, similar to that dealt with here, is shown in Tran Duy Ly's book on New Haven clocks (Ref. 2). Mr. Wyer furnished valuable information concerning the pendulum, as well as for restoration of the movement pallets described in the prior articles. In view of the difficulty encountered in finding an example to use as a reference for reproduction of the pendulum, I concluded it might be of some benefit to make available a description of the procedures and materials I used. The references at the end of this article include my sources for tools and supplies.

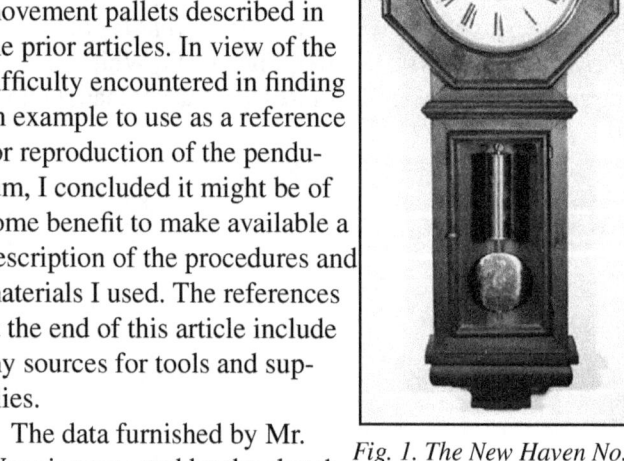

Fig. 1. The New Haven No. 1.

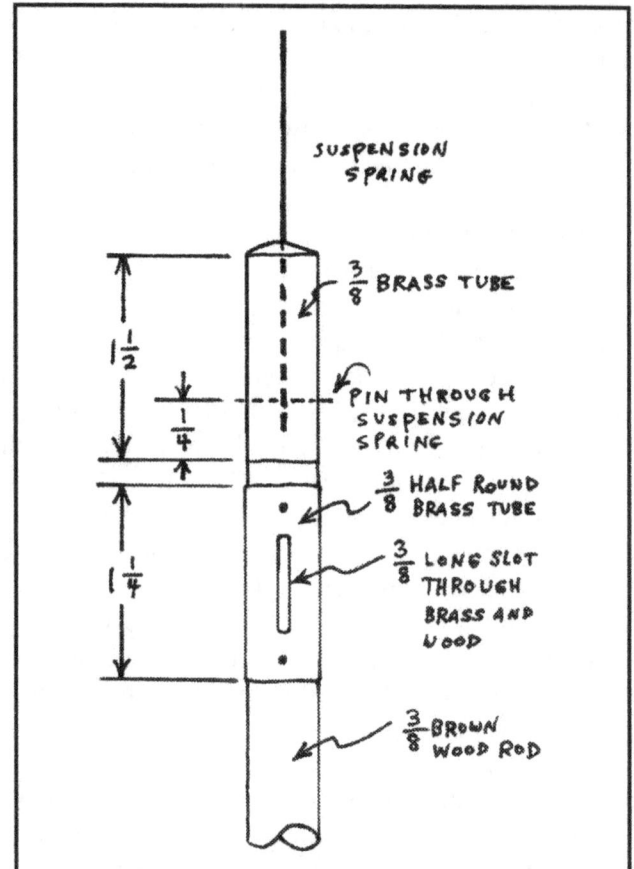

Fig. 2. A working sketch showing Mr. Wyer's data.

The data furnished by Mr. Wyer is presented by the sketch in Figure 2. Figure 3 shows the actual upper components that were ultimately fabricated. These include the tubular suspension spring retainer, the crutch wire wear plate, the suspension spring, and of course the rod to which they were attached.

The first step was to obtain a 3/8" walnut dowel *that was straight*. I ordered a number of 3 ft. dowels from Constantine. (Ref. 3). specifying that straightness was essential. I must here compliment Constantine for sending three very straight dowels, well protected for shipping. Finish was smooth, the diameter was uniform, there were no irregularities; a great source.

It was decided that the 1-1/2" long suspension spring retainer would be made up of two components, a piece of 3/8" O.D. brass tubing and a slotted cap. The brass tubing, obtained from Micro-Mark (Ref. 4) was item #60206 in a series of telescoping tubing. This tubing has been found extremely useful. The cap was machined from available brass stock. It was turned down to slightly less than the I.D. of the tube. To make it easier to follow the discussion of the fabrication of the cap, the completed part is shown by Figure 4.

The brass was bored with a 15/64 drill, slightly wider than the suspension spring. The slot was cut (Figure 5) with a jeweler's saw, making sure that it was cut down to the full diameter of the drill to ensure the internal slot width was wide enough to accommodate the width of the suspension spring. The cap was fitted into the tube and secured with Devcon (Ref. 5) 5-minute epoxy. The end of the cap was rounded off in a lathe with a file and cut off to 1-1/2" length, yielding the retainer shown by Figure 6.

This article originally appeared in the June 2002 Clockmakers Newsletter and is reprinted here with permission.

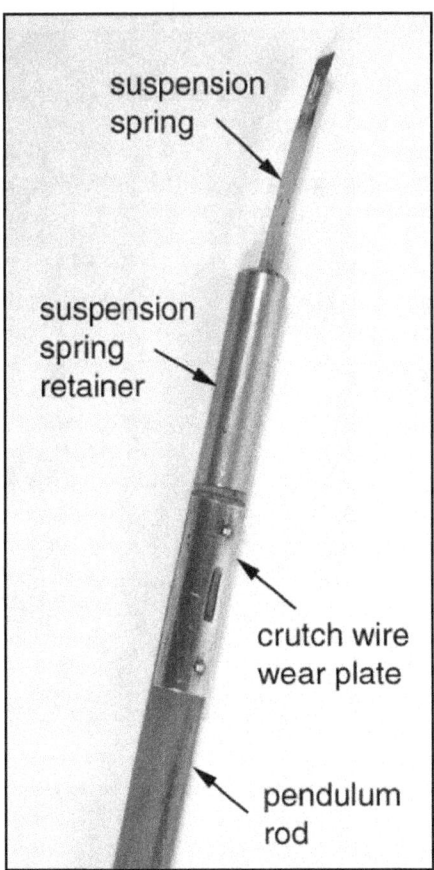

Fig. 3. The completed upper portion of the pendulum.

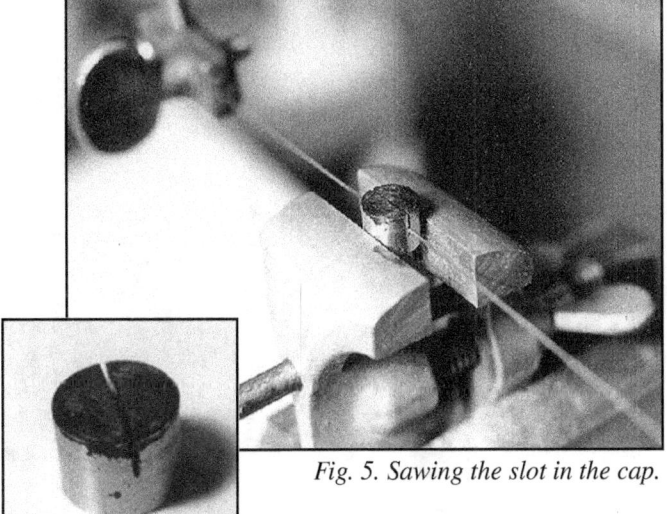

Fig. 5. Sawing the slot in the cap.

Fig. 4. Slotted cap.

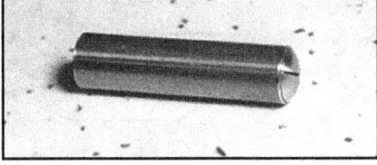

Fig. 6. The completed suspension spring retainer.

Fig. 7. Length of brass tube sawn half away to form the wear plate.

The second item that was prepared was the 1-1/4" long half round brass wear plate shown completed and attached to the rod in Figure 3. While the spring retainer was of 3/8 diameter and the rod turned down to accept the tube I.D., the wear plate was to fit upon the outside of the rod, both conforming to the original pendulum rod. Using again the same piece of 3/8 brass rod as for the suspension spring retainer, the end was coated with layout dye and scribed for cutting. Two holes were drilled to define the two ends of the 3/8" long slot, shown by Figure 2, and to provide an access for the later sawing of the slot. The rear half of the lube was removed with a hacksaw (Figure 7). Using a jeweler's saw, the blade passed through one of the two drilled holes; two closely spaced parallel slots were cut (Figure 8) then dressed with a pattern file. The wear plate was cut to length, cleaned up, and a small hole drilled in each end. This completed the wear plate.

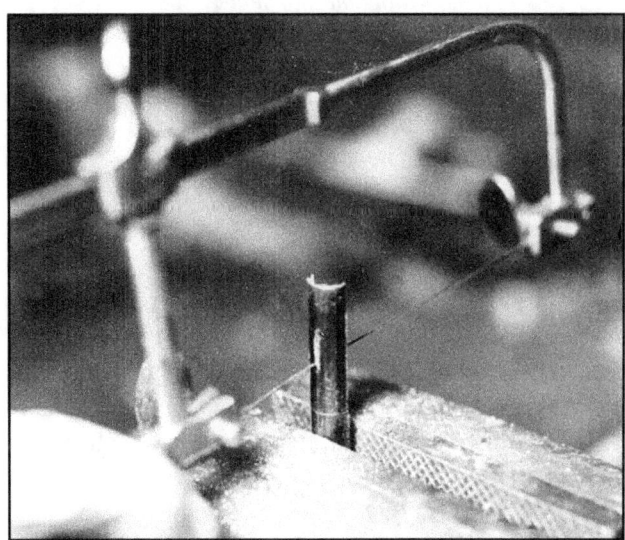

Fig. 8. Cutting the slot in the wear plate.

The next step was securing of the suspension spring; .004" thick, .230" wide, and 1.25" long (from the top of the suspension spring retainer to the bottom of the upward-bent suspension wire through a hole near the top of the spring). The rod was slotted with a jeweler's saw. It was very difficult to cut straight. I have since acquired a .013" thick backsaw. 1-3/16" depth, from a set of four saws, Part No. 35-140, by Zona Tool (Ref. 6); this should be a major improvement). A hole was formed in the suspension spring by laying it on the end grain of a hard wood block and driving a small punch through the spring. A hole was then drilled through the rod, and a taper pin was driven through both the rod and suspension spring. The spring was further secured within the rod with epoxy.

The retainer was slipped over the spring onto the rod, secured with a dab of silicone rubber adhesive. It is hoped that the retainer could be later removed for suspension spring replacement, should this be necessary.

Fig. 10. The new pendulum rod installed on the New Haven movement.

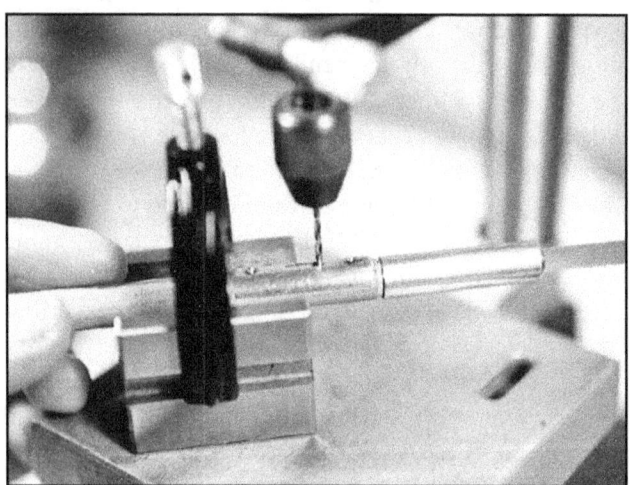

Fig. 9. Drilling the slot in the wood rod.

The next two steps, securing the wear plate to the rod and adding the crutch slot, were rather critical: it was necessary that the crutch slot be centered on the rod, that it be in line with the suspension spring, and *parallel* to it. The wear plate was placed over the outside of the rod, carefully centered and secured with two brass escutcheon pins. To ensure drilling parallel to the spring, the rod was secured in a V-block as shown by Figure 9, ensuring that the suspension spring was perpendicular to the drill table by positioning it against a square placed on the drill table. The slot was then drilled out, through the wear plate; perpendicular to the drill Fig. 10. The new pendulum rod installed on the New Haven movement table hence parallel to the suspension spring. The slot was dressed with a flat pattern file. The completed upper portion of the pendulum rod is shown, suspended from the movement, by Figure 10.

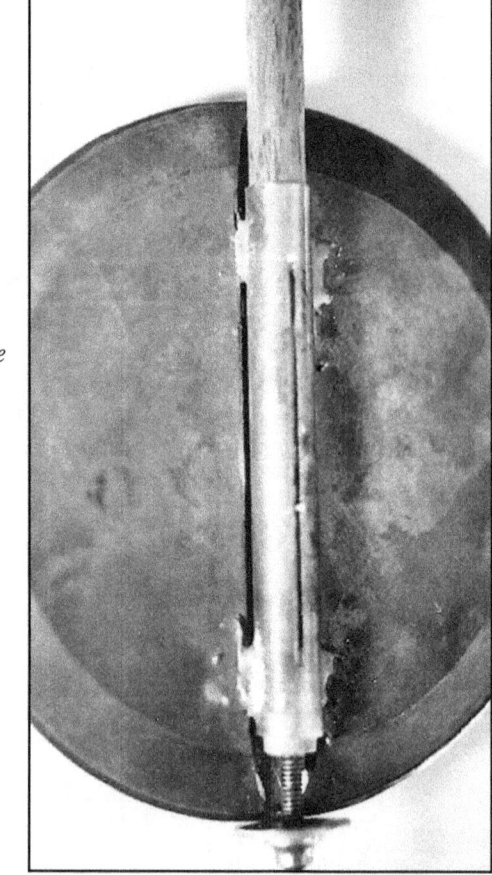

Fig. 11. The rating assembly was added to the new pendulum rod.

The final action was attachment of the original bob to the rod. The bob was temporarily attached to the rod with drafting tape. The rod was attached to the movement, and timekeeping tests run. It was determined that the bottom of the bob should be approximately 29-5/8" from the bottom of the suspension wire (which secured the spring in the pendulum support post). The original rating screw was inserted into the bottom of the rod and secured with epoxy, as shown by Figure 11. A pin was driven into the rod, behind the bob, through a slot in the mounting tube as also shown by Figure 11. This allowed for vertical adjustment and prevented rotation of the bob on the rod.

The completed pendulum is shown by Figure 12. Mr. Wyer confirms the pendulum, as defined by this article, does indeed closely duplicate his original.

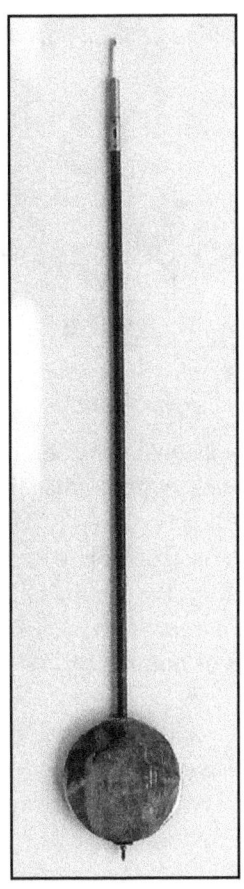

Fig. 12. The completed pendulum.

Acknowledgement
I commend Col. Warren Botz, USAF, Ret., for his interest and patience during the restoration of his clock.

References
1. Jack Wyer, of Centereach, NY, a collector and restorer of high quality clocks, provides photos for Tran Duy Ly's Clock Identification Guides. He has furnished valuable information assisting in the present restoration.

2. *New Haven Clocks & Watches*. Tran Duy Ly. Arlington Book Co., Inc., Fairfax, VA. 1997. Page 146.

3. Constantine, 1040 E. Oakland Park Blvd., Ft. Lauderdale FL 33334. www.constantines.com.

4. Micro-Mark, 340 Snyder Ave., Berkeley Heights, NJ 07922-1596. 1-908-464-1094.

5. Devcon, Germantown, WI 53022. 5-Minute Epoxy, item 14210 available at hardware stores.

6. Zona Tool Co., Bethel, CT 06801. www.zonatool.net. (The item was purchased at Sears.)

7. Dremel, www.dremel.com. Available at hardware stores.

8. Loctite Corporation, North American Group. www.loctiteproducts.com. Available at hardware stores.

RESTORATION OF A NEW HAVEN NO. 1 OFFICE CLOCK
CENTER ARBOR REPAIR

Edwin U. Sowers, III, CMC

This article originally appeared in the July 2002 Clockmakers Newsletter
and is reprinted here with permission.

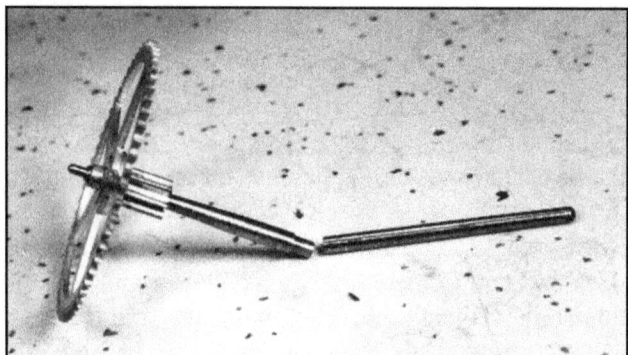

Fig. 1. The broken New Haven center arbor.

This article covers center arbor repairs to a New Haven No. 1 Office Clock. Two other repairs to this clock, also presented in this book, were escapement and pendulum repairs.

The center arbor on which, of course, the hands are located, was broken off immediately forward of the front plate, where a hole had been drilled through the arbor for a pin to position a hand clutch spring. The broken arbor is shown by Figure 1.

The approach selected to restore the arbor was to drill out the ends of the two segments of the arbor adjacent to the break, and insert into the bores in the arbor a section of the shank of the same drill that was used to drill it. Fortunately the arbor was soft enough to drill without the need for tempering.

The drilling was accomplished on my Unimat 3 lathe. With each of the two arbor segments, the broken end was supported by a steady rest, and the opposite end secured in the 3-jaw chuck. A crucial condition that had to be satisfied was centering of the ends of the arbor in the steady rest. Figure 2 shows how this was accomplished with the rear segment of the arbor. A brass tube with a slightly larger inside diameter than the outside diameter of the shaft was fitted into the tailstock chuck, and the tube moved forward to fit over the end of the shaft. This established the centered position of the arbor. The steady rest was then adjusted to retain the arbor in that position.

With the arbor secured, the end was center drilled, and then drilled as shown by Figure 3. Three drills of increasing diameter were used. The drill was flushed with oil and backed out frequently to remove chips; the objective being to preclude wandering of the drill or oversize drilling. Prevention of oversize drilling was necessary to ensure the shank of the drill would fit snugly into the drilled bore.

Fig. 2. The broken pieces were set up in the Unimat 3 lathe and supported by a steady rest.

The relevant dimensional considerations were as follows: The diameter of the arbor adjacent to the break was 0.120". The final drill was size #47 (0.0785"), allowing for a 0.021" wall thickness. The hole was drilled to a depth of 33/64". The length of the pin made from the drill shank was 1/2", slightly chamfered on each end. This resulted in a pin engagement of nominally 1/4" on each side (3.2 times the pin diameter).

The drill shank was cut off to form the 1/2" pin using a Dremel tool with a cutoff wheel, as shown by Figure 4. (Dremel products are available in hardware stores.) Figure 5 shows the pin inserted into the arbor and secured with Loctite 609 cylindrical locking compound (also available at hardware stores).

A similar approach was used to drill the second segment of the arbor. The second segment was fitted over the pin and again secured with Loctite 609.

Fig. 3. After it was center drilled, the arbor was drilled as shown in the photo.

56 • Challenging Repairs to Interesting Clocks

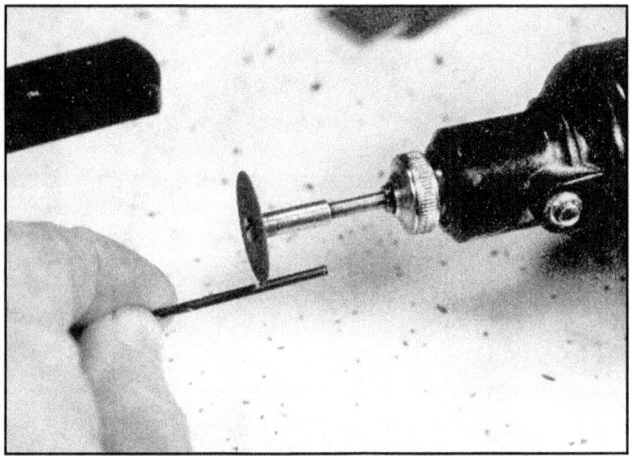

Fig. 4. A Dremel tool was used to cut off the shank of the drill that was used on the center arbor. This created a pin; each of the original broken arbor sections was drilled and slipped onto the pin.

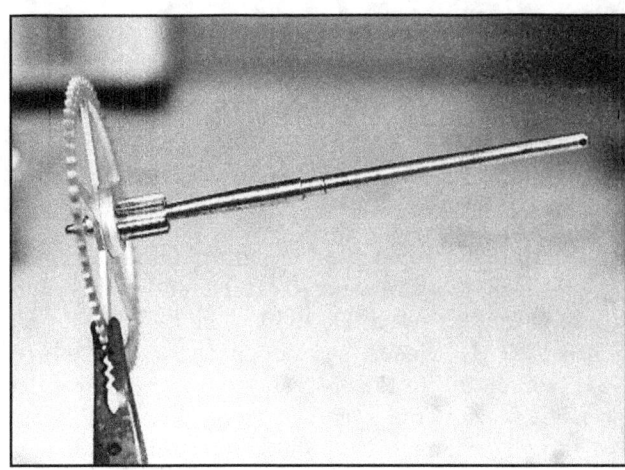

Fig. 6. The repaired center arbor.

The restored center arbor is shown by Figure 6. The joint was solid, with the two segments adjacent to the joint concentric within 0.001". The outer end of the hand segment, 1-3/4" from the joint, was concentric with the wheel segment within .007".

It remained to incorporate a means of positioning the hand clutch spring. The arbor was placed in the lathe again, with the steady rest. Using a thin screw head slotting file, I cut a shallow groove at the joint between the two arbor segments. It was important to avoid cutting into the pin. A snap ring was fitted into the groove. The restored arbor, with the snap ring and hand clutch spring in place, is shown by Figure 7.

Fig. 5. The pin, shown by the arrow, was inserted into one end of the broken arbor, which had been drilled to receive it.

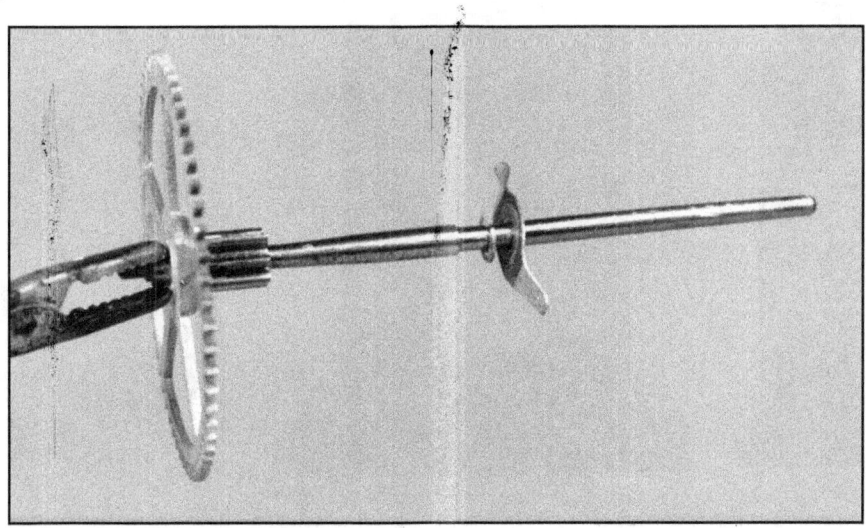

Fig. 7. The finished repair with the hand clutch in place.

The Ingenious Poole Clock
Edwin U. Sowers III (PA)

Figure 1. The author's Melrose model #20 clock.

Arthur F. Poole filed a patent for an "Electric Clock" on January 10, 1924, and received his patent on April 29, 1930.[1] The first patent was #1,756,472. He filed a second patent on January 6, 1927, which more closely relates to the movement described here. This second patent, #1,756,437, was also issued on April 29, 1930. The Poole clock is an ingenious timekeeping device. It involves an electro-mechanical concept that is intended to yield accurate timekeeping through minimizing many of the variables that can degrade clock accuracy.

With most clocks, the gear train drives the pendulum. In this case the reverse is true. The pendulum drives the gear train. When the pendulum swing decreases to a predetermined amplitude, the pendulum is given a sideways impulse to regenerate the amplitude. The only force acting on the gear train is that very small amount delivered by the pendulum through the escapement. With forces being small, no gear train lubrication is required. Friction losses are negligible and viscous losses are eliminated. There is then very little to detract from the accuracy of the oscillating pendulum.

The mechanism for providing an impulse to the pendulum, through the dropping of a gravity arm and resetting of the arm through an electromagnetic and spring return system, is intriguing to one who appreciates intricate electro-mechanical devices.

My Melrose model #20 clock, which is the subject of the photographs in this article and also my source for operational information, is shown in Figure 1. The dial is imprinted with "Poole Mfg. Co., Inc., Ithaca, N.Y., U.S.A." The serial number stamped on the base plate is 12451. Figure 2 shows a rear view of the case, which houses a stack of three D-size batteries that activate the electromagnetic mechanism involved in resetting

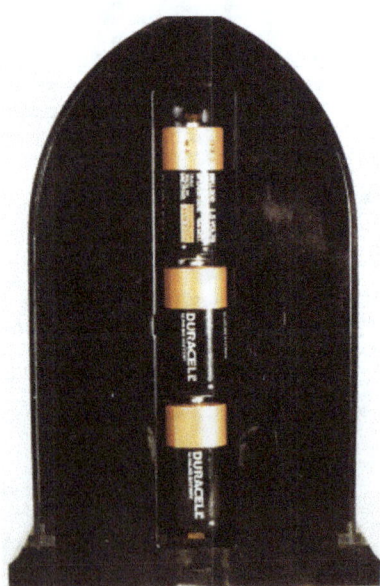
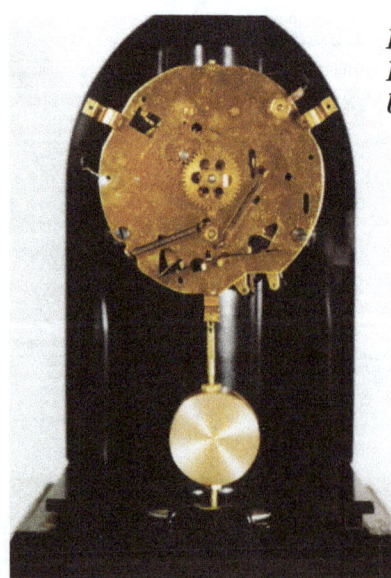
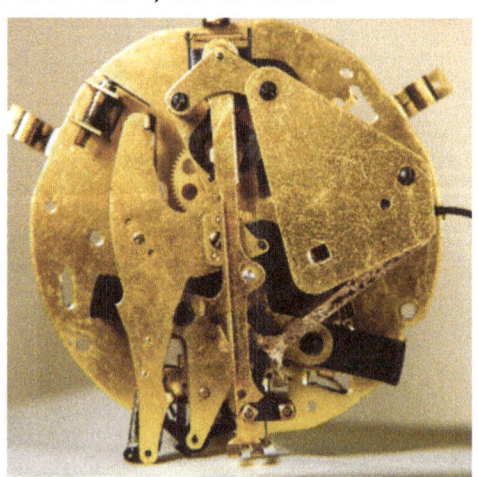

*Figure 2, **left**. Rear view. Figure 3, **center**. Front view with movement mounted. Figure 4, **below**. Rear view of the movement.*

This article originally appeared in the October 2000 NAWCC Bulletin.

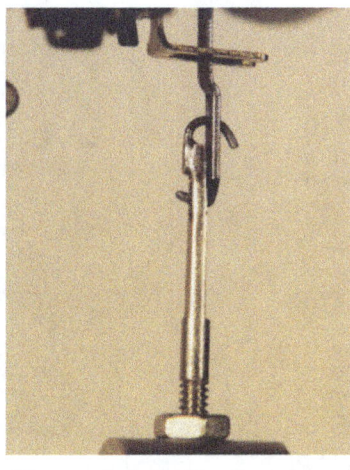

*Figure 5, **left**. Replacement pendulum. Figure 6, **above**. The interconnection to the pendulum rod. Figure 7, **below**. One of the pallets and the pin wheel.*

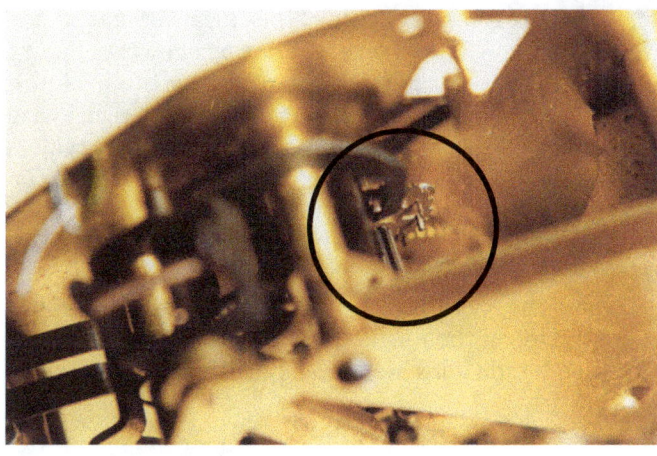

the gravity arm. Figure 3 shows a front view of the movement mounted to the case, and Figure 4 shows a rear view of the movement removed from the case. There are a number of models, some with noticeable variations, such as the use of two rather than one electromagnet and the incorporation of a different toggle than that which is described later in this article. However, the basic mode of operation appears to be essentially the same.

A series of clocks similar to the Poole clock was manufactured by the Barr Manufacturing Company after 1932.[2] The Barr Manufacturing Company was a part of the same parent company as the Poole Manufacturing Company at that time.

This article will describe the following:
- The timekeeping system.
- The gravity arm which re-energizes the pendulum.
- The reset mechanism and the sequence of events involved.
- The electrical circuit.

I have incorporated a section dealing with reliability and maintenance, including a discussion concerning non-lubrication of the movement. I have also briefly summarized some Poole clock historical information.

Timekeeping

The pendulum assembly of my clock was originally missing. My fabricated replacement is shown in Figure 5. The pendulum bob was fabricated from brass bar stock to a 1.57" diameter by .74" thickness, with a weight of approximately 7 oz. The threaded adjusting member was designed to provide for timekeeping adjustment, snug fit to the bob, and very tight interconnection with the pendulum rod. The interconnection to the pendulum rod is shown in Figure 6. It is essential that there be no play or looseness in this interconnection, to optimize conversion of the impulse delivered by the gravity arm into reinforcement of the pendulum swing.

The pendulum and crutch assembly are coupled to a pallet unit which drives a pin wheel. One of the pallets and the pin wheel are shown in Figure 7. The pallet unit and pin wheel essentially serve as the escapement, with the pallets driving the escape wheel. The angled impulse face of the pallet drives the pin wheel forward as the pallet moves into the pin wheel. The width of the pallet fills the space between adjacent pins and locks it in place. As the shown pallet rocks out of engagement, a pallet on the opposite side similarly moves into and locks the pin wheel. A pawl, which is located above the pin wheel, indexes on notches in the pin wheel periphery to ensure correct positioning of the pin wheel for pallet entry. The pin wheel pinion drives through a two-arbor gear train to the center arbor on which the minute hand is fitted, and which, subsequently, through the typical motion works, drives the hour hand. The first driven arbor incorporates an extension for a second hand. As noted earlier, forces are minimal. There was no indication of significant gear train pivot hole wear on the subject clock.

Gravity Arm

The gravity arm is shown in Figure 8. Viewed from the rear, the gravity arm pivots on the right side of the movement. The hidden part of the arm which extends to the pivot pin, is shown by dashed lines. The function of the gravity arm is to transmit a lateral impulse to the pendulum crutch when the arm drops. Figure 9 shows a 0.44" diameter impulse roller attached to the gravity arm resting on a 0.12" diameter pin on the crutch. When the gravity arm is released, the roller rolls down upon the pin as the crutch swings to the left and applies a leftward impulse to the crutch. The weight of the arm, plus a downward acting spring, pro-

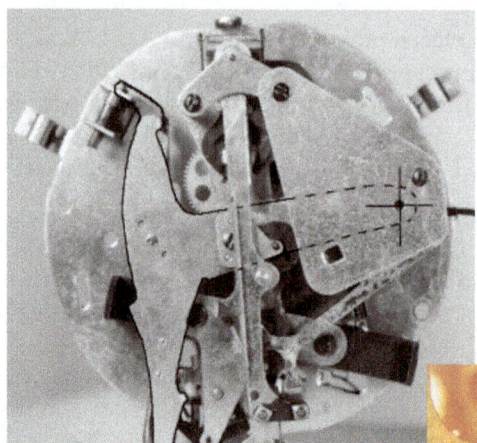

Figure 8, left. The gravity arm, rear view. Figure 9, below. Impulse roller. Figure 10, right. Armature and pad arm.

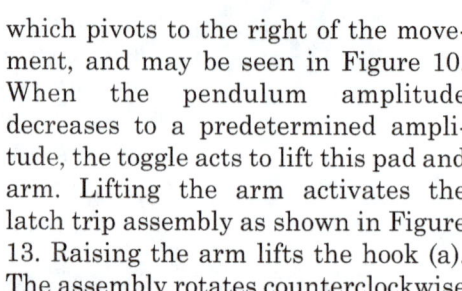

vide the force needed to generate the impulse required to rejuvenate the pendulum amplitude.

Prior to release, the gravity arm is held in its raised position by a latch mechanism incorporated into the armature assembly which is defined in Figure 10. The latch is shown in Figure 11. The gravity arm remains in its raised position until this latch is tripped.

The latch is tripped, and the gravity arm allowed to drop, by the action of the Hipp toggle[1] shown in Figure 12. The toggle is shown with its top edge contacting a 1/8" wide notched pad, which is a member of a long arm which pivots to the right of the movement, and may be seen in Figure 10. When the pendulum amplitude decreases to a predetermined amplitude, the toggle acts to lift this pad and arm. Lifting the arm activates the latch trip assembly as shown in Figure 13. Raising the arm lifts the hook (a). The assembly rotates counterclockwise about pivot (b), this moves latch (c) to the left, releasing the latch from the knife-edged tab (d) affixed to the gravity arm, thus allowing the gravity arm to drop.

The phenomena by which the Hipp toggle leads to tripping of the latch is as follows:

When the pendulum swings at its greater amplitude, the top of the toggle flaps against alternate edges of the pad and slides along the surface as it passes, the

Figure 11. The latch.

Figure 12. The Hipp toggle.

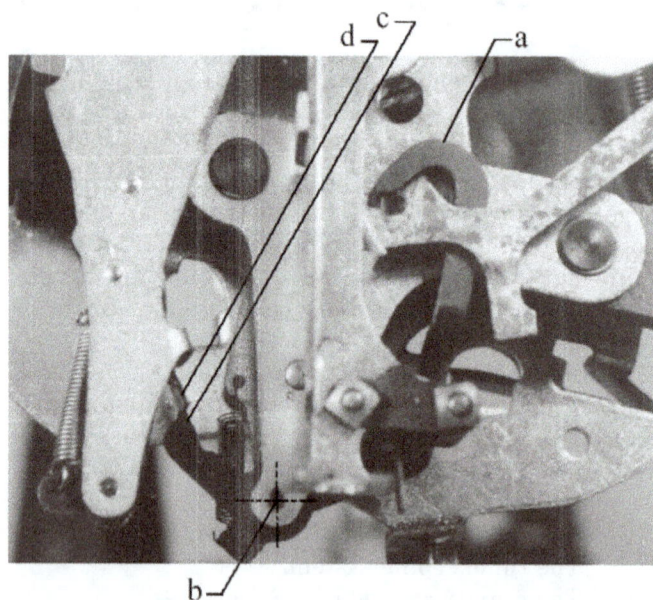

Figure 13. Lifting the arm activates the latch trip assembly.

60 • Challenging Repairs to Interesting Clocks

top of the toggle angling to the right when the pendulum swings to the left, and left when swinging to the right. The toggle is weighted more heavily below its pivot than above, so it will hang vertically in its undisturbed state. Nothing happens as long as the swing amplitude is sufficient for the toggle top to move past the pad on both sides. The top of the toggle has the shape of a knife edge; the left edge is ground at an angle, terminating with a knife edge on the right (viewed from the rear). The pad incorporates a series of notches along its width. Refer now to Figure 14. As the pendulum amplitude decreases, the case will occur where as the pendulum swings to the right, and the toggle top is angled to the left as it slides across the pad, the toggle will not pass beyond the right hand edge of the pad. The pendulum will begin to swing back to the left. As it does, the knife edge of the toggle will catch on a notch in the pad and, as the pendulum continues to swing to the left, will lift the pad as the toggle rotates toward a vertical orientation. Lifting of the pad will cause the latch release mechanism to function, tripping the gravity arm latch. The tripping action will not occur as the pendulum reverses from a leftward swing since the angled edge of the toggle contacts the pad surface rather than the knife edge. The toggle will not catch on the pad notches in this case.

Reset

When the gravity arm falls, a sequence of events commences that ultimately resets the arm to its elevated "reset" position. When the arm drops, the two

Figure 14. Toggle catching on pad.

*Figure 15, **above**. When the arm drops, the two spring-type contact points attached to the gravity arm drop. Figure 16, **below**. The electrical circuit activates the electromagnet.*

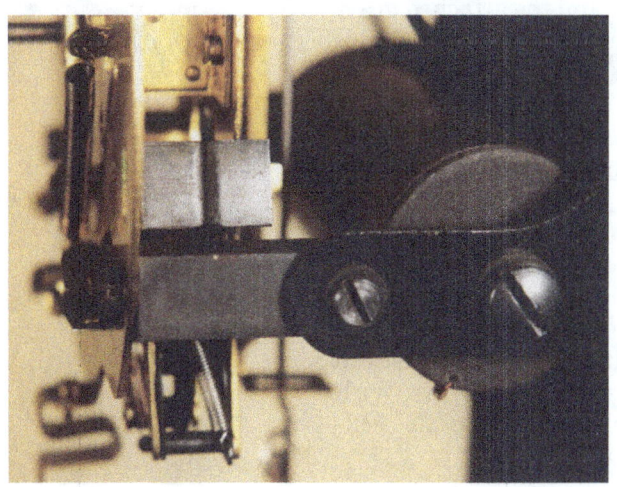

spring-type contact points, shown in Figure 15, which are attached to the gravity arm, drop and close upon the two contact points attached to the clock front plate. This stops the fall of the gravity arm, and by closing the contacts, activates the electrical circuit. It should be noted that the two contacts act electrically in parallel, enhancing the dependability of the reset phenomena.

The electrical circuit activates the electromagnet shown in Figure 16. The rectangular iron bar extending forward from the magnet is immediately magnetized. The left end of the armature (Figure 10), shown above the forward end of the left iron bar of Figure 16, is pulled down <u>vigorously</u>. The other end of the armature is similarly acted upon in an upward direction; the result is a strong counterclockwise rotation (from the rear) of the whole armature assembly about its center pivot point. In driving down the left hand end of the armature, the latch locks under the tab of the gravity arm shown earlier in Figure 11. Note that the end of the armature assembly incorporating the latch is driven <u>down</u> by the magnet to latch under the projecting finger attached to the gravity arm. <u>The gravity arm is then latched to the armature.</u>

Now looking at Figure 17, which views the movement from the front, an arm (e) can be seen projecting through the lower right part of the plate. This is a component of the armature assembly. Since now viewing from the front, this is now the right end of the armature assembly. The projecting arm is driven down <u>vigorously</u> into the leaf spring located beneath

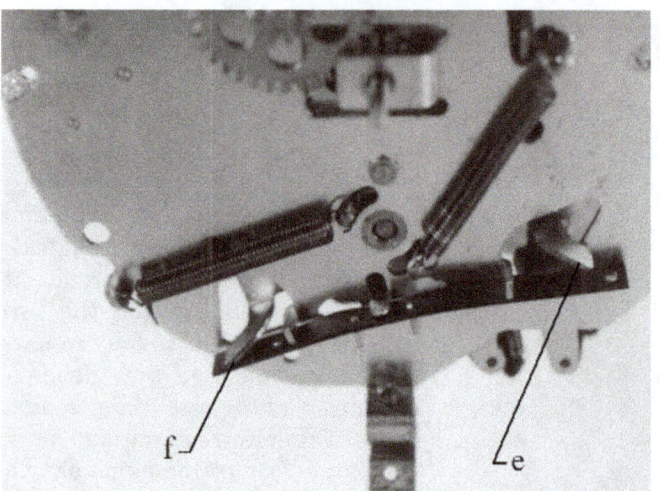

Figure 17. Leaf and coil springs attached to the front of the plate.

The Electrical Circuit

Figure 18 presents a graphic description of the electrical circuit. The lower end of the battery stack is connected to one end of the electromagnet. A wire emerging from the electromagnet is connected to the front plate of the clock movement, hence to all parts of the movement, with the exception of the fixed portion of the contacts which are mounted to the front plate but are insulated from it. The gravity arm contacts are electrically coupled to the movement. A wire attached to the fixed contact fastener nut in front of the plate is returned to the upper, positive end of the battery stack. The mounting of the contacts to the front plate, and the electrical connection to it, are shown in Figure 19.

There is no current flow through the electromagnet and no magnetic activity when the contact points are open.

it. This causes the armature assembly, and the gravity arm to which it is now latched, to bounce in an upward direction. This opens the electrical contact points. The magnetic force immediately ceases.

The two coil springs attached to the front of the plate, shown in Figure 17, are coupled to the armature assembly by means of two tabs projecting through the front plate, and act to rotate the armature in a counterclockwise direction. These springs, which had been overpowered by the magnetic action, now rotate the armature assembly to raise the right hand end of that assembly and the attached gravity arm. The armature rotates until the arm (f), extending through the left of the plate, contacts the left end of the leaf spring. This then stops and holds the armature and the gravity arm in the reset position. It should be noted that it is the upward bounce and the action of the two springs that lift the gravity arm; it is *not* accomplished by the electromagnet.

This then completes the full cycle which regenerates the amplitude of the pendulum swing and returns the gravity arm to its reset position. This reset state will exist until the pendulum amplitude again decreases to the point where the toggle trips the gravity arm. With this particular clock, the pendulum completes 38 oscillations prior to needing a "nudge."

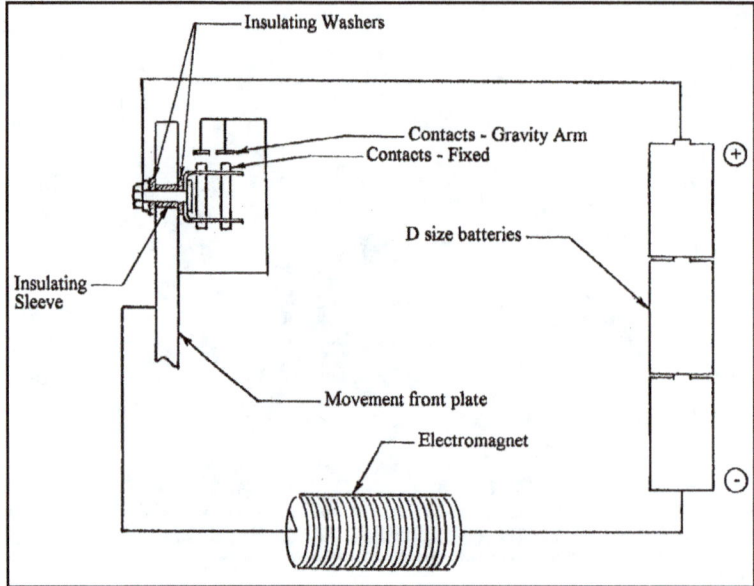

Figure 18. The electrical circuit.

When the gravity arm drops and the points close, the electromagnet is activated. The flow of current is from the bottom of the battery stack to and through the coil of the electromagnet and to the movement. Then through the movement to the gravity arm contact points, through the fixed contact points (insulated from the movement) and then back to the top of the battery stack.

Figure 19. The mounting of the contacts to the front plate and the electrical connection to it.

There is current flow and energizing of the electromagnet for only a fraction of a second during a cycle, and it occurs only when the gravity arm drops and contacts close. The left side of the armature (from the rear) is immediately driven down by the magnet, bounces up, (with the gravity arm latched to it) and opens the contacts, which discontinues the current flow.

Reliability and Maintenance

The Poole clock is a very reliable timepiece, particularly the later models with the Hipp toggle configuration described in this article. Grover[3] reports, "No strain on any wearing part of the clock...the Poole clock will last indefinitely, giving the same accurate, trouble free service month after month, and year after year." Advertising literature touts accuracy of 60 sec/mo.[1] Experience with my Melrose model suggests that following careful pendulum adjustment, this accuracy is approachable.

Grover[3] states also that no oil is required on the mechanism. Turner[1] states that "the moving parts should not be oiled as this will eventually cause undesirable friction." Steven Conover, editor of the *Clockmakers Newsletter*, reports the label of his Patrician model dictates in bold letters, "Important—Never Oil this Clock." The label of my Melrose model incorporates the same instruction. It is probable that the absence of oil is a significant factor contributing to the accurate timekeeping of this clock. While it reduces wear, oil also creates a viscous resistance to motion between two mating parts. This resistance varies with temperature and with the age of the oil, and will have an effect on timekeeping. This effect will be particularly significant where the driving torque which overpowers the viscous resistance is small, as is the case with the Poole movement gear train.

A series of articles covering the repair of Poole clocks is presented by Conover.[4,5,6] He also discusses the two types of Hipp toggles used in Poole clocks and presents further information on Poole clock operation.

Historical Information

Historical information concerning the Poole clock is presented by various sources, with quite a few inconsistencies. The following is a short summary as understood by the author.

The Poole Manufacturing Company began operation in Westport, Connecticut, in 1924, and in 1926 the company was taken over by the Morse Chain Company of Ithaca, NY.[7] Poole clocks were made by Morse until 1934. The Barr Manufacturing Corp. of Ithaca, NY, also a subsidiary of the Morse Chain Company, manufactured clocks similar to the Poole clock, under the Barr name, during the approximate period of 1932 through 1937.[2] The movements of the initial Barr clocks were essentially the same as the later Poole clocks.

Turner[1] presents an extensive study of the Poole clock history, shows photos of various models, and includes a discussion on the definition of models and styles of case by serial number. Bowman[8] expands the information relative to serial number, presenting an extensive list of models and name plate data related to serial numbers.

Acknowledgments

As noted earlier, Steven Conover, editor of the *Clockmakers Newsletter*, has presented a number of articles concerning Poole clocks. It has been my pleasure to share with Mr. Conover an interest in Poole clocks and to discuss with him their fascinating operating concepts.

I also appreciate the help Martin Swetsky, FNAWCC, President of the Electrical Horology Society, NAWCC Chapter 78, gave me in sizing the pendulum for my clock.

The Fascinating "Terry's Patent" Calendar Clock
How It Works

by Edwin U. Sowers III (PA)

Figure 1. Calendar movement only.

Figure 2. Complete clock with dial.

Introduction

How does the calendar movement shown in Figure 1, which looks like two wheels plus a couple of extra parts, and which attaches to a conventional 8-day count wheel movement, create a calendar clock?

It is the calendar movement of a "Terry's Patent" calendar clock. The inventor was William A. Terry, and the patent is no. 4219, reissued December 20, 1870. How did he manage to satisfy all the calendar requirements with such a simple-looking mechanism?

At the end of a 28-day month he deletes day 28, sweeps aside days 29, 30, and 31, and moves the large date hand on to day 1 of the next month. This is done by a "pusher" that is controlled by a cam on the back of a month wheel, which shows the current month through an aperture in the dial. It is this cam that, at the end of each month, determines when the month shall end; it then immediately rotates, ready to do the same for the next month. This is all done, of course, to establish each month to be of 28-day, 30-day, or 31-day length and to move on to day 1 of the next month, and all done by the simple-looking mechanism in Figure 1. I am fascinated by the movement shown and how it works.

There is another Terry patent for a calendar clock, but it differs significantly from the one described here. Mr. A. Lee Smith presented background information on the different clock models and their manufacturers in an earlier *Bulletin* article.[1] However, I have not been able to locate any detailed articles on the operation of these models, one of which I address here.

I am fortunate enough to have purchased one of these clocks. Mine appears to be the Type 1 shown by Smith. My sources for this article are the patent and examination of my movement.

My complete clock is shown by Figure 2. The dial and the month disk are excellent reproductions; see Figure 3. The month disk is displayed through the aperture in the

Figure 3, above. Dial removed showing month disk.
Figure 4, below. Clock with attached calendar mechanism, dial removed.

dial. All of the mechanical components appear to be original. As can be seen in Figure 4, the calendar mechanism is attached to an Ansonia 8-day American count wheel movement that serves to drive the calendar movement.

I first describe the movement and its components and then discuss how, with these components, the calendar movement requirements are met. Note that the calendar movement is not perpetual; it was not designed to deal with a leap year. I found it fascinating to discover how it does what it does. Finally, I present some testing procedures that were helpful to me.

Description of Calendar Movement

Figure 5 depicts the components of the calendar movement, with their operation briefly described in the following:

Day wheel (A) rotates one revolution per day, driven by a pinion on the center arbor of the clock movement. Long pin (C) (also see Figure 13) on the day wheel contacts a tooth on the date wheel (B) and advances it one tooth per day. The date wheel is rotated the number of teeth required to produce a 28-, 30-, or 31-day month.

A short pin (D) is also attached to the day wheel. It rotates under the date wheel and at the end of the month contacts pusher (E) (also see Figure 8) and pushes it into advance pin (F). The advance pin is attached to a spoke of the date wheel, extending a short distance below the spoke. At the end of the month, pusher (E) pushes against advance pin (F) and rotates the date wheel clockwise, eliminating the extra days beyond 28, 30, or 31. Tooth 1 is moved to the index position, and the date hand (not shown) is moved on the dial, past the ending date to day 1 of the following month.

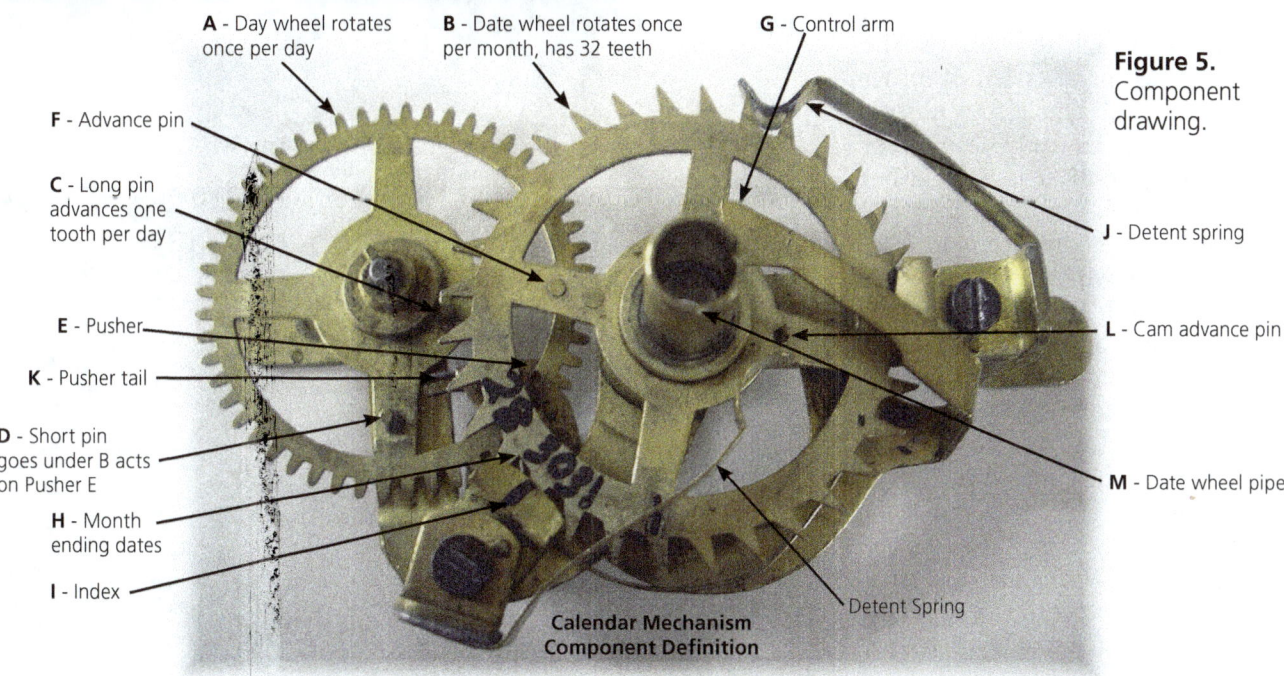

Figure 5. Component drawing.

A - Day wheel rotates once per day
B - Date wheel rotates once per month, has 32 teeth
G - Control arm
J - Detent spring
F - Advance pin
C - Long pin advances one tooth per day
L - Cam advance pin
E - Pusher
K - Pusher tail
M - Date wheel pipe
D - Short pin goes under B acts on Pusher E
H - Month ending dates
I - Index
Detent Spring

Calendar Mechanism Component Definition

Operating Characteristics

The prior section presented Figure 5, which shows the major components of Terry's calendar clock. The function of many of the components are described. The objective of the complete calendar mechanism is to adjust the length of each month to either 28, 30, or 31 days.

The key calendar components are:
1. The cam, on the back of the month disk, which defines what the length of each month shall be.
2. The long pin on the day wheel.
3. The short pin on the day wheel.
4. The pusher.
5. The date wheel advance pin.

How do these components, together, accomplish the objectives of the calendar mechanism? Probably the best place to start is with what happens first. (It will be helpful to follow along with the figures to understand the discussion.)

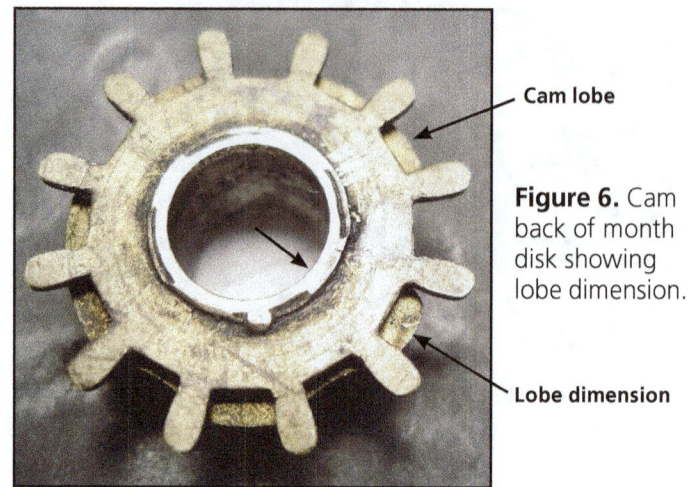

Figure 6. Cam back of month disk showing lobe dimension.

The first thing that happens during the transition from the end of one month into the beginning of a new month is that the cam (Figure 6) on the back of the month disk, establishes the length of that new month. It does that by establishing the position of the pusher E (Figure 5 and Figure 8) for the full month. It is the position of the pusher that determines when the new month will be terminated, which, of course, will establish the length of that month.

The position of the pusher is governed by the lobe dimension, which is defined as the distance from the cam lobe to the inside diameter of the month disk and cam (Figure 6). Basically, this lobe dimension is sensed by the control arm (Figure 7), which rests against the cam lobe during operation. At the other end of the control arm is the pusher, which is located at its ready position for the month (Figure 8). It is this pusher that, at the desired ending day of the month, contacts the advance pin F (Figure 5) on the date wheel and pushes the date wheel forward. This moves forward the attached date hand, from the ending day on the dial, to day 1, thus basically deleting the days following the ending date and terminating the month. The cam lobe is thus the controlling means of the terminating process—by initiating where the sweeping away of the extra teeth begins. Prior to the pusher contacting the advance pin it is at rest at its ready position established by the cam lobe.

Figure 7. Cam and disk on pipe.

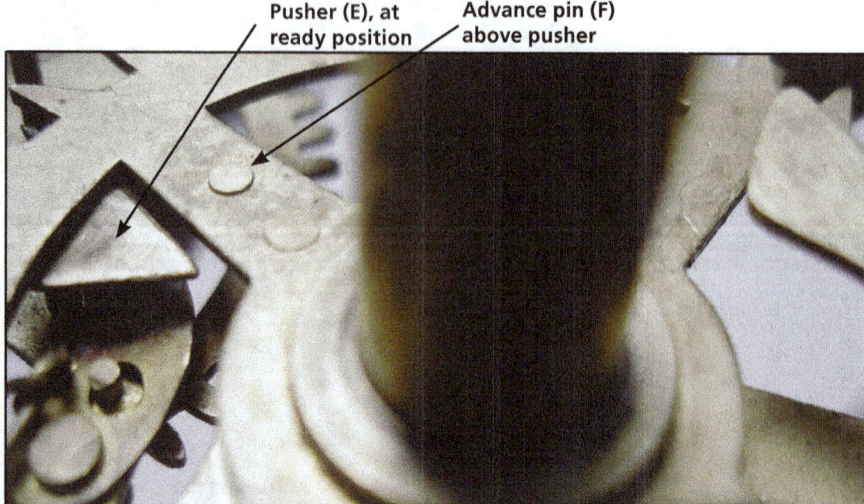

Figure 8. Pusher ready position. Advance pin above pusher.

The ready position of the pusher is located beneath the point where the advance pin (Figure 8) will be located on the ending day of the month. It is a 30-day month, it will be below the pin when the date hand has moved to 31, ending day 30.

Note that I have numbered the teeth on the date wheel that are involved in the month-length adjustments (Figure 13). They relate to the position of the date hand, which is fixed in position relative to the teeth. When tooth 1 is located at the index position, the date hand is at day 1 on the dial. The numbering proceeds clockwise from 1 through 31, 30, to 28 (the ending dates). Each numbered tooth, when located at the index, matches the number of the position of the date hand on the dial. Teeth 29 and 32 are not numbered; they are not month ending dates.

The pusher rests in its ready position most of the time during the month, waiting patiently for arrival of the date wheel advance pin, located on the date wheel. The day wheel rotates one tooth (one day) clockwise each day, slowly moving the advance pin toward the pusher. When the two meet, the length adjustment activity for that month begins. This is the big event, the basic purpose of the calendar mechanism.

Termination Sequence

Following this paragraph by referencing Figure 5 may be helpful. The long pin on the day wheel will advance the date wheel forward one tooth, as from 30 to 31. (Day 30 ends with the transition to 31). The advance pin has now met up with the pusher. It has advanced clockwise from below the pusher to slightly above it. The pusher is waiting in its ready position; it can now contact the advance pin. Now the short pin pushes up on the pusher and the pusher pushes up on the advance pin. The advance pin and the date wheel are pushed upward and in a clockwise direction, moving forward tooth 30, 31, 32, and 1. All of these teeth through 32 are now out of action. Tooth 1 ends up at the index. The date hand has been moved from 30 past 31 and 32 on the dial, to day 1. This all happens in a more or less continual sweep, within less than one revolution of the day wheel, upon which the short pin is located. Note that the date wheel has 32 teeth, with tooth 32 providing space for all of this to happen.

This basic sequence terminates all three months, of 28, 30, and 31 days, all controlled by the cam.

It is the short pin pushing up the pusher into the advance pin that terminates a month. A 30-day month, for example, ends at the end of day 30. At the end of day 30, nearing midnight, the long pin on the day wheel (which rotates once per 24 hours) moves the date wheel forward to 31. (Note that the end of one day and the beginning of the next is the same occurrence.) But the short pin, during the same continuing rotation of the day wheel, moves under the pusher and pushes it up. This is a defining moment.

If the advance pin is there (Figure 8) to be contacted, tooth 30 and all the remaining teeth will be swept forward, ending day 30 and the 30-day month. But if the advance pin is not there, nothing magnificent happens, the pusher will push up into nothing, and will drop back down to its ready position. Note: Proper relative positioning at this point is essential to satisfactory operation.

So the date wheel is designed such that when it is positioned for the end of day 30, the advance pin will indeed be there.

So how about day 28 and 31? At the end of every day, because both the long pin and the short pin are on the 24-hour day wheel, the long pin advances the date wheel one tooth and the short pin pushes up the pusher. During most of the month the pusher accomplishes nothing because there is no advance pin to push upon. But at the end of day 28 and 31, the advance pin will be at the same relative position to the pusher as was the case with day 30. The angular position of the date wheel and advance pin will of course be different because the end of all three months is at a different angular position on the date wheel. For each of the three-month lengths, when the month ending tooth moves to the index position and is advanced one tooth by the long pin, the teeth, the pusher, and the advance pin are all properly positioned.

There is a different cam lobe dimension for each of the three-month lengths. For each 30-day month a lobe with the 30-day lobe dimension must be in the cam control position where it will be sensed by the control arm. A similar requirement, of course, is true for 28- and 31-day months. The lobe dimension is defined as the radial dimension from the sensed surface of the lobe to the adjacent surface of the inside diameter of the month disk. This definition has been chosen to facilitate test procedures to be performed with the month disk removed, to allow a view of the operation.

It was earlier described how a month was terminated when the pusher and the advance pin were in the proper position to accomplish this. The pusher ready position for a given month does not change, and the pusher continues to be raised and dropped to the ready position each 24 hours by the short pin. But by design there is only one time during the month when the pusher can push up on the advance pin. Following the startup of a new month, the advance pin is out of reach above the pusher or below, so cannot be contacted. However, for the 30-day month (or 28- and 31-day months), the one time when the pusher can push up on the advance pin is when the advance pin rotates around to the one correct position where the advance pin is closely above the pusher in its ready position, and this occurs when one of the ending days is adjacent to the index. The fact that the advance pin is there to be contacted is a function of the design of the mechanism.

There remains another step to be considered; the month disk with cam must be shifted one tooth on the cam sprocket next to the cam at the end of the month. To accomplish this there is a spring-loaded pin attached to the date wheel that projects up through a hole in a spoke of the date wheel (Figure 9). It is pushed up by a rise in the surface below while the date wheel is rotating during the transition process to the next month. This pin contacts the sprocket and shifts the disk forward one tooth. The cam is rotated along with the month displayed in the dial aperture.

The timing of the disk movement is rather critical. The cam, at the beginning of the end (of the month) must still be at the original position for the pusher to engage the advance pin for the predefined adjustment made at the beginning of the month. After the tip of the pusher has contacted the advance pin and tilted the tip to the right so it will remain engaged, the cam and disk may then be moved ahead for the next month.

Considerations involved in starting the adjustment process have been addressed. Concluding the process must also be looked into. Every adjustment must end on day 1 of the new month, after starting on the ending day. As the short pin rotates upward and lifts the pusher, ultimately, the pin will drop off the left hand end (or tail) of the pusher tip (Figure 5) and the pusher will drop. So the short pin path and the shape of the pusher were designed so the drop-off occurs when the date hand moves into the day 1 position on the dial. Note that the tail of the subject pusher was sufficiently worn so that drop-off was not always correct. A small piece of angled brass was soft soldered to the tail location to extend it.

Testing and Evaluation

It is very difficult to examine the calendar mechanism to determine if its components are performing correctly, because they are hidden from view by the month disk. Determined to see what was going on under the disk, I took it off, removing the two 6-40 UNF machine screws attaching the calendar movement to the Ansonia movement and then carefully lifted off the calendar movement.

It was realized that in removing the month disk, the component establishing the length of the month, the cam beneath the disk, was gone. However, it was envisioned that spacers of the correct thickness could be placed between the sensing arm and the date disk pipe, providing a successful substitute for direct sensing of the cam lobe by the control arm.

The "cam lobe dimension" was measured as being the distance from the surface of the cam lobe to the adjacent inside diameter of the cam. This is essentially the same dimension as measuring from the lobe to the OD of the pipe onto which the cam and disk are placed. In either

Figure 9. Month disk shifting pin. Advance pin below pusher.

Figure 10, right. Measuring lobe dimensions.

Figure 11, below. Wooden spacers.

case, this dimension is sensed by the control arm and determines the ready position of the pusher tip. These measurements were taken with a dial calipers (Figure 10). Three wooden spacers were prepared one for each of the three cam lobe dimensions, Figure 11. The thicknesses used for each of the three month lengths were:

31 days 0.260"
30 days 0.210"
28 days 0.120" (difficult to determine)

Note that those dimensions apply to my unit and are

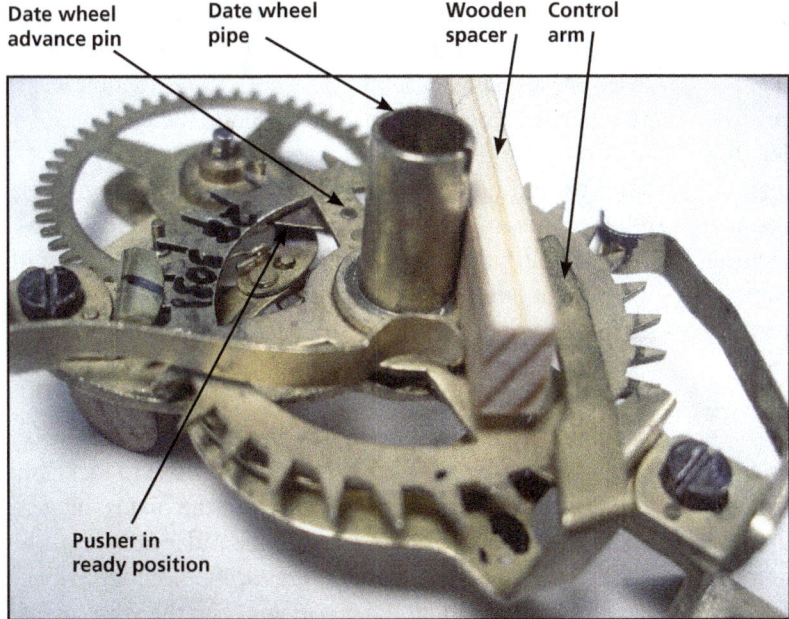

Figure 12. Spacers installed in calendar movement.

Figure 13. Tooth numbering.

disk. It is helpful to clamp one of the mounting brackets into a heavy vise to hold the calendar movement steady. Possible to check for:

1. Smooth and nonjamming rotation of the date wheel by the day wheel, with engagement of the long and short pins.
2. Daily advance of the date wheel.
3. Location of the pusher tip relative to the date wheel advance pin before the short pin engages the pusher; can check the "ready position."
4. Engagement of the short pin with the pusher following advance of the date wheel by the long pin.
5. Engagement of the date wheel advance pin by the pusher.
6. Satisfactory sweep of the date wheel by the pusher the full way to day 1.
7. Drop-off of the short pin by the pusher tail when the date hand moves fully into day 1.
8. Drop back down of the pusher after drop-off.

Prior bending of the control arm may prevent satisfactory positioning of the advance pin relative to the pusher as described in "Termination Sequence." Rebending to correct this is critical and must be done carefully. Ensure that the tip of the control arm remains in position to contact the cam lobes.

I am pleased to report that, by applying what has been learned here to the subject calendar mechanism, it is now working! I remain fascinated; William A. Terry was indeed an amazing fellow. The design of all the components and mechanical logic didn't just happen.

Note

1. A. Lee Smith, "William A. Terry and his Patent Calendar Mechanisms," NAWCC Bulletin, No. 335 (December 2001): pp. 777-781.

presented as a guide only. It would be more exact to take measurements from the applicable cam.

During testing the spacers were placed between the cam lobe and pipe, shown in Figure 12.

Identifying the month ending teeth on the date wheel is helpful in evaluating pusher action. Identify the day wheel hold-down clamp, secured beneath the base of the lower left detent spring and with a felt pen place a mark at the center of the width; this is the index point. Now position the date hand at the day 1 position on the dial. Identify the day 1 tooth adjacent to the index point. Identify with a felt pen, clockwise, teeth 1 and 31, 30, and 28, with 31 closest to 1 (Figure 13). Tooth 29 and 32 can be left blank.

Now, by installing the appropriate spacers and by rotating the day wheel, you can check quite a few operations. If the spacers are correct, the result should be an indication of what you can't see under the

USING THE BUSHING MACHINE
Edwin U. Sowers III, CMC

Some writers have presented a rather negative narrative narrative relating to bushing machines. I am experiencing highly satisfactory results in using a bushing machine, or tool, with the addition of some steps I have always considered essential. These steps relate to carefully filing worn pivot holes to reestablish the original pivot hole center, prior to use of the bushing tool. I would consider it most unlikely to achieve reliable results with the procedure described by Mr. Penman, where no such preparatory centering is mentioned.

By recreating a round hole, centered closely upon the center of the original pivot hole, the bushing tool centering point, and then the reamer, can be closely centered upon the original pivot hole. This then enables centered positioning of the bushing. Side loading, and the effect of "wobble" due to manufacturing clearance between the reamer vertical shaft and its support, described by Mr. Penman, are minimized.

The procedure I have been using with quite satisfactory results is defined below. It presumes the use of a Bergeon, KWM, or equivalent bushing system. There are obviously some variances where a hand held tool is used.

Locate Worn Pivot Holes

Before disassembling the movement, let down the mainsprings. Next, define the location of worn pivot holes. This is accomplished for each gear train by rotating the great wheel clockwise and counterclockwise. Note those pivots which exhibit significant back and forth motion. Check both front and back plates. Check again by similarly rotating the 2nd and 3rd wheel. Record in a logbook the location of worn pivot holes, as T3F (time train, 3rd arbor, front). This is a preliminary listing which will be confirmed by an examination of the pivot holes following cleaning.

Check Pivots and Repair

After disassembling and cleaning the movement, check all gear train components, including a careful inspection of all pivots. Where pivots are worn or bent, dress, straighten or replace *before* bushing. Clean and polish as required. In addition, correct any problems with damaged wheels, pinions, or arbors.

Inspect Cleaned Plates/Confirm Wear Locations

Check the cleaned plates to ensure pivot holes are clean. Inspect each pivot hole. Pivot holes that are round normally do not require bushings. Pivot holes which are noticeably oblong should be bushed. Escape wheel pivot holes are a special case; they do not always exhibit wear by elongation of the hole. This is due to the varying load caused by the oscillating escape motion. Escape pivot holes exhibiting any looseness should be bushed, especially where dealing with deadbeat or half deadbeat escapements with thin pallets. Confirm correctness of the list of worn pivot holes, modifying if necessary. This updated list now establishes those pivot holes which require bushing.

Mark Plates to Define Direction of Filing

Having defined the pivot holes to be bushed, the next step is to determine in which direction to file to reestablish the original centers. Reinstall between the plates the gear trains exhibiting wear, and secure the pillar nuts or pins. Rotate the great wheels in the *operating* direction. Note the direction in which the pivots move in the worn pivot holes; this is the direction in which wear has occurred. Make a mark with a felt tipped pen *directly opposite* from the direction of wear; *this is the direction in which filing will take place.* Disassemble.

Filing Worn Pivot Holes

Figures 1 through 3 define a sequence for filing a pivot hole to reestablish very nearly the original pivot hole center. Visually establish the amount of wear, **w,** as shown by Figure 1. On the opposite side, where the mark was made, file towards the mark an amount equal to **w,** as shown by Figure 2. The center has now been reestablished midway between the two ends of the elongated hole. A high quality round tapered file, 6" long from tip to handle end, and of a 4 or 6 cut, works well. Now round out the hole to a diameter equal to the width of the elongated hole of Figure 2, as shown by Figure 3. It is necessary to file equally on both sides to retain the center. With experience, filing to achieve the results of Figures 2 and 3 can be combined. The handle of the file must be sloped towards the hole center to achieve a straight walled hole. Do not make the hole any larger than necessary. It is most important that the hole configuration be optimum on that plate surface where positioning with the bushing tool centering point will occur. Dress the holes lightly with a countersink to remove any burrs. *This filing to reestablish the hole center is the key to correct positioning of a bushing.* It should be noted that high quality clock repairing is a precise endeavor, requiring care, and in many cases, good visual observation and manual dexterity. Such is required here.

This article originally appeared in the May 1998 Clockmakers Newsletter *and is reprinted here with permission.*

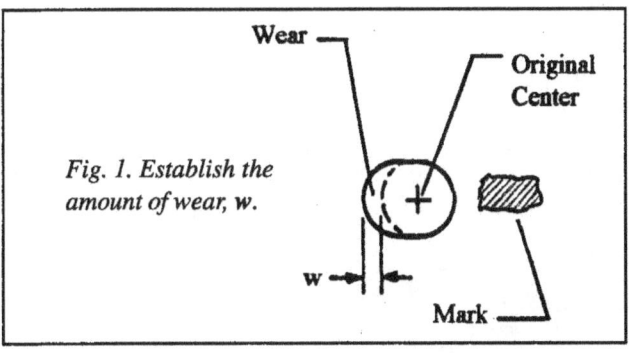

Fig. 1. Establish the amount of wear, w.

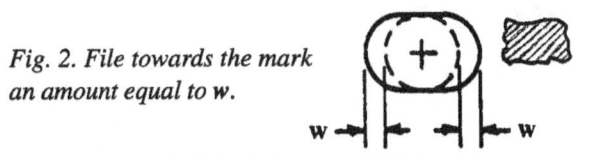

Fig. 2. File towards the mark an amount equal to w.

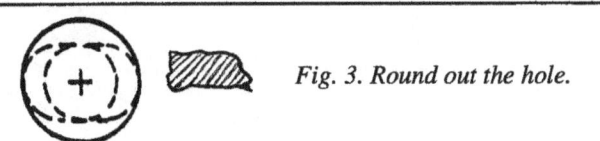

Fig. 3. Round out the hole.

Bushing

Following the filing of all holes, the plates can be installed in a bushing tool, and the centering point can then locate the plate for reaming holes which will be centered very closely to the original pivot hole centers. Reaming is accomplished without forcing the bushing tool vertical shaft sideways and initiating bushing tool wear. Additionally, the effect of minor play or "wobble" in the shaft upon position accuracy will be minimized. The procedures for installing bushings are well defined in many reports and texts.

Testing

Following bushing, each train where bushing has been accomplished must be checked. Install between the plates all arbors where bushings have been installed, as well as the arbors immediately preceding and following those arbors. Secure the pillar nuts or pins. Spin the gears to ensure free movement. Hold the plates horizontally and lift each arbor; *ensure that each arbor drops freely.* If the results of this test are positive, and necessary wheel, pinion, arbor, and pivot repairs have been made, the consequence should be a free-running movement.

REPAIR OF A CONE CUP SCREW
Edwin U. Sowers III, CMC

This article originally appeared in the May 2004 Clockmakers Newsletter *and is reprinted here with permission.*

My Seth Thomas lever octagon Locomotive Clock, shown by Figure 1, had suffered from erratic operation for some time. Timekeeping was irregular and very much affected by orientation. I expected the cause was internal wear of the rear cone cup screw[1] (Figure 2). The cup screw, identified by the arrow, serves as the bearing for a cone pointed end of a balance staff, on which are located the balance wheel and hairspring of a lever escapement.

An assortment of cup screws was available from a supplier. However, all of the threaded outside diameters were significantly smaller than the threaded hole in the plate of my clock.

Solution: insert a new, small cup screw into the original larger one, which did fit into the plate. To do this required

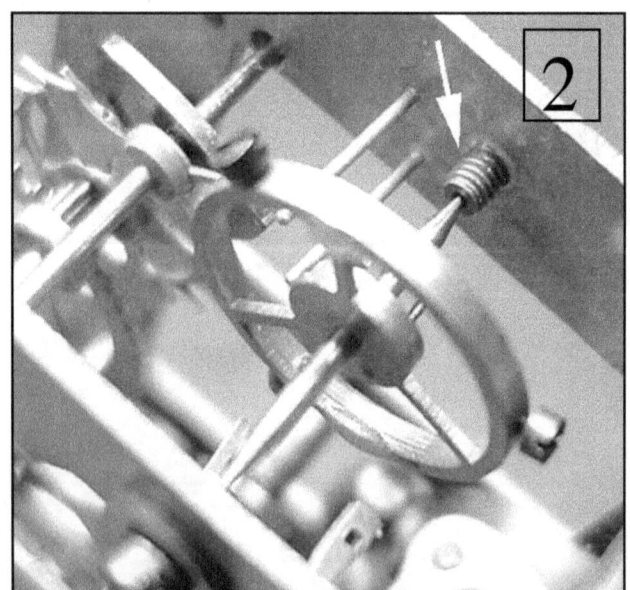

tempering and drilling of the original, reducing the diameter of the new one to fit into the original, and securing the new into the old. Figure 3 shows the original screw and the new one. The new one was included in the PM Co. Item C-226 assortment.[2] The cone ends of the screws are shown by Figure 4.

The new screw was not small enough for the full diameter to fit into the original, so the nut end of the new was ground down to a suitable diameter. Figure 5 shows the new screw mounted in the lathe, being ground manually with a Dremel grinding wheel. The screw was held in the 3-jaw chuck with a piece of slotted brass tubing placed upon it for improved holdability. The screw with the end ground down to .064" diameter is shown by Figure 6.

The original screw was tempered by placing it in a small copper tempering pan and heating it to a gray color

with a propane torch, Figure 7. It was checked with a file to ensure adequate hardness reduction for drilling. The screw was inserted into a brass sleeve, similar to that for the new screw, but larger. The intent here was primarily to prevent damage to the threads. In this case the sleeve was made from a piece of brass bar, drilled #28 (.1405"), the next larger drill size to the .137" thread diameter of the screw. It was slotted with a Dremel cut off wheel in the manner shown by Figure 8, to ensure compression upon the screw for secure holding in the lathe.

The screw was fitted into the sleeve, Figure 9, and placed in the lathe, Figure 10. It was drilled, Figure 11, to a diameter of .0635" with a #52 drill. This was intentionally less than the .064" diameter to which the new screw had been ground. The new screw was again placed in the lathe and carefully stoned down for a close fit into the original screw. It was secured into the original with Loctite RC/609. Figure 12 shows the complete reworked cup screw.

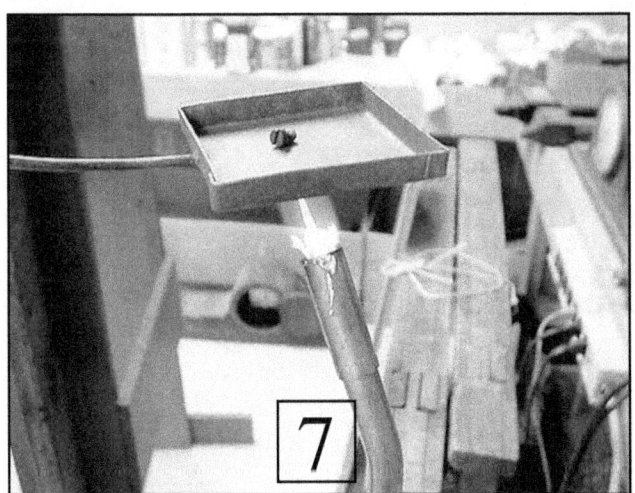

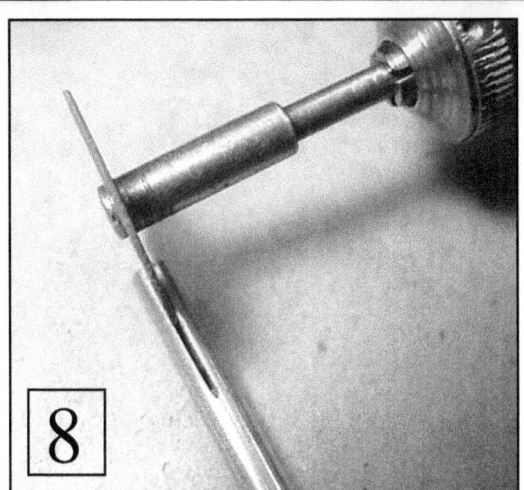

Challenging Repairs to Interesting Clocks · 73

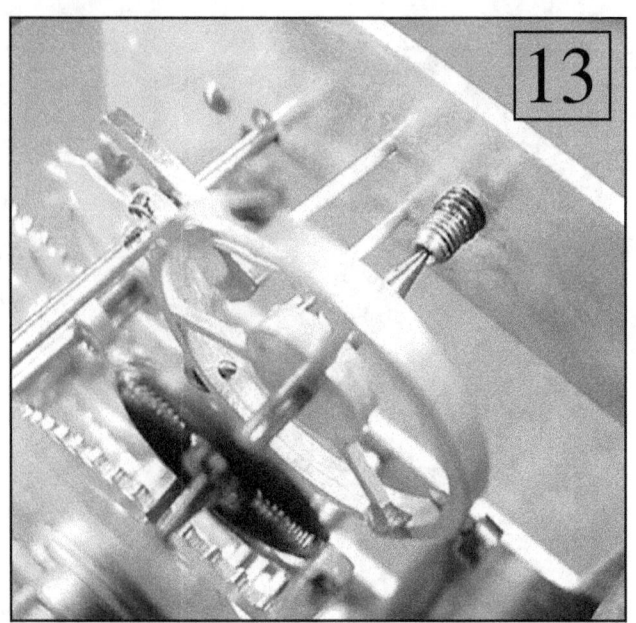

The reworked cup screw was installed in the movement plate and the balance wheel staff put in place, Figure 13. The assembled movement, Figure 14, exhibited the expected performance improvement, demonstrating the success of the repair technique.

[1] Laurie Penman, *Practical Clock Escapements.* (Shingle Springs, CA 95682, ClockWorks Press, Int. Inc. 1998), pp 161, 162.

[2] PM Co. of NY, Inc., www.pmclocks.com. The 25-piece assortment was still available in 2012 at $11.05 plus shipping.

CUCKOO MUSIC MOVEMENT REPAIR

Edwin U. Sowers III, CMC

This article originally appeared in the August and September 2003 Clockmakers Newsletters *and is reprinted here with permission.*

Cuckoo clocks are among the most common clocks in American homes. They are often treasured above more valuable clocks because of how they were acquired; sometimes through someone in the military service in Germany, or perhaps purchased during a family visit to the Black Forest area of Germany.

Quite a few include a music movement. A cuckoo clock with two, rather than one, door, and three chains can be expected to house a music movement and a colorful music man in lederhosen. Following the cuckoo sequence, the music man emerges from one of the doors and a delightful tune commences.

This article deals with the repair of the music movement. There are cases where music movements can, and should, be replaced, rather than repaired. Where teeth are missing, or the movement is severely worn, replacement may be the best option. There are, however, cases where a mechanically suitable movement is not available, or where a replacement for a present movement with a much desired tune cannot be acquired. In such cases repair of the music movement may be the only option. This article does not deal with repairs such as the installation of bushings, which are essentially the same as for typical clock movements. These repairs are well described elsewhere.

There are many different music movement configurations, different mounting means, and different control mechanisms. The more common types are dealt with here. While there are many variations, the basic principles of sound generation and controls are quite similar. The Figures presented are photographs taken of a number of different movements.

A typical music movement in a case is shown by **Figure 1.** The movement is attached to a mounting board which is secured to the underside of the top. **Figure 2** shows a close up of the same movement, with the sprocket wheel on the left which is turned by a weighted chain, and with the rotated pin drum to the right of the sprocket wheel. The cuckoo, behind its emergence door, can be seen immediately below the music movement. The music man, behind his door, is to the right of the cuckoo. A critical component can be clearly seen—the *music movement activation wire* extending from the vertical *music movement activation lever* on the right to the music movement on the left. The music movement activation lever is mounted within the cuckoo movement, and it is acted upon by that movement to pull upon the wire and activate the music movement.

Challenging Repairs to Interesting Clocks · 75

3

4

A typical movement, removed from the case, is shown by **Figure 3.** The sound generating fingers are part of a comb, which is attached to the music movement base. The fingers are positioned close to the pins on the rotating drum. The fingers are lifted by the drum pins, and when released, commence vibration, thus creating musical notes. The pins are critically spaced about the drum and act upon appropriately located tuned fingers to create the desired melody.

Figure 3 also shows a problem occasionally encountered: a broken tooth. This can seriously degrade the music, particularly with a music movement having a small number of teeth. Replacement of the music movement may be necessary. Steps will be noted to minimize the chance of this happening.

The following will be addressed by this article:
1. Music movement removal, cleaning and oiling.
2. Damper inspection and repair.
3. Comb installation and adjustment.
4. Operation of music movement controls.
5. Installation and adjustment of controls.
6. Conclusions.

1. Music Movement Removal, Cleaning and Oiling

Since a music movement is normally dealt with at the same time as the cuckoo movement, both movements must be removed from the case. There are, however, a number of steps to take first. Before removing the chains, and with the weights in place, activate the music movement. Listen for squealing as the drum rotates and the drum pins lift up and release the comb fingers. If considerable squealing occurs, there is a high probability that some dampers should be replaced. This subject will be discussed in detail.

Remove the whistles and bellows lifting wires and mark them R & L for reassembly location. The lifting wires can be identified on a piece of attached tape. Examine the music man to determine how it is moved forward and how adjustment to the timing of its emergence is made, should this be necessary upon reassembly. Remove the chain hooks and rings by opening chain links. De-couple the music man from his emergence door by bending open the wire hook attached to the door. The mounting of the music man and the emergence components, including the emergence cam to the right of the sprocket wheel, are shown by **Figure 4.** De-couple the music movement activation wire, shown by Figure 2, from the music activation lever by bending open the hook. Dismount the cuckoo by loosening the screw on its base and remove the cuckoo movement hands. Now the cuckoo and music movements may be removed. From this point on, attention is directed exclusively to the music movement.

The mounting board, to which the music movement is attached, must first be removed from the case, then the music movement removed from the board. Having removed the music movement, you can now clean it. A word of caution: while handling the music movement, *do not rotate the pin drum backwards*. This can cause serious damage. The correct rotation is such that the drum pins *lift up* on the fingers. The number of acceptable approaches to cleaning are limited. The reason for this is the need to prevent damage to the dampers attached to the underside of the comb fingers. I have found a soft inexpensive artist's paint brush dipped in kerosene works satisfactorily for cleaning, using it to brush dirt and old oil from moving parts. Hold the movement such that the contaminated solvent does not run over the dampers. Clean pivots, drum bearings, gears, linkages, and all governor components. Gently blow dry with an air hose, ensuring air is not directed towards the dampers. Make sure the chain wheel click works reliably, and that teeth are not stripped from any of the gears. Failed clicks can frequently be repaired. Stripped gears are not readily repairable. Check for wobble of the governor gears; if extreme, it may be necessary to replace the governor or bush the existing governor.

Use a good quality clock oil to lubricate the drum bearings and pivots, including those on the governor. I prefer the natural LaPerle Clock oil, but the industry has changed over to synthetics, and readers must use what is available.

I apply a small amount of Moebus 8200 Lubricant (Ref. 1) to the governor helix gear, where it is contacted by the drive wheel.

2. Damper Inspection and Repair

If no significant squealing occurred during the check before disassembly, there is possibly no need for damper repairs. If, however, there was considerable, and annoying, squealing, corrective action should be taken. It is appropriate to double check the magnitude of the problem at this point by rotating the drum by hand, in the direction to lift up on the fingers. (Sounds are amplified and made more readily distinguishable by placing the music movement on a cigar box.) If the presence of squealing is confirmed, and corrective action is necessary, the comb must be removed.

Before proceeding to repair of the dampers, it is appropriate to describe how they function. **Figure 5** shows an array of dampers. They are slightly narrower than the comb fingers, are securely attached to the underside of the fingers, and terminate flush with the tips of the fingers. To understand the function of the dampers, first consider what happens without them. A finger is set into vibration by being plucked with a drum pin. As a drum pin contacts the tip of a finger, it lifts it and then releases it. When released, the finger vibrates. Now if a second pin contacts the finger while it is still vibrating, the finger will buzz, or squeal, against the pin. Since a steel finger is vibrated against a metal pin, the generated squeal can be quite noticeable. Now look at what happens when a damper is present. If a pin moves up to a vibrating finger, it first contacts, and pushes up on, the damper. The damper isolates the pin from the metal finger, and dampens out any residual vibration. As the pin continues to push upward, it bends the damper around the tapered end of the finger, and ultimately moves past the end of the damper onto the underside of the metal finger tip. Since the finger is no longer vibrating, there is no squeal. When the pin releases the finger, the desired vibration is produced.

It is an excellent step, prior to removal of the comb, and unless you are fully familiar with the music initiation and stopping mechanism, to take close-up photos of the position of the music movement controls for future reference. Examine the initiation and stopping mechanism and clearly understand how it works and how adjustments are made, while the relevant hardware is still in place. Review Section 4 which deals with this subject.

Figure 6 shows the two screws which secure the comb. The screw on the left also secures the control mechanism, which will come off when this screw is removed. Note the clearance between the tips of the fingers and the drum surface. It will be necessary to reestablish essentially the same clearance upon reassembly. Remove the two screws and the comb. Inspect the dampers. Dampers are usually attached from the lowest frequency finger, with the largest lead tuning weight, through to approximately the end of the tuning weights. The higher frequency fingers do not require dampers since their vibration ceases before contact with a succeeding drum pin.

Figure 7 shows newly installed dampers, and, by contrast, what is frequently encountered. (The missing new damper on the left was removed due to unsatisfactory installation.) The old dampers show typical problems: they are worn, shortened at the tips, and are bent. Looking closely at the old damper tips, it can be seen where the left side of the damper tips have been worn away by the drum fingers. If most of the dampers are in good condition with few missing, only the missing dampers should be replaced. If quite a few of the dampers are seriously worn, bent, or missing, complete replacement is in order. To remove dampers, pull them off with tweezers. Carefully scrape off residual adhesive with a sharp pointed Exacto knife. Clean the teeth with alcohol on a cotton swab.

6

7

After cleaning, new dampers can be installed. The dampers on cuckoo music movements are usually thin plastic strips. The dampers I have used successfully come in sets of four, as shown by **Figure 8.** They are available from Nancy Fratti, who can be contacted through her web site (Ref. 2). The dampers may be removed from the set of four with a sharp single edged razor blade, cutting onto a piece of glass. There are a number of suitable adhesives. The one that has worked satisfactorily for me is Duro Super Glue liquid. Figure 8, not gel, and a new tube (Ref. 3). Applying the dampers is a rather delicate process. I use thin tipped tweezers and a thin pointed probe. Holding the damper with a tweezers, as shown by **Figure 9,** touch it to the tip of the adhesive tube, with a small amount of adhesive projecting. Immediately place the damper on the bottom of a finger. With the probe, **Figure 10,** shift the damper as necessary to center it on the finger, and ensure it is parallel to the finger. The inside end of the damper should fit up against the tuning weight, **Figure 11.** The outer tip of the damper must extend beyond the end of the finger. Don't let adhesive run into the spaces between fingers. When arriving at the final fingers to which dampers are to be applied, with the smaller tuning weights, a bit of ingenuity may be required. Be sure each damper remains in position until the glue is set.

After all the dampers are applied, looking like those to the right on Figure 11, and with the glue thoroughly set, the tips must be trimmed. Lay the ends of the fingers on a piece of glass, top side up, with the ends of the fingers only extending over the edge onto the glass. The dampers, on the bottom of the fingers, must be laying flat on the glass. Holding the comb in that position, cut down with a new, sharp, single-edged razor blade, held against the ends of the fingers, and perpendicular to them, **Figure 12.** Cut off all the damper ends. The finished job should look like **Figure 13,** with the tips of the dampers even with the tips of the fingers.

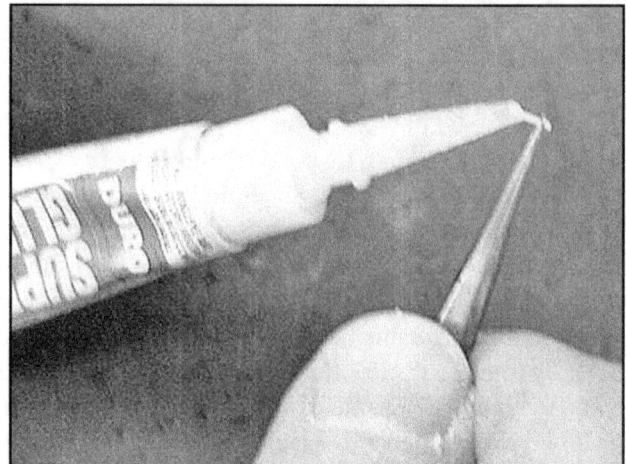
9

3. Comb Installation and Adjustment

The comb with its repaired dampers can now be replaced. A 4 or 5 power eye loupe, with a head spring to hold it in place, and a good light source, are extremely helpful in adjusting the comb.

Replace the two screws, with no attached control components. Lightly tighten down on the two screws. Tap on the comb heel, (solid rear of the comb), on both ends, and on the sides of the comb heel (not on the fingers), with a light hammer, as a clockmaker's staking hammer, to bring the fingers close to the pins and centered upon them. Make sure the lowest frequency finger faces the last pin on that end of the drum. It will probably be necessary to adjust the screw tightness during the process. Now, through a careful process of tapping the comb heel, move the comb in to where the fingers are lightly plucked when the drum is rotated (lifting up on the fingers only).

Adjustment now becomes more critical. The two screws should be rather snug, so that light taps with the hammer cause very small comb movements. Continue to minutely move the comb inward. Frequently rotate the drum slowly and listen to ensure that high frequency notes and low frequency notes are compatible, and that all of the notes are being played. The lower notes should sound somewhat louder than the higher ones. Tapping on the sides of the comb heel

8

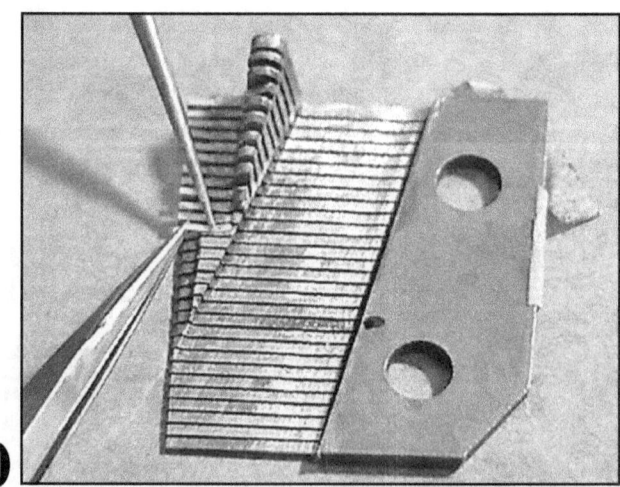
10

may be necessary to keep the pins centered on the fingers. Be aware that tapping on the rear of the right side will slightly rotate the comb and shift the finger tips to the left, and vice versa.

Be sure the fingers are not being lifted excessively. It is not unusual to move the comb in too far, at which point the screws must be loosened, the comb moved back, and the process resumed.

A few comments can be made concerning comb adjustment. If the comb fingers are moved in too far relative to the pins, the fingers will be lifted too high before release; the sound will be harsh, the torque required to rotate the pin drum will be excessive, and finger breakage will ultimately occur. If the fingers are not moved in sufficiently, the tune will be weak and uneven, with probably some notes missing. Achieving a satisfactory adjustment is very much a matter of judgment.

When satisfied with the results, firmly tighten both screws. Rotate the drum to be sure tightening did not affect the setting. While this process has proven satisfactory for me, there may well be other successful approaches.

4. Operation of Music Movement Controls

To be able to install and adjust the music movement controls, it is essential to first understand how they work. This will be discussed by the following.

The best place to start is with the means by which the music movement is stopped. The drum has a hole (in some cases two), in the end of it. A stop hook drops into this hole as the drum rotates, **Figure 14.** (There is usually a groove, or some other means to guide the hook into the hole). With the shown stopping mechanism, this does not, in itself, stop the music movement. The drum continues to rotate with the stop hook in the hole, and pulls the hook along with it. Connected to this hook is a mounting bar to which a stop finger is attached. The stop finger is pulled upon until it moves forward into the path of the rotating fly; *this stops the movement,* as evident from **Figure 15.** The feature which allows the hook to pull the stop finger forward is the slot in the mounting bar, Figure 14. The mounting bar is secured by a shoulder screw passing down through the slot (shown by the arrow in Figure 14). The slot allows for a limited travel. A

11

14

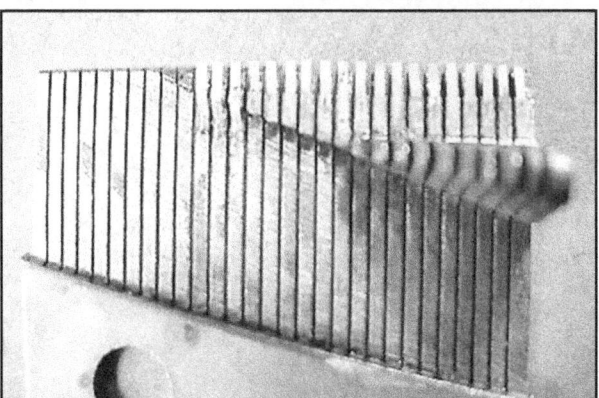
12
13

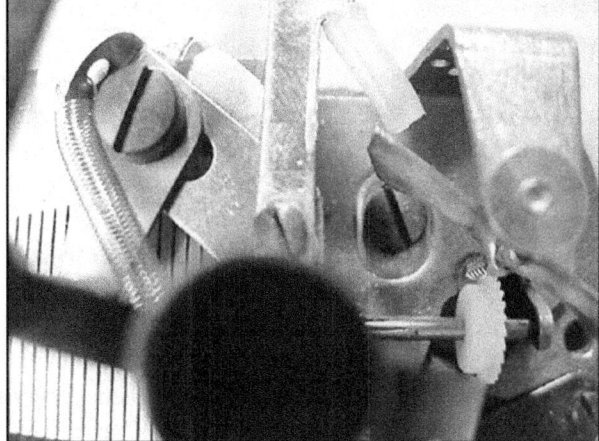
15

common, and simpler, music movement control is shown by Figure 3. Here the mounting of the controls is fixed-pivoted; the stop hook is not pulled upon by the drum hole. When the stop hook drops into the hole, the stop finger is immediately rotated into the fly and stops drum rotation.

Starting the movement requires that the stop hook be pulled out of the drum hole and the stop finger moved away from the fly. Looking back at Figure 2, the music movement *activation lever* is shown, along with the activation wire attached to it. The other end of the wire is attached to the music movement *unlocking lever,* shown extending towards the top of Figure 3. As can be seen by this Figure, pulling to the left upon the unlocking lever pulls the stop hook out of the drum hole and the stop finger out of the path of the fly.

Now, the music activation lever which implements the unlocking sequence is attached to the arbor of the *cuckoo movement lifting lever.* When the lifting lever is raised to initiate cuckoo warning, the activation lever is rotated with the arbor, it pulls upon the activation wire and the unlocking lever; the stop hook is pulled from the drum hole, and the stop finger is rotated out of the path of the fly. This unlocking, then, occurs at the same time as cuckoo warning, the beginning of the cuckoo cycle.

When the lifting lever drops, the unlocking lever and the stop hook are released. The hook is spring loaded, so it snaps back against the drum, adjacent to the hole. (In the case of the slotted mounting bar, the hook is also pulled back from the hole.) In this state, the stop finger remains removed from the path of the fly.

Since the music movement stop hook and stop finger are disengaged at the beginning of the cuckoo cycle, at the initiation of cuckoo warning, and the start up of the music movement is to commence at the end of the cuckoo cycle, there must be a means to inhibit the unlocked music movement until the cuckoo cycle is completed. The mechanical logic here is ingenious. This inhibiting is accomplished by a wire attached to the *rack hook arbor.* When the rack hook is raised, the wire is rotated into the path of the fly, **Figure 16.** Consider the action of the rack hook. It is raised by the lifting lever, hence lifted at the same time as the stop hook is pulled and the locking finger releases the fly. The rack hook remains raised during the cuckoo cycle (resting upon the rack), with the wire inhibiting the fly, then drops at the end of the cycle, when it falls off the end of the rack. Drop of the rack hook causes the wire to move out of the path of the fly, permitting the drum to rotate. So, at the end of the cuckoo cycle, the music movement commences operation, as is desired.

5. Installation and Adjustment of Controls

Following the previously described repair and adjustment of the comb, the controls may be replaced and adjusted. The controls are secured by the left hand (low frequency) comb screw. Ensure that the right hand (high frequency) screw is *tight,* to ensure the comb remains fixed. Then remove

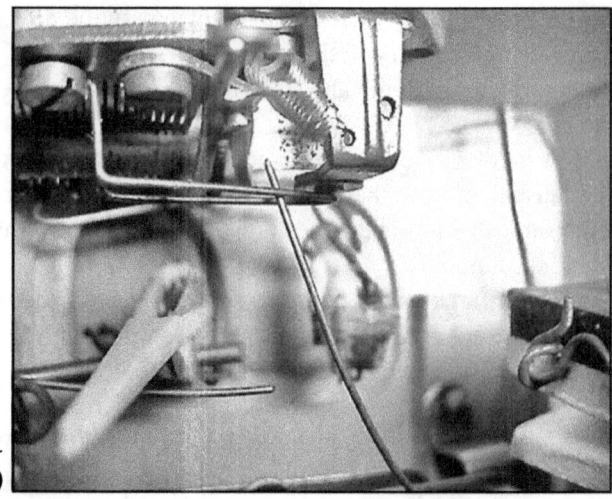

the left hand comb screw. Mount the control bracket, with attached spring, **Figure 17,** replace the screw and lightly tighten it. Now is the time when understanding the operation of the controls becomes important.

The bracket, secured by the left hand screw, supports the stop hook and mounting bar with the stop finger attached to it. The bracket must be positioned so that while the drum is rotating, the spring-loaded stop hook must drop into the drum hole, the hole must pull the hook and bar forward, simultaneously moving the finger into the path of the fly, and must do this before the hook runs out of allowable travel. If the hook runs out of travel, and it stops the drum, the hook will be jammed in the hole and cannot be pulled out to again release the drum. *It is the finger interfering with the fly which must stop the drum.* With a fixed-pivoted control, the bracket must be adjusted so the spring-loaded stop hook drops fully into the hole and the stop finger rotates into the path of the fly. Note: The controls must be adjusted to stop the drum immediately following the end of the tune. There is a pin-free section of the drum which precedes the beginning of the tune; this allows for start-up of the movement before pins are encountered.

For initiation of drum rotation, pulling upon the unlocking lever must pull the stop hook out of the drum hole. It is essential that the spring attached to the stop hook (Figure 17), functions to accomplish the following: When the

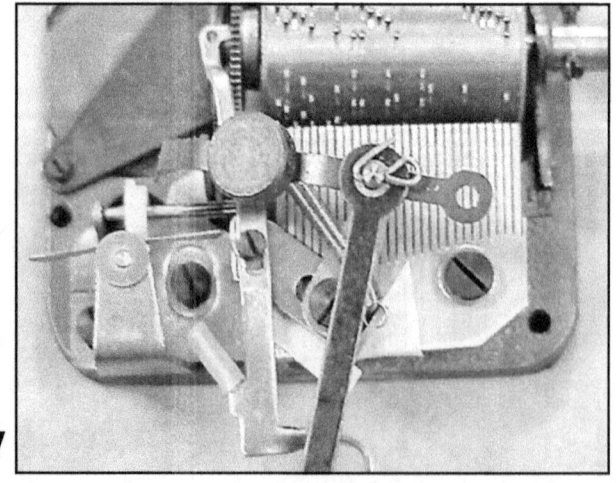

unlocking lever is released, the stop hook must snap back against the end of the drum. The hook must end up to the side of the hole, or back of it; *it must not fall back into the hole.* In the case of the slotted mounting bar, the bar must also be snapped backwards, within the limits of the slot, moving the stop finger hook away from the fly. With the hook resting against the *end* of the drum, the *stop finger must be removed from the path of the fly.*

When the above adjustments are completed, the cuckoo and music movements must both be installed, interconnected, and adjusted. (Install the cuckoo when installing the cuckoo movement.) Before installing either movement, add the chains. After installation add the chain hooks and rings. The activation wire which had earlier been disconnected, must be reconnected by directing it through the hole in the music activation lever and bending the end over as shown last by Figure 2. At this point it is best to place the clock on some type of a test stand, as shown by **Figure 18,** where the back is open, the hands are in place, and the weights can be mounted, with some drop for the weights provided.

The next step is to adjust the music activation lever with the clock on the test stand. Add both the cuckoo and music movement weights (not the time weight) and raise them. Rotate the minute hand towards the hour position and observe the unlocking lever and the stop hook. The pull by the music activation lever upon the unlocking lever must cause the hook to be pulled out of the stop hole and slightly beyond the end of the drum. When cuckoo warning is released and the lifting lever drops, the unlocking lever must rebound towards the cuckoo movement and the hook must rebound to the drum end, not into the drum hole. Ensure the stop finger has rotated out of the path of the fly. Move the minute hand towards the half hour position. The lever will be pulled, but less than for the hour position. Here the hook may *not* be pulled out of the hole and the fly may *not* be released. The lever, then, must be bent as necessary to pull out the hook on the hour, but *not* on the half hour. If there are two holes, which indicates the music movement is to be activated on both the hour and half hour, the hook must pull out fully from both holes, on the hour and half hour.

When the drum rotates so the hole in the end lines up with the stop hook, the stop hook must have adequate freedom to drop fully into the hole.

The inhibit wire must also be adjusted. Move the minute hand towards the hour position. At the same time as the stop hook is being pulled, the inhibit wire must move into the path of the fly. Bend or otherwise adjust the wire so that it moves beyond the fly edge by approximately 1/32" to 1/16". It is essential that the wire moves in front of the fly to prevent it from turning when the hook is pulled out of the hole. As the cuckoo sequence takes place, and the rack hook to which the wire is attached moves up and down, the wire will slide back and forth on the fly blade. The wire must not release the fly. When the rack hook drops at the end of the cuckoo cycle, the wire must move away from and release the fly. The wire must be bent, or otherwise adjusted, so these conditions are satisfied. The adjustment of the wire so that the wire restrains the fly during the cuckoo cycle, but then releases the fly at the end of the cuckoo cycle can be very critical. It is essential that there is no fly rotation during the period where it is to be restrained. If this is not accomplished, lock up of the stop hook in the drum end hole can occur.

Rotate the hands around the dial a few times and observe the cuckoo and music movement operations, to ensure they are both performing satisfactorily, at both the hour and the half hour positions. Connect the music man to his emergence door. If necessary adjust the music man cam on the drum arbor, shown by Figure 4, so he emerges as music commences.

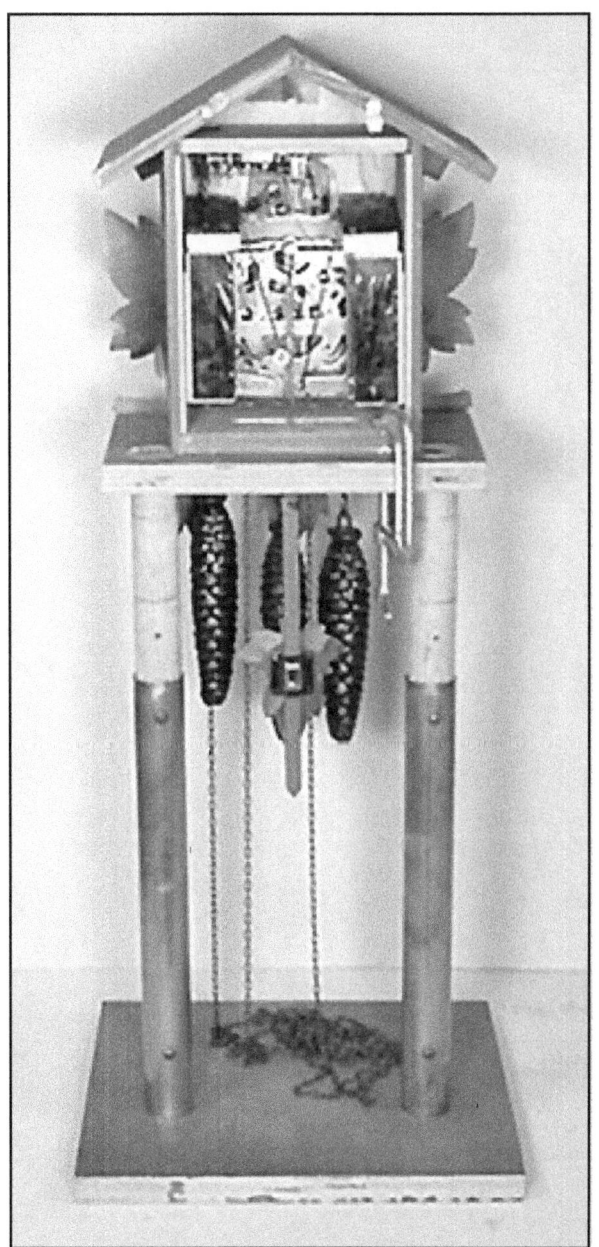

18

It remains to install the cuckoo whistles and lifting wires, adjust bellows lifting as necessary, then test the whole clock long enough to be sure everything is working reliably. It is advisable to be aware that linkages and levers that are bent as part of the adjusting process can relax and shift a bit, which can belatedly lead to malfunctions, and the need for minor readjustment.

Conclusions

The repair of music movements may be required when repairing a cuckoo clock. Cleaning and oiling of a music movement is discussed. Procedures for inspection and repair of the dampers are provided, and suggestions for adjustment of the comb are given. A thorough description of the operation of the controls is presented, and an organized procedure for their adjustment is given. The repair and maintenance of cuckoo music movements is a fascinating endeavor for the most learned clock enthusiast.

References

1. Moebius 8200, 20 ml, 10074, Moebius, Swiss made. Available from most clock parts suppliers.
2. Nancy Fratti, www.nancyfrattimusicboxes.com.
3. Duro Super Glue, available from hardware stores.

FABRICATION OF A CUCKOO CLOCK CHAIN WHEEL LOCKING SPRING

Edwin U. Sowers III, CMC

This article originally appeared in the July 1999 Clockmakers Newsletter *and is reprinted here with permission.*

Cuckoo clock movements are ingenious mechanisms that frequently present unique problems. I recently worked on a hunter style cuckoo clock with a Regula movement. The movement is shown in Figures 1 and 2. The cuckoo chain wheel would not lock. Examination established that the friction drive spring was broken. The suppliers from whom I purchase parts no longer supply replacement springs. Fabrication of a spring appeared the most direct solution.

I removed the chain wheel brass retaining collar, shown on a similar wheel in Figure 3. Measurements taken of the failed unit showed the spring diameter to be approximately 0.020" and the arbor diameter to be 0.148".

Requirements to be satisfied by the new spring were:

1. The spring wound on the arbor had to fit within the inside diameter of the chain wheel bore, and it had to support the chain wheel on the arbor with neither binding nor undue looseness.

2. The wound spring had to fit snugly onto the 0.148" arbor diameter.

3. The spring had to be wound and installed so the spring tightened on the arbor and turned the great wheel in the weight driving direction, and loosened on the arbor in the reverse direction to accommodate winding.

The original steel spring wire was of 0.020" diameter,

Fig. 1. Front view of the Regula movement.

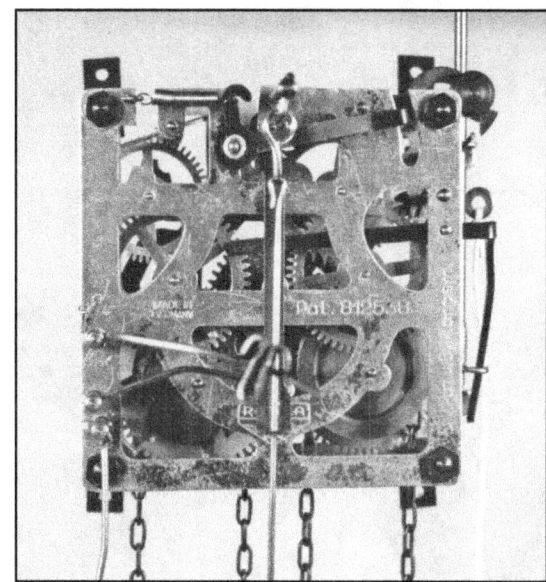

Fig. 2. Rear view of the movement.

B&S wire gauge size #24, which is available from suppliers. Since the original spring adequately centered the chain wheel on the arbor, it was concluded that a similar replacement spring of the same diameter would satisfy the first requirement.

Fig. 3. The chain wheel retaining collar is shown holding the black steel chain wheel on the arbor.

It required some trial windings to establish the diameter of the arbor onto which to wind the spring. The wire was wound onto different diameters of nails positioned in the chuck of a Unimat-3 lathe, with the end of the wire hooked into a drilled hole, as shown by Figure 4. The wire was held tight with the right hand and the chuck turned with the left, as shown by Figure 5. Following winding, the spring, when released, assumed a larger free inside diameter than that upon which it had been wound. It was established that a nail diameter of 0.115" yielded a free inside diameter that fit snugly onto the 0.148" chain wheel arbor. In my case this was realized with a 6-penny common nail. This then provided the means to satisfy the second requirement.

Fig. 4. A nail is gripped in the lathe chuck.

Fig. 5. Winding the wire spring in the lathe.

Fig. 6. The completed spring installed in the chain wheel.

A bit of thought was required to ensure the spring was wound in the correct direction. Figure 6 shows the completed spring installed into the chain wheel. The great wheel was to be driven in the counterclockwise direction as shown by the arrow. The chain wheel, which would ultimately be reversed for final installation, would then drive the great wheel in that direction.

To look at the manner in which the spring functions, consider the chain wheel as shown in Figure 6. If placed on the arbor in the orientation shown, the clockwise wound spring will drive the great wheel in a clockwise direction. With the wound spring fitted snugly onto the arbor, turning the chain wheel clockwise will wind the spring more tightly on the arbor, locking it onto the arbor and thereby driving the great wheel in a clockwise direction. Turning the chain wheel counterclockwise will have the reverse effect, unwinding the spring and releasing it from the arbor, so the chain wheel can be rotated freely to allow for lifting the weight and thus winding the clock. As noted, the chain wheel was reversed upon final installation to drive the great wheel counterclockwise, satisfying the final requirement.

When winding the spring I wound the wire inward towards the chuck, and counterclockwise as indicated by Figure 5. It would seem to simplify determination of the winding direction to always wind the wire to wrap outward from the chuck. If then desiring a clockwise lock and rotation, as with the spring attached per Figure 6, the wire must be wound clockwise (by turning the chuck counterclockwise). If counterclockwise locking is desired, wind counterclockwise.

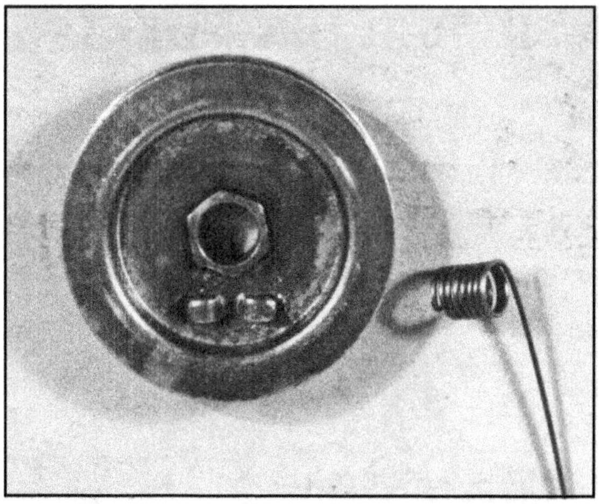

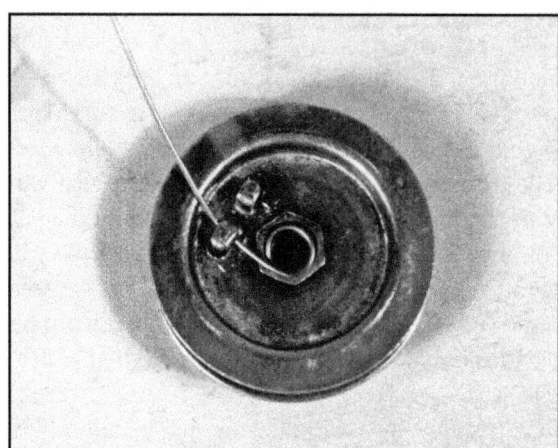

Fig. 7. The chain wheel is shown with the new spring.

Figures 7, 8, and 9 show the steps involved installing the spring. The wound spring shown by Figure 7 had been wound longer than the width of the chain wheel at the bore location. The left hand end, incorporating the hook which fit into the winding arbor, was cut off to a length slightly less than this width with a large sidecutting pliers. The wire spring was fit into the bore as shown by Figure 8 and secured around the tabs on the chain wheel, yielding the spring fully installed as shown by Figure 9.

The final step was to reverse the chain wheel from the position shown by Figure 6, fit it onto the great wheel arbor, and replace the brass retaining collar, applying Loctite to ensure a permanent fit. The chain wheel/great wheel unit was installed in the movement, and has been performing as intended.

Fig. 8. The spring fitted into the wheel bore.

Fig. 9. The spring is shown installed.

REBUILDING DEADBEAT ESCAPEMENT PALLETS

Edwin U. Sowers III, CMC

This article originally appeared in the November 1997 Clockmakers Newsletter *and is reprinted here with permission.*

Fig. 1. Herschede tambour chime clock, Pendulum Model 10.

Fig. 2. The movement.

I encountered an interesting problem with a Herschede tambour clock with Westminster and Canterbury chimes, as shown in Figures 1 and 2. The deadbeat pallets were severely grooved, as shown in Figure 3. The wear was too severe to be corrected by stoning; the width of the pallets was not great enough to relocate the pallet/escape wheel contact area; and a replacement part could not be located. The solution selected was replacement of the worn pallet material, leaving intact as much of the original pallets as possible.

Figure 4 shows the exit pallet and the location of material replacement. The location of **A** on the locking surface was slightly above the uppermost contact point of the escape wheel teeth. **B** was slightly above the original tip of the pallet. Cutting the pallet along the surface **A-B** removed the grooved surface, and the replaced material then furnished completely new contact surfaces for the escape teeth. I concluded that this approach offered the following significant advantages:

- Negligible reduction of rigidity and strength.
- Retention of the original pallet configuration.
  The rear surfaces of the original pallets were left virtually intact to provide references for shaping the concentric locking faces.

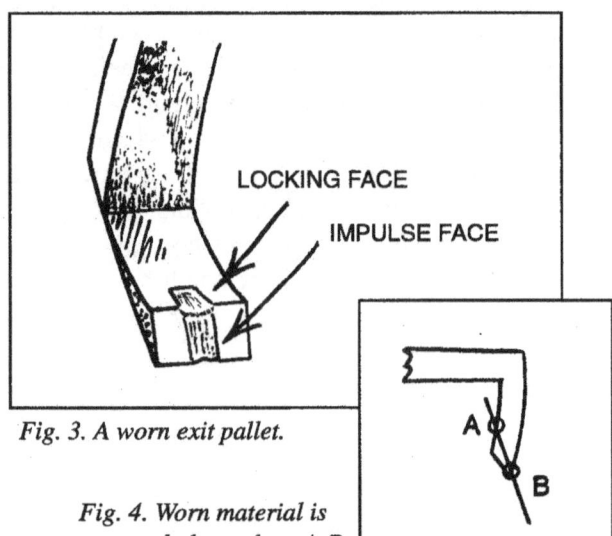

Fig. 3. A worn exit pallet.

Fig. 4. Worn material is removed along plane A-B.

Summary of the Procedure

1. Take measurements of the pallet assembly.
2. Grind off the worn material, along the plane **A-B** with a Dremel tool and cutoff wheel.
3. Soft solder a hardened carbon steel piece to the pallet.
4. Roughly shape the pallet with a Dremel cutoff wheel and sharpening stones.
5. Test and complete the shaping of the pallet.

Tools and Materials

- Dremel Moto Tool
- Dremel cutoff wheel
- Soldering gun, at least 1.1 amps
- Hardened carbon steel, as a section from the tang of an old butcher knife
- Tix solder, low melting point of 275° F.
- Sharpening stones, including a thin round-edged stone as the Morton, Bear Brand, Medium India Oilstone M824, and an Arkansas stone
- Dial calipers

The procedure described in this article covers the rework of an exit pallet; the procedure is similar for an entrance pallet.

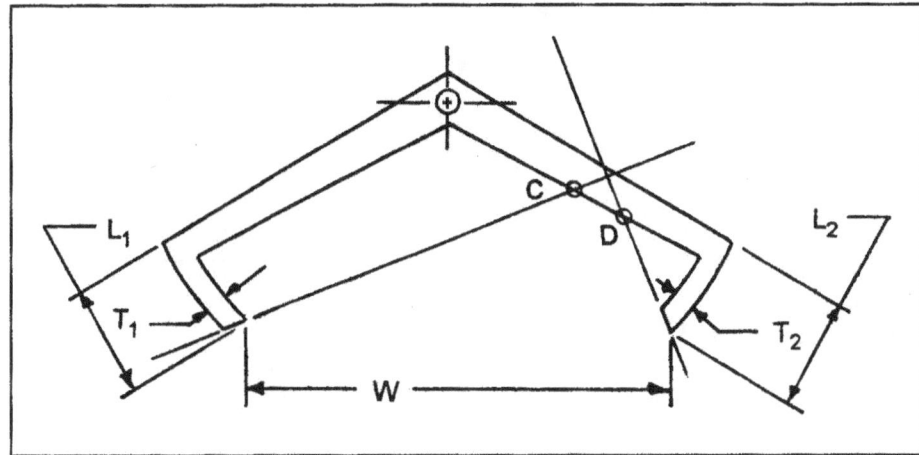

Fig. 5. Measure the pallets.
L_1 entrance pallet
L_2 exit pallet
C and D reference positions
T_1 entrance pallet thickness
T_2 exit pallet thickness
W width between pallet release points

Take Measurements

Trace the outline of the pallet assembly on a sheet of paper attached to a cigar box with a hole in it through which to pass the lower section of the arbor and the crutch. From non-worn locations on the pallet assembly, take measurements as shown by Figure 5.

Using dial calipers, measure the lengths of the entrance and exit pallets, L_1 and L_2, taking the measurement perpendicular to the back edges of the pallet body. As accurately as possible, draw extended lines parallel to and through the impulse surfaces. Points **C** and **D** provide references for positioning a stone when removing material from the impulse surfaces. Measurement of pallet thickness T_1 and T_2, and width **W** between pallet release points, should also prove helpful.

Grind Off the Worn Pallet

Using a Dremel tool and cutoff wheel, grind off the worn portion of the pallet through plane **A-B** as shown in Figure 4. Positioning of the Dremel tool is shown in Figure 6. The ground surface must be flat to ensure a solid solder joint.

Solder Replacement Material to the Pallet

Form a piece of replacement material approximately 1/2 inch long and 1.5 times the pallet width. Thickness must be sufficient to form the end of the pallet. A piece may be cut from a butcher knife tang with the Dremel cutoff tool. The material may be hardened and left glass hard.

Tin both the pallet and replacement material with Tix solder. Mount the pallet body in a heavy vise for stability, with the ground surface facing upward, and horizontal. Place the replacement material strip on the pallet and hold in place with a pointed tool, as a scriber, centering the point above the center of the ground surface. This allows the replacement strip to flatten against the pallet surface when the solder flows.

Heat the pallet and the strip with a soldering gun. Remove the gun as soon as the solder flows. Since the Tix solder has a melting temperature below tempering temperatures, there should be little loss of hardness if not heated significantly above the solder melting temperature. Hold the strip in place until cool. Pull on the extended end of the strip to check joint adhesion. Figure 7 shows the replacement strip soldered in place.

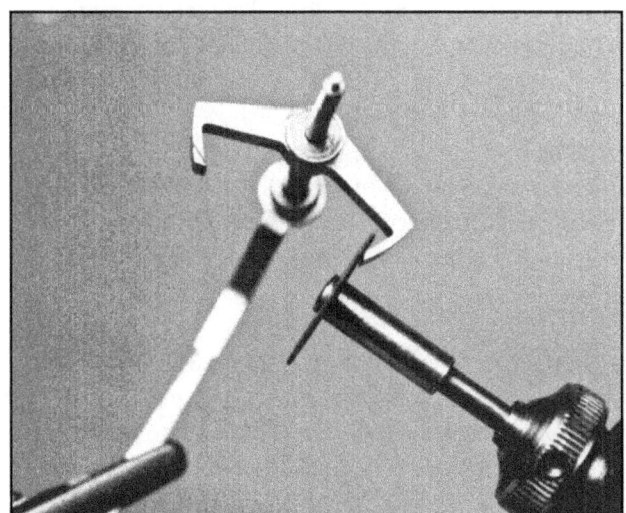

*Fig. 6. Grinding off the worn portion of the exit pallet with a Dremel tool and cutoff wheel. The surface is ground along plane **A-B** (see the text and drawing, Figure 4.)*

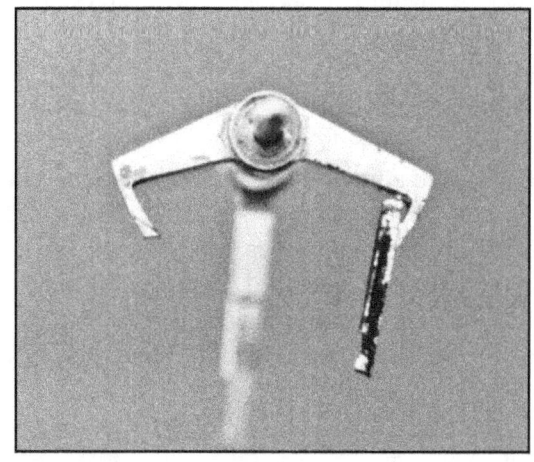

Fig. 7. Strip soldered in place.

Roughly Shape Pallet

Using the Dremel tool and cutoff wheel, roughly shape the pallet end. Remove material gradually so as not to overheat and melt the solder. Figure 8 shows a pallet roughed out with the cutoff wheel. Continue further rough shaping with a sharpening stone.

Stone the new rear surface of the pallet, obtaining a good blending of the new section of the rear surface to the original, removing no material from the original surface. Continuity of the curvature can be checked with a draftsman's circle template.

Stone the locking face to a thickness of .003" to .004" greater than the original, and stone the impulse face to achieve a pallet length of approximately .008" longer than the original pallet length. It is essential to leave adequate material for subsequent testing and final forming.

Stoning the locking face of the exit pallet will prove to be more difficult than for an entrance pallet, due to the convex curvature and reduced accessibility. The thin round edged oilstone defined earlier appears suitable. Use a hand vise to firmly hold the pallet body. Use the back edge of the pallet as a guide for curvature of the locking surface and as a reference surface for measuring thickness. When stoning the impulse surface, direct the cutting surface of the stone toward point **D** of Figure 5 to assist in achieving an angle close to that of the original pallet. Do not round the corner where the locking and impulse faces intersect.

Test the Pallet and Complete the Shaping

Following rough shaping, measure and record L_1, L_2, T_1, T_2, and **W**, install the pallet unit into the movement, adjust for the best equality of drop and best lock that can be realized, and test. The pallets must be shaped and adjusted through a sequence of testing, then stoning and adjustment to obtain adequate and nearly equal, drops, and satisfactory lock. References 1 and 2 present detailed discussions relating to the operation and adjustment of deadbeat escapements. A summary of some information which may prove helpful is presented in the appendix, "Deadbeat Pallet Shaping and Adjustment Considerations", preceding this article.

Both drops must be sufficiently large so there is no impingement of either pallet on any escape wheel teeth. Lock should ultimately be such that escape teeth initially contact the pallets slightly above the impulse surface onto the locking face, with no recoil occurring .Lock initially will be greater than desired due to leaving the pallets longer than original during rough shaping. When stoning the impulse face, it is essential to maintain the desired impulse angle.

After each stoning, take and record all the dimensions defined by Figure 5. When the pallet unit is installed, adjusted, and tested, note the resultant changes in drop and

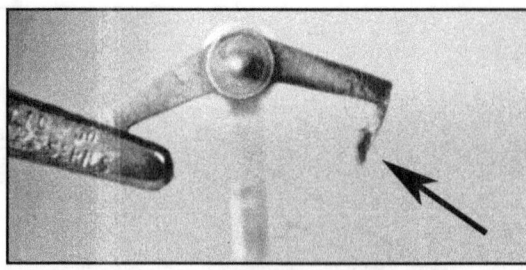

Fig. 8. New pallet end at arrow.

Fig. 9. The pallet unit shown with the re-worked exit pallet.

lock resulting from the dimensional changes. By proceeding gradually, a trend can be determined and will serve as a guide to continued refinement. As the original dimensions are approached, be extremely careful not to remove too much material. It is important not to over-shorten the pallets as satisfactory lock cannot then be obtained.

When initially working to equalize drop, it may be found that interference between pallets and teeth occurs, particularly with the exit pallet contacting the tooth tip or rear of the tooth when the pallet is rotated towards the escape wheel. This may relate to the excess length of the pallets and suggest the need for some initial shortening.

Changes made during stoning and testing are interrelated. Proceeding gradually, recording measurements and observing results, will yield optimum results.

When satisfactory escape performance is achieved, finish stoning with a fine stone, such as an Arkansas stone, moving parallel to the direction of escape tooth movement. This may be followed by a fine emery board moving again in the direction of tooth movement. Care must be exercised not to round the locking face/impulse plane corner.

The procedure described here defines a hand accomplished means for forming the pallets, which has yielded quite satisfactory results. Figure 9 shows the unit I re built, which has been functioning well upon installation into the movement. Shaping of the pallets may also be accomplished by means of a lathe with appropriate grinding wheels and fixtures, as described by Reference 1.

References

1. Joseph G. Baier, James L. Tigner, Marvin E. Whitney, *Questions and Answers of and for the Clockmaking Profession,* American Watchmakers Institute Press, Cincinnati, Ohio, 1981.

2. Charles Terwilliger, *The Horolovar 400-Day Clock Repair Guide,* The Horolovar Company, Bronxville, N.Y, 1984.

APPENDIX A to the preceding article
Rebuilding Deadbeat Escapement Pallets
Edwin U. Sowers III, CMC

This article originally appeared in the December 1997 Clockmakers Newsletter
and is reprinted here with permission.

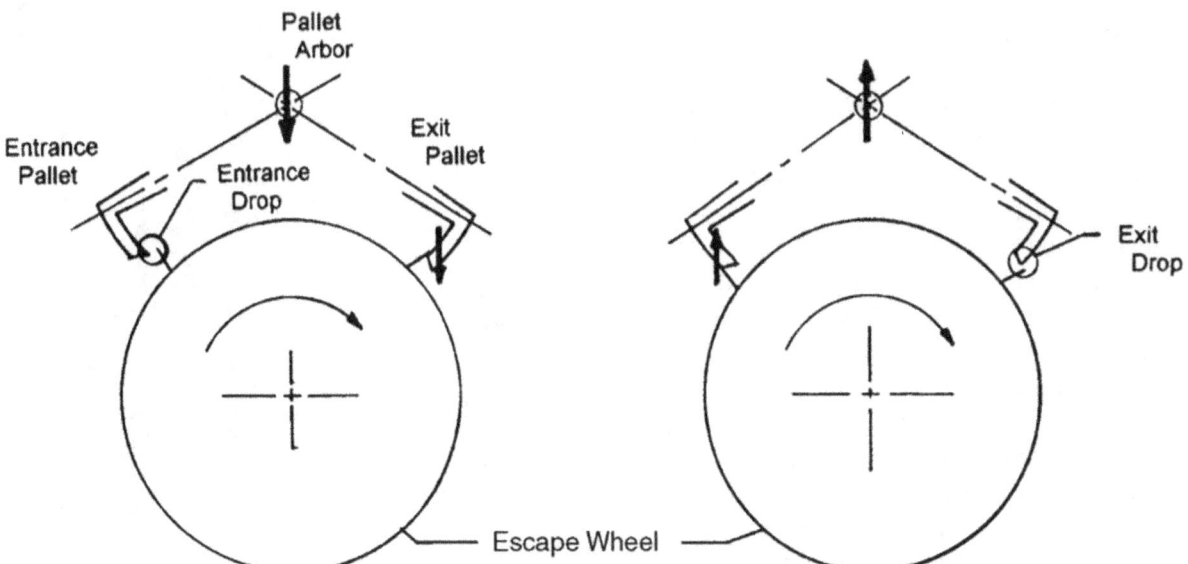

Entrance drop occurs when a tooth is released by the tip of the entrance pallet, and the escape wheel rotates until a tooth contacts the exit pallet.

Exit drop occurs when a tooth is released by the tip of the exit pallet, and the escape wheel rotates until a tooth contacts the entrance pallet.

Entrance Drop is Increased by:

1. Moving the pallet arbor towards the escape wheel, thus moving the exit pallet downward and allowing the escape wheel to rotate further before a tooth contacts the exit pallet. (Moving the arbor away from the escape wheel has the opposite effect.)

2. Removing material from the locking surface of the exit pallet.

Exit Drop is Increased by:

1. Moving the pallet arbor away from the escape wheel, thus moving the entrance pallet upward and allowing the escape wheel to rotate further before a tooth contacts the entrance pallet. (Moving the arbor towards the escape wheel has the opposite effect.)

2. Removing material from the locking surface of the entrance pallet.

The concept of defining drop as free movement of the escape wheel tooth from the pallet which released it is described in the book *Questions and Answers of and for the Clockmaking Profession* (Ref. 4 from the preceding article).

Summarizing some of the shaping and adjusting considerations:

Drop Adjustment

Pallet arbor moved *towards* the escape wheel:
Entrance drop increased
Exit drop decreased.

Pallet arbor moved *away* from the escape wheel:
Entrance drop decreased
Exit drop increased.

Material removed from locking surfaces:
Removal from entrance pallet increases exit drop
Removal from exit pallet increases entrance drop

Lock Adjustment

Pallet arbor moved *towards* the escape wheel:
Lock increased on both pallets.

Pallet arbor moved away from the escape wheel:
Lock decreased on both pallets.

Pallets shortened (while retaining impulse angle):
Shortening either pallet acts to decrease both locks.
Warning: over-shortening precludes adequate lock.

Note: Be aware of interactions among changes, e.g., moving the pallet arbor to improve drop also affects lock.

CLOSING A DEADBEAT PALLET
Edwin U. Sowers III, CMC

This article originally appeared in the January 1999 Clockmakers Newsletter *and is reprinted here with permission.*

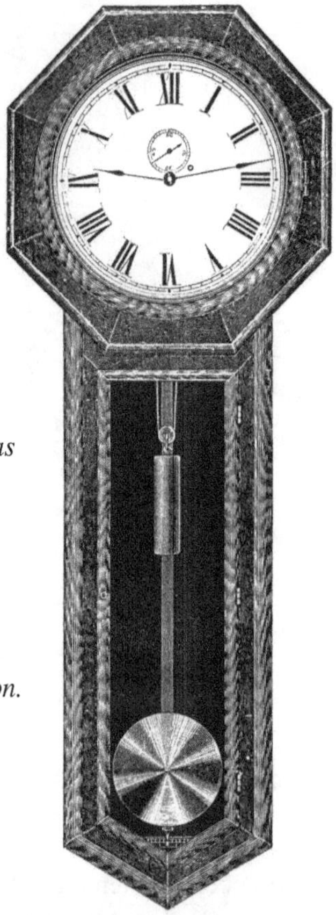

I recently encountered a challenging escapement problem. The clock involved was a Seth Thomas No. 18 Regulator. The case was of oak, 54 inches deep, with a 14 inch dial, and incorporating a No. 61A, eight-day, deadbeat, time only movement. The clock and the movement are shown in Figures 1 and 2.

The problem related to adjustment of the deadbeat escapement. Correct engagement of the pallets with the escape wheel could not be realized. Upon adjusting to obtain a lock of .010 to .015 inches, a slight nicking of the exit pallet upon the back of the adjacent tooth occurred. The condition is depicted by Figure 3. Moving the pallet arbor away from the escape wheel enough to eliminate this problem led to inadequate lock.

It was apparent that the solution was to slightly close the spacing between the pallets. It was expected that a closing of .004 to .005 inches would be required; the final value would be determined by testing. However the complete pallet unit was hardened. To incur any significant stress by closing the pallets would probably have broken the pallet unit. Tempering the unit near the arbor, while maintaining the original hardness of the pallets proper, was required.

Prior to any tempering it is necessary to first obtain a clear, shiny surface on the sides of the unit, so the color change, which defines the temperature and degree of tempering, can be observed.

This can usually be accomplished with 400 or 600 grit wet or dry paper.

To preserve the hardness of the pallets proper, parallel jaw machinist clamps were firmly secured to both of the pallets, as shown by Figure 4.

It must be noted that tempering of a hardened steel component to a softness allowing bending without breakage, is not a risk free endeavor. A judgment call is required in achieving the correct temperature, as determined by the observed color. If underheated, the piece will remain too hard. If overheated, approaching a cherry red, it will probably be hardened and brittle. If tempered to the point where the steel part can be easily filed, tempering should be adequate. It is urged that the extensive discussion of heat treatment given by Reference 1 be studied.

As with many other repair actions, irreversible damage can be inflicted if done improperly. However, in some cases, the solution to problems leaves no suitable alternatives to sensitive repair actions. The author and Clockmakers Newsletter can not be held responsible for any problems encountered in performing the repair procedure described here.

Fig. 1. Seth Thomas No. 18 Regulator. The illustration is from the catalog "Seth Thomas Clocks", 1909-10, from the Charles Partridge collection.

Fig. 2. The No. 61A movement on a test stand.

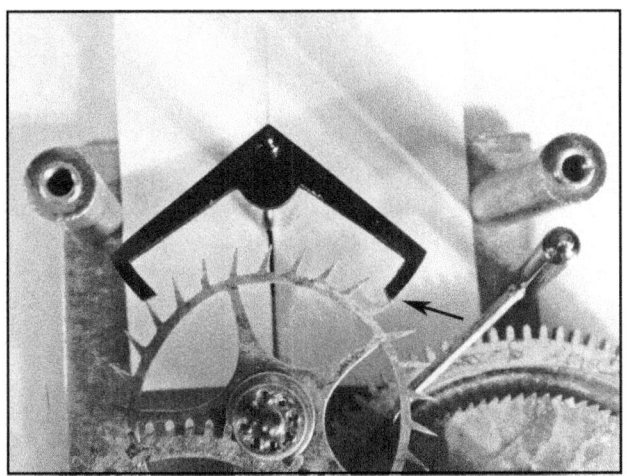

Fig. 3. The exit pallet (at arrow) is shown nicking the back of an escape tooth.

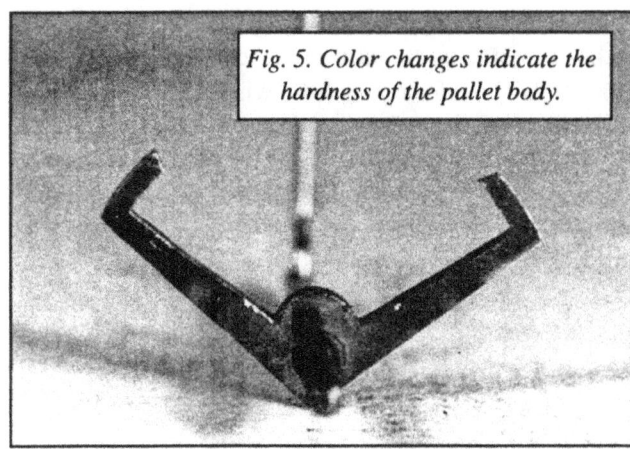

Fig. 5. Color changes indicate the hardness of the pallet body.

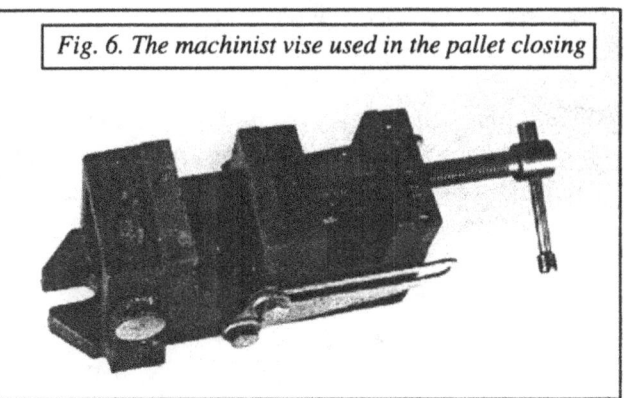

Fig. 6. The machinist vise used in the pallet closing

The exposed portion of the pallet unit was heated with a propane torch. The heating was continued until a *gray color* was achieved, then the torch was immediately removed. When cooled, it was possible to file a nick in the pallet unit with the corner of a sharp file, an indication that adequate tempering was achieved. The successfully tempered pallet unit, with the pallets still hard, is shown by Figure 5. It is, unfortunately, impossible to clearly show the color change in a black and white image.

To close the pallets, the unit was inverted and placed on the opened jaws of a heavy machinist vise. A Sears 2-1/2" vise, of 8-1/2 lb. weight, as shown by Figure 6, was used. The jaws were covered with a few layers of drafting tape to protect the arms of the pallet unit. The space between the two inside edges of the pallets was measured with a dial calipers. The jaws were positioned to contact the pallet arms to the inside of the still hardened pallets. It was expected that .004 to .005 inch closing would be required. A brass bar was placed on the pallets, as shown by Figure 7, then struck with a hammer. The strength of the blow was gradually increased until closing occurred. It was surprising, and somewhat disturbing, that a rather heavy blow was required to obtain results. A closing of .005 inch was achieved, established by dial caliper measurements.

Fig. 4. Clamping the pallets to protect them from heat.

Fig. 7. Closing the pallet unit.

The pallets were installed in the movement and adjusted for the correct lock. It was established that the closing was too great to allow for equal drop, while retaining the correct lock.

The pallet unit was reversed and placed right side up over one jaw of the vise, in a straddled fashion as shown by Figure 8. The brass bar was placed on the top and struck with a hammer. The total closing was reduced to .003 inches. The unit was then reinstalled in the movement and adjusted. Both correct lock and adequate and equal entrance and exit drop were realized.

Satisfactory operation of the clock was achieved. A detailed discussion on the operation and repair of deadbeat escapements is given by Reference 2.

References

1. *Questions and Answers of and for the Clockmaking Profession.* Baier, Tigner, and Whitney. American Watchmakers Institute Press, 1981, Cincinnati, OH, pp. 201-207.

2. Tigner, pp. 169-184.

Fig. 8. Opening the pallets slightly to the final span.

ADJUSTING DROP WITH A RECOIL ESCAPEMENT

Edwin U. Sowers III, CMC

Drawings by Steven G. Conover

This article originally appeared in the August 2007 Clockmakers Newsletter *and is reprinted here with permission.*

Drop is defined here as the small movement of an escape wheel tooth immediately following release by an adjacent pallet. The tooth moves ahead of the releasing pallet. The basic fact to keep in mind is that the drop of one tooth is determined by the pallet on the opposite side of the escape wheel.

Exit Drop

Observe Figure 1. The exit pallet is about to release the exit tooth. Look at the entrance pallet. When the exit tooth is released, the escape wheel will rotate clockwise and the entrance tooth will run into the entrance pallet. This will stop rotation of the escape wheel. The amount the exit tooth moved past the tip of the exit pallet is the exit drop. So the entrance pallet did indeed establish the exit drop.

So to change the exit drop, one must do something to the entrance pallet. Moving up the pallet arbor with respect to the escape wheel arbor will move up the entrance pallet with respect to the entrance tooth. Upon exit release, the entrance tooth will have to move further to contact the entrance pallet, increasing escape wheel rotation and movement of the exit tooth beyond the exit pallet. The exit drop, then, is increased by moving up the pallet arbor. The exit drop is reduced by moving the pallet arbor down.

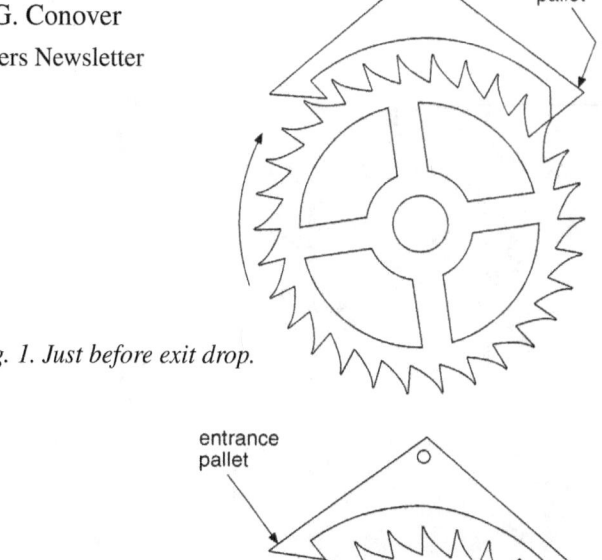

Fig. 1. Just before exit drop.

Fig. 2. Just before entrance drop.

Entrance Drop

The situation with the entrance drop, with the recoil escapement, is different from the exit drop. Figure 2 shows the entrance pallet nearly ready to release the entrance tooth. A major difference exists here with the shape of the exit pallet. The contact surface of the pallet is essentially vertical. Moving the pallet arbor up or down will have little effect on the angular position of the escape wheel when the exit tooth contacts the exit pallet, so will have little effect on the entrance drop. This is true for most recoil escapements which have pallets shaped essentially like that shown by the Figures. This means the entrance drop cannot be significantly changed; it is fixed by the shape of the pallet unit.

How Adjust?

In view of the previous discussion and the limitations described, how then does one adjust? The basic objective of drop adjustment is to minimize both drops while permitting all escape wheel teeth to pass by both pallets. However, in the case of the recoil escapement, since little change can be made in the entrance drop to decrease it, the desire for both drops to be nearly equal becomes the primary consideration. The entrance drop becomes the reference, and the pallet to escape wheel distance is adjusted to match the exit drop to the entrance drop. In many cases the result is that both drops are satisfactory.

However, in some cases, desired adjustment cannot be realized and can necessitate a change in the shape of the pallet unit, usually by spreading or closing the pallets to change the distance between pallet tips. Bending a solid pallet body brings the risk of breakage. Generally, avoid attempting it! However, steel slips can be added to solid pallets to compensate for wear, and strip pallet units can be reshaped by bending.

Facts to Keep in Mind

When adjusting escapements, keep in mind that small adjustments can have large effects. Be sure that when moving the pallet arbor upwards adequate lock is not lost. By moving the pallets down too far, the exit pallet can nip the rear of the exit tooth as the pallet rotates downward—and more obviously, teeth can hang up on the pallets, not being released.

It must be noted that not all recoil escapements are vertically oriented, that is, with the pallet arbor directly above the escape wheel arbor. The whole escapement can be angled off to one side. However the adjustment process is the same, with the pallet arbor being moved towards or away from the escape wheel arbor.

Multiple Repairs to a Mainspring Barrel

by Edwin U. Sowers III (PA)

Figure 1. The Gustav Becker wall clock

A mainspring barrel with three significant, simultaneous, problems is not frequently encountered. Such was the case, however, for the time barrel of a Gustav Becker wall clock, shown in Figure 1.

The problems were:
- Two bent teeth
- A loose barrel cover
- A significant bulge in the barrel shell adjacent to the mainspring hook

It is expected that the first two were related. It appears that the cover may have worked loose, shifted out of the barrel, and allowed the barrel to cock. Examination of the teeth suggests that the cocked barrel caused excessive loading of the teeth that resulted in their bending. The bent teeth can be seen at the top in Figure 2. It is not clear whether the bulging was related to the two prior problems.

The problem initially addressed was the bulge in the barrel shell. It was considered that the most aggressive step should be resolved first, before dealing with the more precise procedures involved in correcting the bent teeth and loose barrel cover.

Barrel Bulge

Figure 3 shows the barrel with the bulge in the shell at the location of the barrel hook. A number of problems can stem from this condition. It can cause problems in positioning a new mainspring over the end of the hook, and in keeping it there while inserting a new mainspring into the barrel. A second, and serious, problem can be a loosened barrel hook.

A very basic tool was used in correcting the deformed barrel; a 1-1/8" diameter steel bar with a 1/4" diameter hole, 1/8" deep, centered 1/4" from the end of the bar. The bar was actually a heavy 14-1/2" long cold

Figure 2. Two severely bent barrel teeth.

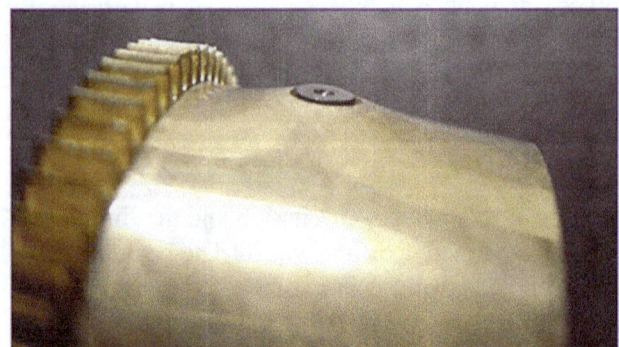

Figure 3. Bulged barrel shell.

This article originally appeared in the February 2005 NAWCC Bulletin.

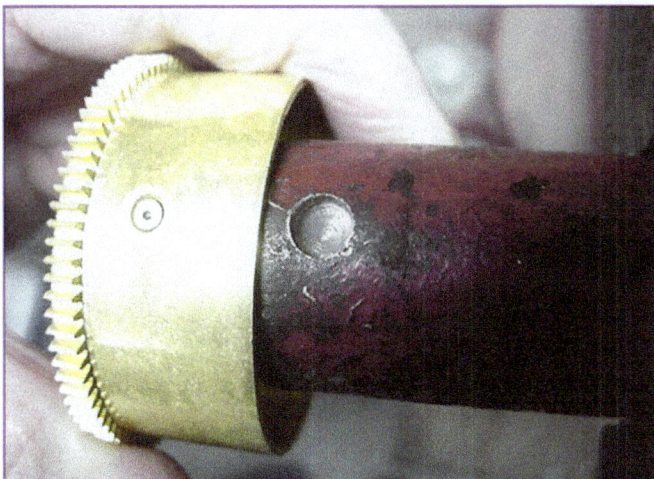

Figure 4. Bar used as anvil.

Figure 5. Straightening shell on the bar.

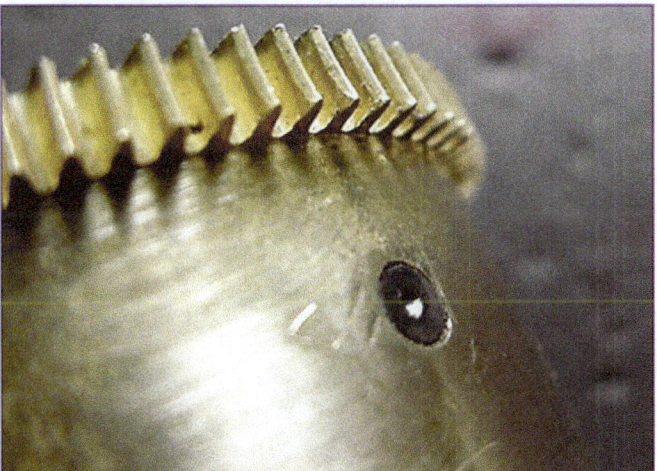

Figure 6. Barrel shell after straightening.

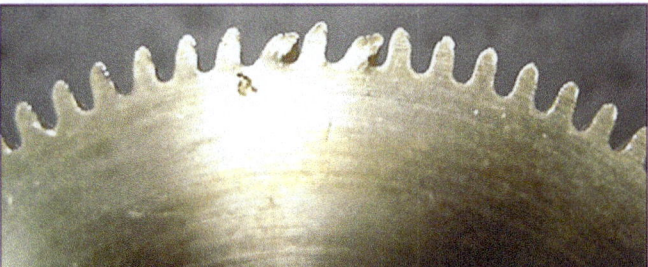

Figure 7. Closeup of the two bent barrel teeth.

Figure 8. Barrel marked for teeth removal, with tooth donor barrel on right.

heavy hammer, not shown), using the bar as an anvil upon which to shape it. (It is essential that whatever is used as the anvil must be of significant mass.)

To ensure that the hook was secure, the inner end of the hook was placed upon the outside diameter of the bar, and the exposed rivet end was hammered with a medium weight ball-peen hammer.

The reshaped barrel is shown in Figure 6.

Bent Teeth

Figure 7 shows a close up of the bent barrel teeth. It was apparent that the two badly bent teeth could not be straightened. Corrective action was replacement of the two bent teeth, along with the relatively straight tooth between them.

Figure 8 shows the damaged barrel on the left, along with the barrel on the right from which replacement teeth were removed. The donor barrel was of a smaller diameter than the damaged barrel. The circular pitch of the teeth, however, was the same for both; the tooth shape for both, and the spacing, thus being essentially the same. While the radius of the pitch circle (and of the tooth tips) for the smaller barrel was less than for the larger barrel, there was no significant discontinuity since only three teeth were involved. The damaged barrel is shown blued and scribed for removal of the three teeth.

A close-up of the teeth marked for removal is shown in Figure 9. The approach was to cut out a section from the great wheel as scribed, with a continuation of the same width back into the barrel shell. I prefer parallel-sided cutouts for tooth replacements, where a single

chisel. The bar, with the barrel placed upon its end, is shown in Figure 4.

A heavy vise was used to hold the bar in a horizontal position. The barrel was placed over the end, with the hook fitting into the hole. Figure 5 shows the barrel shell being reshaped with a heavy brass bar (and a

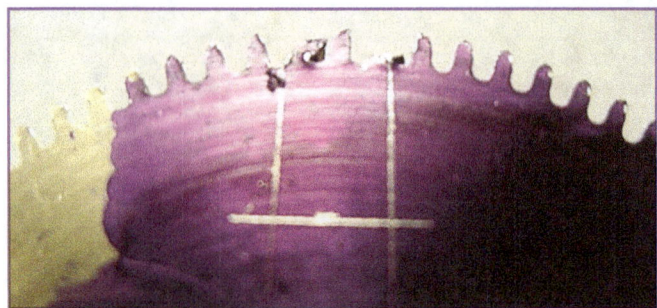

Figure 9. Close-up of 3-tooth segment scribed for removal.

Figure 12. Square file removing material, approaching scribed lines.

Figure 10. Barrel secured in tilted vise for sawing.

Figure 13. Preliminary filing completed.

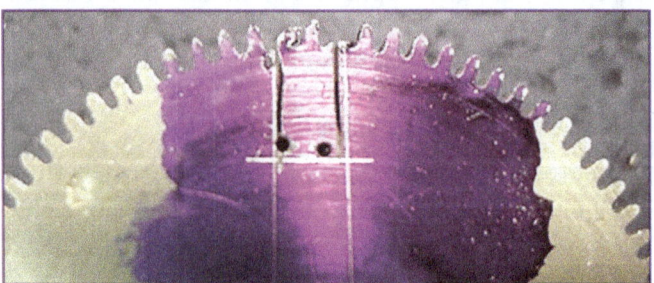

Figure 11. Saw cut made inside of scribed lines.

tooth up to 3 or 4 are replaced. In my experience this contributes to a tight, strong, accurately positioned tooth repair.

Figure 10 shows the cutting out of the damaged teeth with a jeweler's saw; the blade installed to cut on the back stroke. It is important to use a heavy vise for this operation to avoid shifting and saw-blade breakage. The vise used was tiltable, which permitted suitable positioning of the barrel for sawing. Figure 11 shows each of the scribe marks to be centered on a tooth space. The saw cuts are made inside the marks; finishing to be done by filing, which is more accurate. Two holes were drilled near the bottom of the saw cuts through which to insert the saw blade to cut out the bottom of the slot and to extend the side cuts up and behind the teeth into the barrel shell.

Figure 12 shows the cut into the barrel shell and filing of the cutout towards the scribe lines. Note that filing proceeded to slightly inside the scribe lines. The intent was to leave adequate material to ultimately match the replacement segment into the slot for a tight metal-to-metal fit. Completion of preliminary filing of the cut-out is shown by Figure 13.

The next step was to cut out the 3-tooth repair segment from the donor barrel. Most of the cutting was done with a Dremel cut-off wheel, Figure 14. The removed segment, cut intentionally oversize, is shown in Figure 15, and shown beside the cutout in Figure 16. The replacement segment was held in a hand vise, Figure 17, and filed to size. Both the cutout and the insert were carefully filed to obtain a snug fit, all around. The snug fit was essential for two reasons. First, for metal-to-metal contact for strength; solder being used basically to keep the insert in place; sec-

Figure 14. Cutting out donor segment with Dremel cut-off wheel.

Figure 15. Donor 3-tooth segment removed.

Figure 16. Donor segment cut over-sized.

Figure 17. Finish filing segment for close fit.

Figure 18. Flowing Tix solder with alcohol burner.

Figure 19. Installed segment viewed from inside barrel.

ondly, so the insert could be tapped into place, and remain in position for subsequent soldering.

Soldering was accomplished with Tix solder and flux, and an alcohol lamp. Small pieces of solder were laid on the inside joint, and heat was applied with an alcohol lamp as shown by Figure 18.

The segment was positioned to be essentially flush on the inside, Figure 19. The outside was filed flush and teeth touched up as required. The completed repair is shown by Figure 20. Note that a slight gap was left at the bottom of the insert so that final positioning

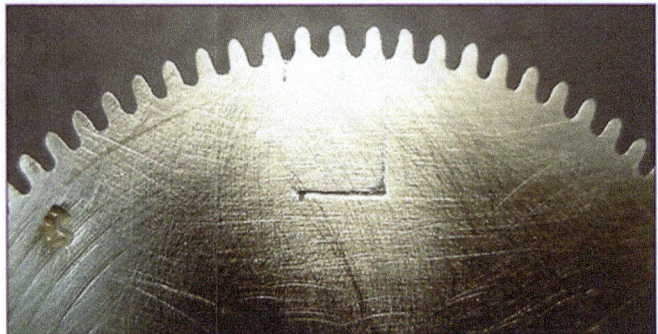

Figure 20. Outside of segment, finished to match with barrel.

Figure 21. Bolt with collar sized to mount cover in lathe.

Figure 22. Stretching outside diameter of cover.

Figure 23. Truing cover in lathe.

Figure 24. Checking cover concentricity with dial indicator.

could be directed to matching the tips of the inserted teeth to the barrel teeth.

Loose Cover

The first step in resolving the loose cover problem was to confirm that indeed there was inadequate interference between the barrel diameter and the barrel cover diameter. Measurement of the cover diameter and of the barrel groove diameter was taken with a dial calipers. The diameter of the cover was 1.796" while that of the barrel groove was 1.796" to 1.798" (slightly out of round). The cover diameter was obviously too small for an adequate interference fit into the barrel groove.

The apparent solution was enlargement of the barrel cover diameter. The approach to increasing the cover diameter was to first hammer the cover to deform it to a larger diameter, and then to turn it down to a suitable diameter.

Figure 21 shows a bolt with a tight-fitting sleeve that was prepared to mount the barrel cover in the lathe. The sleeve was turned down to the diameter of the arbor hole to facilitate machining the cover O.D. concentric to the arbor hole. The width of the sleeve was less than the width of the cover (including an inward facing collar), to permit securing the cover against the bolt head with a nut.

The cover was hammered upon an anvil as shown in Figure 22. The cover, mounted on the described bolt and secured with the shown nut, was placed in the lathe and machined to a diameter of 1.806", (.009"

Figure 25. Test installation of cover into barrel.

approximate interference), see Figure 23. Presence of a continuous diameter, and concentricity, were confirmed by a dial indicator, as shown in Figure 24. The diameter was further carefully reduced by filing the rotating cover and checking the fit with the barrel until a satisfactory interference was achieved. It was not possible to precisely predefine the desired interference due to the unknown effects of the barrel shell out-of-roundness. The inner edge of the cover was slightly chamfered to enhance the force fitting of the cover into the barrel. The cover inserted into the barrel is shown in Figure 25.

With the barrel again performing its function in the Gustav Becker movement, it is expected that the rejuvenated cover will serve faithfully for years to come.

Maintaining Power

Edwin U. Sowers III, CMC

This article originally appeared in the August 2004 AWCI Horological Times *and is reprinted here with permission.*

Maintaining power is an approach used to prevent the loss of torque to a movement during winding. Maintaining power is normally incorporated into a weight driven regulator which is intended to be an accurate timepiece. The clock movement including maintaining power, which will be discussed by this article, is from the Seth Thomas #2 Regulator shown in Figure 1. The continuation of torque during winding enhances timekeeping accuracy by maintaining continuous operation of the escapement during winding.

In the absence of maintaining power, the torque generated by the weight cable wrapped around the drum is transmitted directly to the great wheel (through the drum click wheel acting upon a click attached to the great wheel). Consider this torque to be counterclockwise (CCW). Now, during winding, the drum must be cranked in the opposite direction – clockwise (CW). The drum click wheel will back away from the click, so no torque will be delivered to the great wheel. All the gearing becomes slack, escape wheel rotation ceases, and there is no impulse to the pendulum.

When maintaining power is added, a large ratchet wheel, as shown in Figure 2, is placed between the click wheel and the great wheel. The click wheel now acts upon a click attached to the ratchet wheel rather than directly upon the great wheel. It is the maintaining power components that then transfer torque from the ratchet wheel to the great wheel. The key component is a spring, located between the ratchet wheel and the great wheel, and which is connected to both.

Figure 3 shows the spring located within a groove in the great wheel. A downward directed hook on the upper left-hand end of the spring fits into a hole in the great wheel. There is an upward facing hook on the right hand end of the spring. This hook fits into the upper hole of the ratchet wheel (on the left) when it is turned over and placed down upon the great wheel. Now with the ratchet wheel in place on the great wheel, turning the ratchet wheel CCW acts upon the spring to wind it CCW and to rotate the great wheel in the same direction, delivering the desired CCW torque to the great wheel.

Figure 1

Figure 2

Figure 3

Figure 4

Figure 5

Figure 6

In Figure 4 a pin can be seen extending upwards below the center of the great wheel. The pin fits into the slot in the ratchet wheel when it is turned over upon the great wheel (Figure 5); it limits the rotation between the two wheels. As the ratchet wheel is rotated CCW by the weight torque, and the spring is wound, the pin should move towards the center of the slot, away from both ends. During weight driven timekeeping the pin should contact neither end of the slot, so there is no transmission of torque between the ratchet wheel and the pin. The spring is then the only component connecting the ratchet wheel and the great wheel; it is the spring *only* that delivers torque from the ratchet wheel to the great wheel, and thus rotates the great wheel.

The next consideration is the manner in which torque is maintained during winding. It is for this period that the maintaining power function is incorporated into the movement. There are two primary components. One is the long pawl arm, pivoting between the plates, shown in Figure 6, which acts upon the small teeth on the outside diameter of the ratchet wheel, to prevent the ratchet wheel from backing up in a CW direction. The second component is the prior described spring.

Now, when winding commences, weight induced CCW driving torque ceases. The spring, however, has been kept in a constantly wound state by the pawl, the ratchet wheel rotating CCW under the pawl, while driving the great wheel, and the pawl continuously re-latching as the ratchet wheel turns. Return now to Figure 3. *The upper right-hand end of the CCW wound spring is locked in place in the hole in the ratchet wheel, and the ratchet wheel is locked in place by the pawl. The left-hand end of the spring, fitting into the great wheel, now continues to deliver torque to the great wheel.* It will provide torque to the great wheel as it unwinds, rotating it CCW, until the great wheel pin within the ratchet wheel slot (Figure 5), runs into the right hand end of the slot. By this time, however, winding will be completed. The weight will then again provide the torque to rewind the spring and drive the great wheel.

For the maintaining power to function properly there are requirements placed upon the spring. The strength and shape at the spring must be such that the weight torque will rotate the ratchet wheel CCW (Figure 5) so that the pin moves towards the slot center.

To check maintaining power operation, first *ensure satisfactory weight driven movement operation.* Also, make sure free rotational movement exists between the ratchet wheel and the great wheel (no binding). Make certain that the pawl properly engages the ratchet wheel. Should corrections be necessary, disassembly of the maintaining power components will ultimately be required.

Secure the movement in its normal operating position, with pendulum attached, the ratchet pawl unhooked, and the cable unwound. Attach the weight, engage the ratchet pawl, wind a few turns, and remove the crank. Check the pin in the slot. Ensure the weight torque has rotated the ratchet CCW so the pin has moved away from the right-hand end of the slot, towards the center, but not into the left end. Make sure the movement is operating satisfactorily. Next, lift the weight and be sure the spring torque maintains movement operation.

In the first case, if the pin has not moved away from the right-hand end of the slot, the spring is too stiff; it will be necessary to close the spring somewhat for maintaining power to function. Correct the spring until, with the weight in place, the pin moves close to the center of the slot. If the pin moved into the left-hand end of the slot, the spring is too weak, and might not be able to maintain movement operation when the weight is lifted, or when the movement is wound. Spread open the spring until the pin moves to the center of the slot. If the pin is positioned near the center of the slot with the weight in place, satisfactory movement operation should be realized when both weight driven and when being wound.

Now, if when the weight was lifted, movement operation did not continue, it is probable that a mechanical problem existed. Check the pawl for free and effective latching, and be sure there is no binding between the ratchet wheel and great wheel. With a bit of persistence and an understanding of how maintaining power works, satisfactory operation can be achieved.

There are other maintaining power configurations. However, the two basic components, the latching ratchet wheel, and the great wheel driving spring, will be present in some form.

HOUR WHEEL TOOTH REPAIR

Edwin U. Sowers III, MSME, CMC

This article originally appeared in the August 2001 Clockmakers Newsletter *and is reprinted here with permission.*

Beware! Observe Figure 1. Do *not* allow this to happen to you. If you work on a tall case clock with a moon dial, and with a dial advance wheel and tab as shown in Figure 1, make sure the tab does not run into the snail. Should this occur, expect to lose a tooth. Figure 1 shows that the hour wheel and attached snail are driven by the motion works hour pinion. The moon dial advance wheel is driven

by a wheel directly behind the snail. When the tab jams against the snail, the advance wheel and hour wheel are both immediately locked. The motion works hour pinion will frequently continue to rotate and will snap off a tooth on the hour wheel, as shown by Figure 2.

This was not the first such occurrence with this clock. Figure 3 indicates this had already happened three prior times. (The fourth tooth, the one to the left of the massive tooth repair on the right, is the tooth with which I dealt.)

To prevent this tooth breakage, it is essential to ensure that as the tab approaches the snail, it passes by the 1:00 o'clock segment and enters into the space to the right of it, in the 9:00 to 11:00 o'clock region. After setting up the

advance wheel relative to the snail to achieve this, it is a wise exercise to rotate the movement sufficiently to cause a full revolution of the advance wheel, to make sure there is no interference at any position.

Having issued the warning to prevent tooth breakage, I think it may be of interest to follow through a procedure for replacing a tooth, should this become necessary. This improvement.

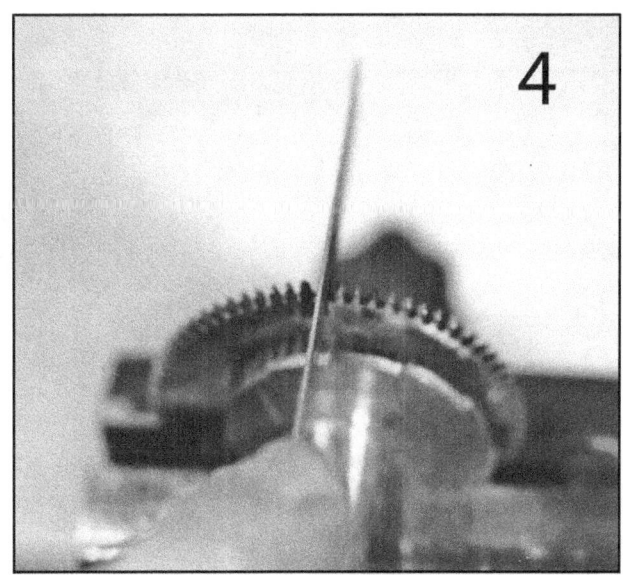

Challenging Repairs to Interesting Clocks · 103

The procedure I followed in replacing the tooth is presented in the following. This procedure can also be used on between-the-plate wheels, being careful not to notch more deeply than necessary, to prevent weakening of the wheel rim.

Filing the Slot/Fitting the Brass Stock

It is my conclusion that the most secure installation of a replacement tooth is achieved by closely fitting a piece of brass flat stock into a straight, parallel sided notch in the wheel, then securing the strip in place with soft solder (silver soldering will soften and weaken the brass). With a tight fit, the function of the solder is basically to hold the tooth in place, not to absorb any significant stress. By inserting the tooth stock into the wheel a depth of 2 to 2-1/2 tooth widths, and ensuring good contact for the full depth, I have never had a tooth failure.

A piece of 1/32" thick brass, half hard, was selected for the tooth stock, with the 1/32 dimension to be the width fitting into the slot. A slot of less than 1/32 width was cut in the wheel with a 0.018" thick screw head slotting file,

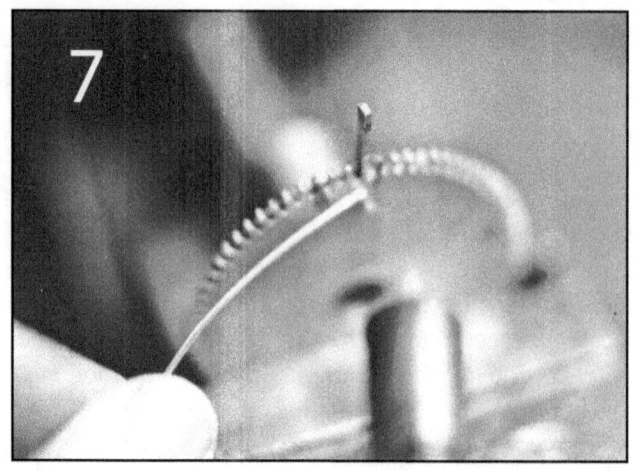

and a flat pattern maker's file ground down on one side, towards the end, to remove the teeth from one side and to thin the file. The hour wheel/snail assembly was firmly secured in a vise, as shown by Figure 4, and well lit, to assist in accurate formation of the slot. An eye loupe was used in the final stage of filing, when the notch was carefully fitted to the tooth stock. Figure 5 shows the groove and Figure 6 the tooth stock tapped into the slot with a light hammer. The snug fit not only yielded a strong joint, it also positioned the tooth stock for soldering.

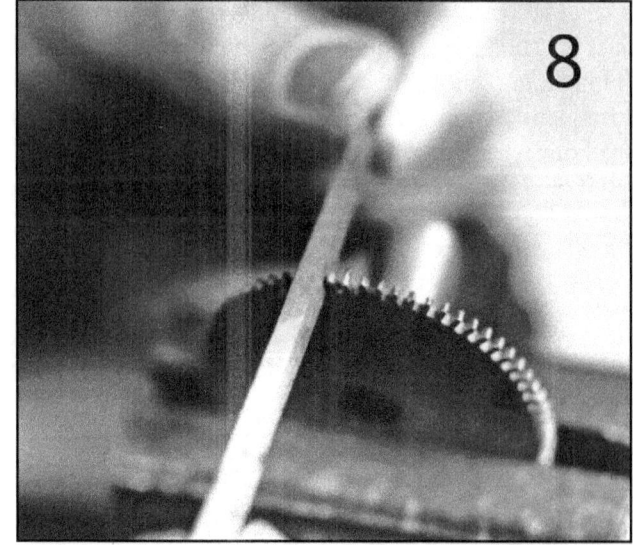

Soldering the Tooth in Place

Figure 7 shows soldering of the tooth with a propane torch, using Tix® solder and flux. Both products are available from most clock part suppliers. It is important to heat the wheel only to the temperature where the solder flows, to prevent softening of the brass. (The melting point of Tix solder is less than the annealing temperature of the brass.) It is desirable to cleanse the soldered area with a baking soda solution to remove all traces of flux and prevent corrosion.

Hand Shaping the Tooth

The 1/32 tooth stock thickness was suitable for the final tooth thickness with little need for thinning. The outer end was cut off with a jeweler's saw, and filed down to a length slightly greater than that of the adjoining teeth. The tip of the tooth was shaped with a barrette (triangular shaped back) pattern maker's file, as shown by Figure 8. The back of the file was ground down to achieve essentially a knife edge on both sides. This provided more maneuverability of the file while shaping the tip of the tooth.

Both sides of the tooth were trimmed down to the thickness of the hour wheel as seen by Figure 9. Wetordry 400 then 600 grit paper was used to finish all surfaces of the tooth. The finished tooth is shown by Figure 10, it being the tooth identified by an arrow.

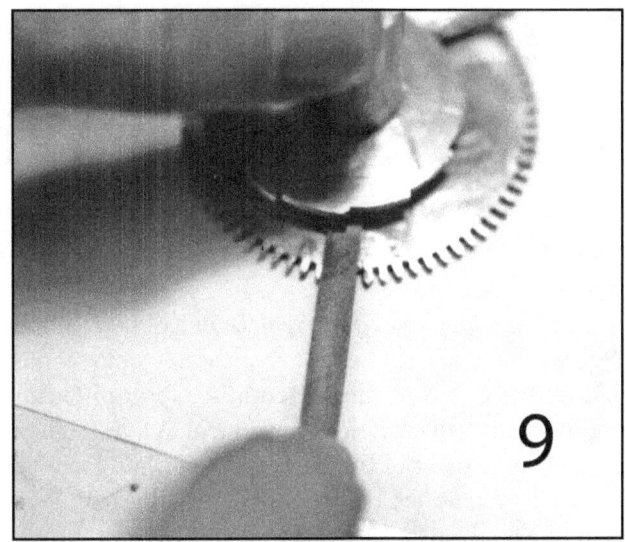

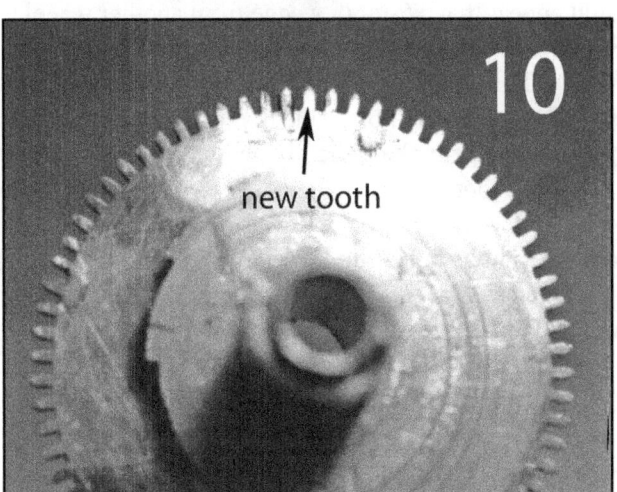

Creating a Six-Tooth Segment for a Tall Case Hour Wheel

Edwin U. Sowers III, CMC

This article originally appeared in the October 2003 AWCI Horological Times *and is reprinted here with permission.*

It is not uncommon to replace one or two teeth in a wheel. It is more of a challenge to replace a 6-tooth segment. The need for such a repair arrived in the form of the snail hour wheel on a tall case clock movement. A five-tooth segment had, at some prior time, been inserted into the wheel, as shown by Figure 1. Looking at Figure 2, it is not obvious how reliable advance of the snail could have occurred. It would appear that a 5-tooth wedge from another wheel had been imprecisely over-soldered onto the snail wheel.

The 5-tooth segment had to go. The plan was to then insert a properly fitted brass blank into the wheel and hand form suitable teeth along the periphery.

The tooth to the right of the 5-tooth segment, shown by Figure 2, was incomplete. It was decided to remove that tooth also and install a 6-tooth segment. Figure 3 shows the old segment removed and the cut made to remove the sixth tooth. All three surfaces of the cutout were carefully filed to ensure a straight edge for each.

A tracing was made of good teeth on the wheel, as shown by Figure 4, to define the spacing of the teeth. As noted by the Figure, the wheel outside diameter (OD) was 2.237" and the root diameter 2.013". The nominal shape of the new insert, Figure 5, was laid out on the plate which had been colored with DYKEM bluing (Reference 1). The insert had been cut from an old German clock plate of adequate hardness, and of 0.070" thickness—the same as that of the hour wheel.

As can be seen the two sides of segment were radial, leading to essentially a wedge shape. When installing up to 3 teeth, I prefer a straight, parallel sided insert; a tight and strong insert can more easily be achieved in this manner. However, when dealing with the present 6 teeth, the two teeth outside and next to the insert would be undercut and weakened with a straight-sided configuration; this approach would also remove more of the wheel material than desirable.

The wedge was cut out, oversized, with a jewelers saw, Figure 6. By careful filing the segment was fitted into the hub as shown by Figure 7. The objective was to establish full metal-to-metal contact along each side. The depth of insert positioning was established by the *sides, not the bottom*. A slight clearance was allowed along the bottom edge to ensure a tight fit on both sides. The stresses between the insert and the wheel hub, after soldering, should be through metal-to-metal contact, not born by the solder; the solder serving basically to keep the insert in place.

Figure 2

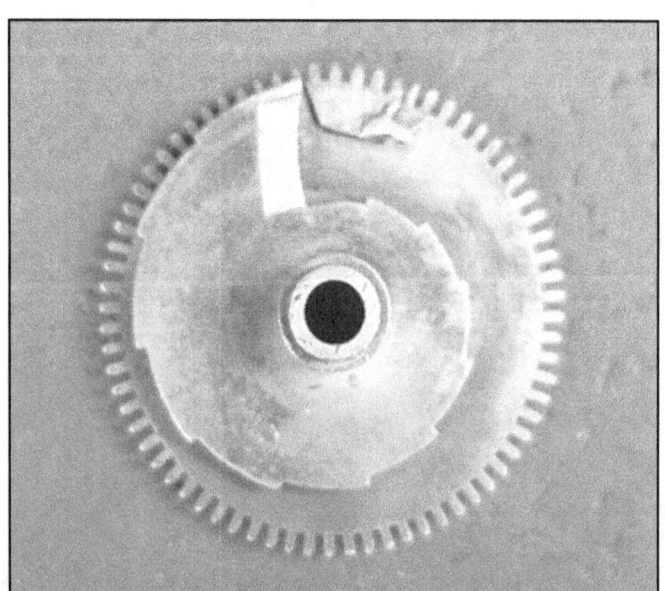

Figure 1

Figure 3

Now with the insert accurately shaped to fit into the hub, the insert was soldered into place with Tix Solder (Reference 2). This solder has a low melting point which reduces the chance of annealing the hardened brass with overheating. The insert was tapped snugly into place with a hammer and secured by a parallel-jawed machinist's clamp, as shown by Figure 8. Tix soldering flux was applied and small pieces of Tix solder were laid along the intended solder joint.

Figure 4

Figure 5

Figure 6

Figure 7

Figure 8

Figure 9

Heat was applied from below with an alcohol burner. Immediately upon flowing of the solder, the heat was removed, preventing overheating and softening of the brass. To solder the right-hand side, and not melt the solder on the left, the clamp was tightened down into the soldered left side, to serve as a heat sink. Soldering was accomplished in the same way as with the left side. After soldering, a solution of baking soda in water was brushed onto the soldered area to neutralize the acid-based flux. The secured insert is shown by Figure 9. The projecting end of the insert was sawed off and filed down to slightly larger than the wheel OD.

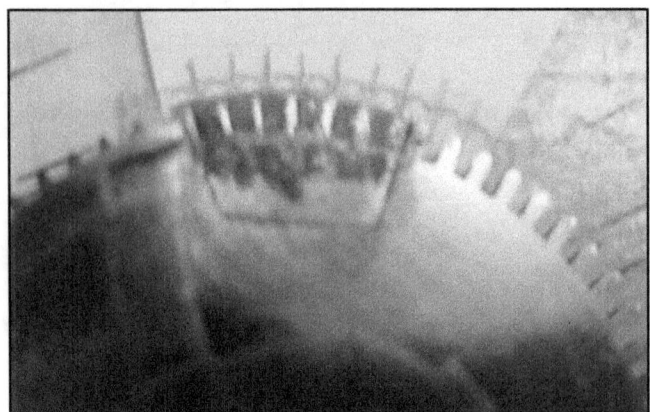
Figure 10

Figure 11

Figure 12

Figure 13

The next step was to mark the insert for filing out the teeth. To the prior described tracing of satisfactory teeth on an index card, radial lines were extended outward from the tooth gap locations, as shown by Figure 10. The insert was blued. The tracing was laid behind the insert, with the tooth tips coincident with the tracing OD. The location of the space between teeth was scribed into the bluing as shown.

A favorite Swiss slotting file, 0.7 mm (0.028") thick, #2 cut, with teeth in the outer edges only, was used for the initial filing of the between-teeth spaces, Figure 11. Similar files can be obtained from Grobet (Reference 3), their FL 31.16 Series Joint Round Edge Files, in thickness from 0.016" to 0.059". Further finishing was accomplished with a flat pattern maker's file, ground down on one side to reduce thickness and also to allow for filing with one side only, without damaging the adjacent tooth. The teeth were carefully filed to the same width as the original with the spacing being equal. The tips of the teeth were rounded, using a barrette pattern maker's file.

While rounding the teeth, the tips were cut back to achieve the 2.237" OD, measuring from each tooth across to a tooth on the opposite side, using a dial caliper. During final finishing of the teeth tips, the spacing was checked for uniformity with a number drill a few sizes larger than that which would fall down between the teeth. The finished teeth are shown by Figure 12.

The snail unit, with repaired hour wheel teeth, is shown returned to the movement by Figure 13.

References

1. DYKEM Steel Blue Layout Fluid, Felt Tip Applicator, I.T.W. DYKEM, Olathe, KS 66061. Available from MSC Industrial Supply Co., 1-800-645-7270.
2. Tix Solder, Allied Mfg. Corp., Bozeman, MT. Available from clock parts suppliers, as Merritt's Antiques, 1-800-345-4101 or S. LaRose, Inc., 1-800-752-7673.
3. Grobet File Company of America, Inc. Available from Merritt's Antiques.

Ratchet Teeth on a Tallcase Date Wheel a Novel Repair Technique

by Edwin U. Sowers III (PA)

This article originally appeared in the August 2011 NAWCC Watch & Clock Bulletin.

Repairing a tallcase moon dial or a date hand can occasionally become more of a problem than the movement.

I recently was faced with a date hand that did indeed have a problem. The date wheel to which the hand was attached had a few teeth with lost tips. As a consequence these teeth were short, as shown in Figure 1. The date wheel was advanced once per 24 hours by an advance pin on the moon dial wheel that contacted a tooth on the date wheel, Figure 2. The advance pin engaged a full-length tooth by less than 1/32", so a short tooth was completely missed, with no advance of the date wheel.

A replacement could be machined, but the expense for a few teeth did not seem justified. Replacement of the teeth was another option, but removal of full teeth was considered excessive.

Figure 2. The date wheel, bottom, and moon dial wheel top. Date wheel advance pin attached to moon dial wheel.

Figure 1. Short tooth due to broken tip.

Figure 3, right. Conceptual sketch of repair solution.

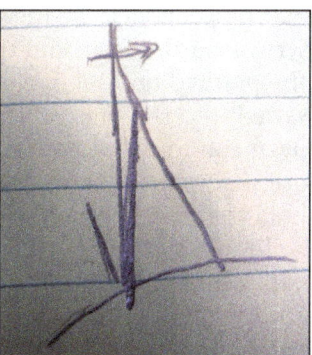

The chosen solution is shown by the conceptual sketch in Figure 3. The concept was basically to cut back the leading edge (contacted by the advance pin) at an angle and to build it up with an extending tapered piece of brass. The tapered insert would be pushed against the remainder of the original tooth at the top, and the bottom would be secured by a pointed tip inserted into a notch sawed into the hub with a jeweler's saw, with the whole held in place by soft solder.

The first step toward accomplishing this chosen solution was to make a tracing on a 3" x 5" card (with a sharp pencil) of a section of undamaged teeth, to serve as a reference for the desired shape. A hole for the mounting pipe of the date wheel was cut into the card, the wheel was placed on the card, and the teeth were traced; the results are shown in Figure 4.

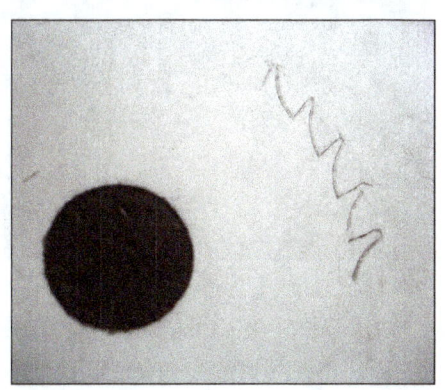

Figure 4. Tracing of undamaged teeth.

The leading edge of the teeth were initially tilted forward somewhat. The conceptual drawing shows the leading edge tilted back, to allow for a greater robustness of the upper portion of the insert. To accomplish this objective, the leading edge was filed to tilt it backward, Figure 5. As shown by the figure, a tapered piece of

Figure 5. Tapered insert with notch for pointed tip.

half-hard brass, with a point at one end, was prepared as the insert. A notch was cut into the hub parallel to the leading edge of the filed-back tooth. The structural concept here is to solder the insert to the modified tooth with the pointed end inserted into the slot, and with the upper portion pushed solidly against the tooth. The force of the advance pin will push against the upper end of the insert, which is supported by the original tooth. The tip of the tooth will be above the original tooth so a torque will be generated, acting to push the bottom of the insert forward, away from the base of the tooth. However, the pointed bottom of the insert is fixed within the slot sawed into the hub. So the forces are absorbed basically by metal-to-metal contact between the insert and the original tooth. The function of the solder is basically to hold the insert in place.

To secure the inserts onto the teeth, first a hole for the date wheel pipe was cut into a 3" x 5" card, and placed on a heavy drill press vise. The date wheel and insert were placed on top. A 250-amp Weller soldering gun was used, with Tix solder and flux, Figure 6. The dissipation of heat to the date wheel (which acted as a heat sink) made soldering somewhat difficult). The excess solder was removed with a file and scraper. The file was repeatedly cleaned with a brass wire brush to prevent the file from loading with solder.

Figure 6. Soldering the insert to the tooth.

110 • Challenging Repairs to Interesting Clocks

The teeth were carefully shaped with pattern files. The date wheel was held by a hand vise, as depicted in Figure 7, during the filing. During the process they were

Figure 7. Hand vise holding date wheel, as used during tooth filing.

checked against the tracing of original teeth, Figure 8. Tooth length was checked against untouched teeth, measuring with dial calibers from a tooth tip to the far side of the date wheel pipe. It was essential that the repaired teeth were not shorter than the untouched teeth, to ensure adequate contact with the date wheel advance pin.

Figure 8. Restored teeth compared to tracing.

Three finished teeth are shown in Figure 9, with the advance pin contacting the center tooth.

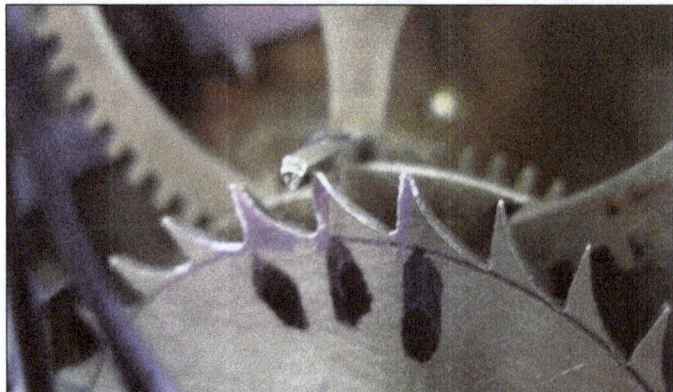

Figure 9. Three finished teeth with advance pin.

Now with the inserts solidly attached and the teeth shaped, the final step was to be sure that each of the rebuilt teeth would be contacted by the advance pin, advanced one tooth only, and not jam. To ensure that this occurred reliably, the date wheel was added to the movement and the moon dial, with the pin, was rotated. One tooth was a bit too long and advanced two teeth. The tooth tip was filed back slightly, correcting the problem. The advance pin was bent down slightly to increase engagement with the teeth. Continued tests showed consistently satisfactory operation.

The procedure here was applied to a ratchet-type tooth as found on moon dials, date wheels, and escape wheels. It may also be found applicable to a wheel tooth with damage to its driven face.

A number of positive features associated with this technique should be noted: the failed tooth is not removed, it is used to support the new tooth, formation of a deep weakening slot in a wheel rim is not required, dimensions of the repairs are not critical (except, of course, in shaping the repaired tooth) and finally, the repair is structurally sound.

A New Face
Successfully Installing a Paper Dial — Edwin U. Sowers III, CMC

This article originally appeared in the October 2002 AWCI Horological Times *and is reprinted here with permission.*

It is amazing how easily one can install a paper dial, look at it when finished, and realize the results are not what you expected.

The following will describe a procedure I have found successful and have used to replace the 10" dial of the Ansonia Drop Octagon Clock shown by Figure 1. The following steps are addressed:

1. Establishing the case center line and defining identification points for the 12:00 and 6:00 positions of the dial.
2. Preparation of the dial for cutting.
3. Cutting the dial to the correct size.
4. Gluing the dial to the pan.
5. Cutting out the dial holes.

1. Case Center Lines

The first requirement is to secure the dial pan in the position in which it will ultimately be located. With the dial pan in position, place a 2" piece of tape across the expected top and bottom of the pan. The next step is to determine the vertical centerline of the case. To do this, place a metal straight edge on the upper surface of the case, as shown by Figure 2, with one edge going through the center of the center arbor hole in the pan, and through the center of the top and bottom of the case. The pan center hole in the photograph, which is difficult to see due to the shadow to the right of the straight edge, is above and to the left of the clearly visible winding arbor hole. As shown by Figure 3, the center of the top had been earlier identified by a line on a piece of tape. The bottom was defined by the point of the bottom of the case.

Figure 1.

Figure 2.

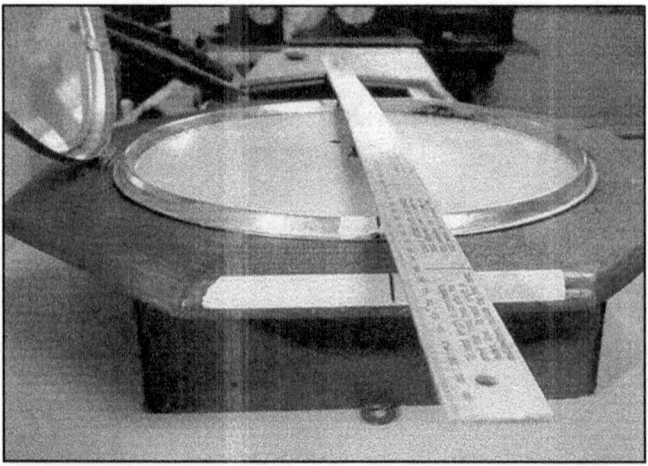

Figure 3.

In some instances the three positions defining the centerline, the pan center arbor hole, the center of the top and bottom of the case, do not line up perfectly. A bit of judgment then comes into play. Do *not* modify the center hole position. Rotate the straight edge slightly about the center hole position to achieve the most visibly acceptable compromise.

Once a satisfactory case center line is established, make a mark on the tape at the top and bottom of the dial pan along the edge of the straight edge. This defines where the case centerline crossed over the top and bottom of the dial, as shown by Figure 3. These marks define the 12:00 and 6:00 clock positions for placement of the dial on the pan. This is a crucial step in the process.

2. Dial Preparation

The next essential step is to determine the center of the dial. Now this seems simple since a center is usually printed on the dial. However, this is not always accurate, and if used could ultimately lead to a cut out dial with a non-uniform border about the chapter ring. It is best to ensure you have a correct center.

The center can be defined through use of a compass. Set the compass to a radius approximately 1/32" less than the radius from the printed center to the chapter ring. Place a piece of drafting tape over the center. From each of the four quarters, place the compass needle *on* the chapter ring and draw a short radius adjacent to the center. The results will be four closely positioned marks about the center as shown by Figure 4. At the center of these marks is the true center relative to the chapter ring. As an example, Figure 5 shows a radius drawn from the 3:00 position (a dial that had already been cut out was used for this illustration).

Now measure the desired outside diameter of the dial to establish the cutting radius (½ the diameter) as shown by Figure 6. With a dial pan of the style shown, having a raised border about it, plan on a space of 1/32" to 1/16" between the edge of the dial and where the upward formed edge of the pan begins, all around the dial. There is a practical reason for this; it is not wise to assume

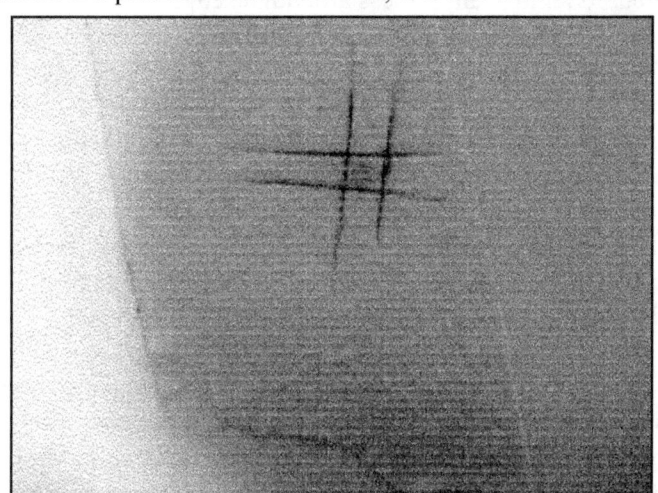
Figure 4.

Figure 5.

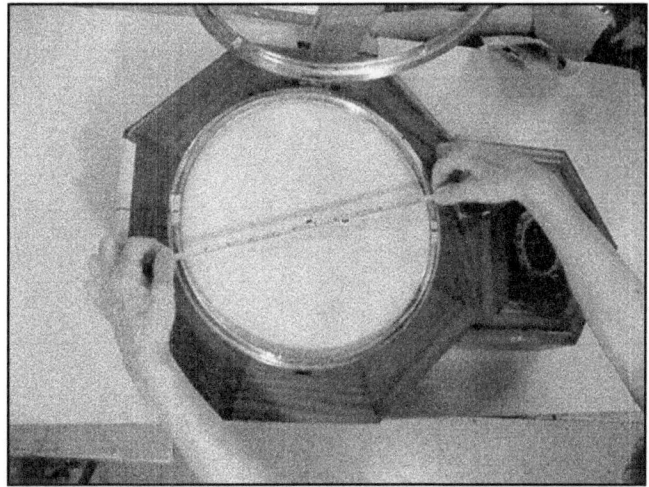
Figure 6.

Figure 7.

that you will always be able to center the dial on the pan perfectly. It is much better to have a slight gap about the dial to accommodate some placement error, than to have a larger dial that bends up onto the pan edge (a not uncommon disaster).

3. Dial Cutting

I used a dial cutter as shown by Figure 7. There are a number of such cutters available; the source of this one is not known. Establishing the correct radius setting of the

Challenging Repairs to Interesting Clocks • 113

Figure 8.

Figure 9.

Figure 10.

cutter has not, for me, been a one-step process. I have found it necessary to make a few trial runs with some heavy paper, as the butcher's wrapping paper shown by Figure 7, to zero in on a suitable setting.

Fasten the paper to a piece of artist's poster board with drafting tape. Set the cutter to the radius determined in Section 2. Cut out a test piece and fit it on the pan. With a few tries one should arrive at a satisfactory cutter radius setting.

The next step is to cut out a dial. Secure the dial to the poster board, center the compass point in the center of the four lines of Figure 4, and carefully cut out the dial (see Figure 8). Ensure that the cutter blade is sharp. Make sure the point does not slip out of its hole, and that the dial paper is cut through completely around the edge. Hopefully, placing the dial on the pan will establish that a perfect dial has been cut, ready for installation. If not, a minor adjustment to the compass radius may be required and another dial cut.

I have had good experience with Henry Cove Base Adhesive, shown by Figure 9. It is the adhesive used to secure plastic base molding in kitchens and bathrooms. It does allow for some movement, does not bleed through the dial, and securely attaches the dial when dry.

When ordering dials I have found it judicious to order 2 or 3. They are not expensive. It is a wise precaution to have a backup, should a dial prove to be slightly wrong in size, or ruined by slippage of the dial cutter. Trial dials may be saved for later sizing tests with smaller dials.

4.   Dial Gluing

Prior to applying the dial, be sure the pan is clean, free of dust, and smooth. If rust is encountered, removal of the rust and cleaning of the pan is required, application of a primer is desirable.

There are many types of adhesives proposed for dial installation. The ideal adhesive must allow for some shifting of the dial while positioning it, then when dry must securely attach it to the pan, and must not bleed through into the dial. Contact cement, which is frequently recommended, does well in permanently securing the dial, does not bleed through, but does *not* allow for any shifting of the dial for final positioning. This deficiency causes major problems.

Apply a thin layer as uniformly as possible to the dial pan with a brush, as shown by Figure 9. Be sure there is no excess glue applied toward the edges where it would be squeezed out when pressing down on the dial. Use a damp cloth to remove any excess around the edge.

Lay the 12:00 position of the dial lightly onto the dial pan, lining up with the marked tape, and leaving the desired gap above the dial. Lightly lay the dial down on the pan, gradually from top down, centering on the sides at 3:00 and 9:00 positions. Finally lightly lay down the lower (6:00) position. Do not press down yet. Ensure 6:00 lines up with the marked tape and that 12:00 is still correct. Check for best consistency of the edge space for each quarter. At this point the dial can be carefully lifted and shifted if necessary.

When satisfied that the dial is positioned satisfactorily, equal space at the edges, top and bottom and also both sides, the dial can be pushed down onto the pan. Lay a sheet of clean paper on the dial (to keep it clean) and work the dial down onto the pan *from the center toward the edges*. Force

Figure 11.

out any air bubbles that have been trapped under the dial. With a damp cloth, wipe away any adhesive that may have been squeezed out around the edge of the dial. Any adhesive on the dial surface can usually, before the glue dries, be removed carefully with a damp cloth (do not rub aggressively). Glue around the outside of the dial can similarly be removed. The dial satisfactorily glued to the pan is shown by Figure 10. Note the line up of the 12:00 and 6:00 dial locations with the positioning marks on the tape attached to the dial.

5. Treatment of Dial Holes

When the adhesive has set up, the dial holes for the center arbor and winding holes can be cut out. A sharp, tapered knife as shown by Figure 11 works well. First push the knife through the dial *from the back* to ensure it is located at a hole. Then carefully cut around the edge of the hole from the front. Make a clean, sharp cut all around, with the knife edge *held firmly against the hole edge*. This is essential for a good appearance, particularly where grommets are not inserted. Sloppy holes degrade the appearance of the whole dial. Grommets are frequently installed in winding holes, frequently not in the center holes. Be sure that if grommets are used that they fit the holes snugly and that the tabs at the rear are properly bent down.

Conclusion

There is always the question of when to replace a dial. Most agree that it is desirable to retain the original dial; the more valuable the clock, the more this is true. However, the time does arrive with many clocks where the dial becomes badly stained, torn, or illegible and should be replaced (except for an extremely valuable antique clock). When this state occurs, an attractive installation of the dial makes a world of difference in the appearance of the whole clock. Now what clock does not deserve that! To view the results of the procedure, revisit Figure 1.

Acknowledgments

The Ansonia Drop Octagon Clock, on which the dial was replaced, and of which the photographs were taken, has been returned to the Quentin, PA, United Church of Christ. It was restored for the church under the direction of Mrs. Deborah Smith.

Practical Repair and Restoration

CLOCK CASE REPAIR
Edwin U. Sowers III, MSME, CMC

When repairing clocks, I consider it appropriate to address the complete clock—both the case and the movement. To restore a movement to excellent condition and then put it back into an unattractive case for return to the owner, is not a very elegant endeavor. This observation, of course, excludes high-value collector-quality clocks where case work may significantly degrade value.

In many instances cleaning and waxing the case and polishing the bezel can greatly enhance the appearance of a clock. I have found Black Wax, available from Merritt's Antiques,* to work well for cleaning, being careful to stop rubbing before removing too much patina. If the appearance is too glossy, the case can be wiped with paint thinner and a softer wax applied. Howard Feed-N-Wax, which contains bees wax and orange oil, provides a soft lustre which is appropriate for many clocks. This can be obtained at various antique outlets.

Nevr-Dull is well suited to polishing bezels and other brass components. With this impregnated padding, one can polish to a mellow state short of a bright new appearance. If the brass is extremely dirty or is coated with discolored lacquer, light rubbing with 0000 steel wool prior to use of Nevr-Dull has proved helpful. Nevr-Dull can be secured from Merritt's.

In contrast to situations where the above touch-up procedures are applicable, there are instances where damage to the case has occurred which requires repairs. The objective here is to make repairs in such a way as to blend into the rest of the case. The repair should not be obvious and certainly should not look new if the clock is old.

The following describes a repair I made to an attractive Seth Thomas walnut parlor clock, shown in its restored state in Figure 1. The upper right ornamental member was broken, as shown in Figure 2.

The first step was to cut away the broken wood and create clean surfaces perpendicular to the rear surface of the part. A piece of wood, of the same material, was

---

*Editor's Note: Merritt's Antiques is located in Douglassville, Pennsylvania. Other vendors may be found in the NAWCC MART under the categories "For Sale Other" or "Service."

Figure 1. The repaired Seth Thomas parlor clock.

Figure 2. The broken upper right ornamental piece.

Figure 3. Forming a replacement piece of wood.

Figure 4. Tracing the matching part to create a template.

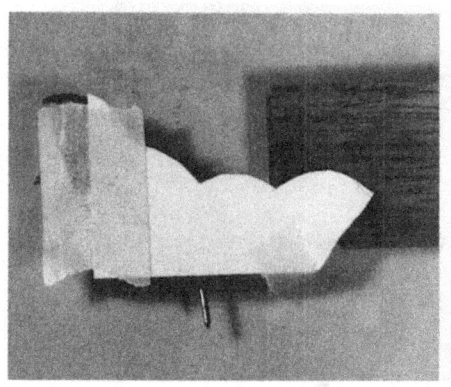

Figure 5. Tracing the new replacement piece.

Figure 6. The shape was filed and sanded.

Figure 7. The piece was color-matched using Grumbacher oil paints burnt umber and raw umber.

formed at one end to match the prepared surface of the broken part, as shown by Figure 3. The grain direction matched that of the original. The thickness of the piece was slightly greater than that of the original.

The two pieces were of configurations difficult to clamp for gluing. They were consequently positioned and forced together by nails driven into a flat board; this is also shown in Figure 3. Waxed paper was first placed on top of the board to prevent adhesion of the glue to the board. All nails but one to the right were put into position prior to gluing. Elmer's Glue-All Multi-Purpose Glue was liberally applied to the mating surfaces of the two pieces. The right-hand nail was then driven in such as to force the two pieces together.

Next the shape of the matching part on the opposite side of the clock was traced onto an index card as shown in Figure 4. The card was held in position with drafting tape. The card was cut out to serve as a template for the component to be repaired. The template was taped to the repair part as shown in Figure 5 and a tracing made onto the new replacement material.

The defined shape was then cut out with a jeweler's saw, slightly outside the tracing. The shape was refined and matched to the original part as shown in Figure 6, by filing with pattern files and sanding. The groove was cut in with an Exacto knife.

The added piece was color-matched to the original part as shown in Figure 7. Color-matching was accomplished by use of Grumbacher oil paints, burnt umber and raw umber, mixed together as required and worked into the wood with a small brush and by hand. More than one application of color was required. Prior to initial and subsequent applications, Plaid "Patricia Nimocks" CS200305 artists' clear acrylic gloss sealer was lightly sprayed on the surface (a brief dusting—considerably short of wetting the surface). This, or equivalent, spray is available at art supply sources. When coloring was completed, the part, when thoroughly dry, was protected with a few light coats of the sealer and lightly brushed with 0000 steel wool.

The finished part was glued to its base as shown in Figure 8, and glued and taped to the clock as shown in

Figure 8. The finished replacement piece.

Figure 9. Considerable glue was used, with excess removed from external surfaces with a paper towel.

The completed project is shown close up in Figure 10, and the completed clock in Figure 1.

Whether touching up a case or repairing it, there are some overall considerations I view as relevant. An old clock should look old—and well cared for. A clock that may have served the human race for more than 100 years deserves to retain the patina which developed through those years. A majority of clocks benefit from an application of a mellow wax which incorporates bees wax; some more elegant clocks look best with a gloss finish, which can be enhanced by a high-gloss paste wax. A high-gloss finish can also be achieved if the case is properly cleaned with Black Wax. Original paper dials should be retained if at all possible. Brass work should be polished, but not made to look new; some tarnish remaining in recessed areas contributes to that desired old, cared-for look.

This article originally appeared in the October 1999 NAWCC Bulletin.

Figure 9. The finished piece was glued and held onto the clock with masking tape.

Figure 10. The completed project.

A Case Study—
Reproduction of the Missing Rosette

by Edwin U. Sowers III, CMC

This article originally appeared in the February 2004 NAWCC Bulletin.

I received the attractive walnut New Haven "Tagus" mantel clock shown in Figure 1 for repairs. I had been told that the movement needed attention. However, one look at the case clearly exposed a further matter suggesting attention; the space at the top of the case above the dial, shown in Figure 2, was glaringly empty.

A check of *New Haven Clocks and Watches* by Tran Du Ly[1] showed that the vacancy was originally filled with a rosette, similar to the two on the sides, but slightly larger.

How to create a rosette! I had earlier reproduced a missing furniture ornament by casting a replica of the desired ornament, using a matching piece that remained as the pattern. The process involved making a mold from the matching piece, using it as the pattern, then casting a replica from the mold.

The Synair[2] casting system I had used for the furniture repair was expected to be applicable to the reproduction of the missing rosette. Although the rosette would be slightly smaller than the original, it would be quite satisfactory.

This article will describe the casting procedure as applied to the creation of a rosette. The following steps will be discussed:
Preparation of a mold
Preparation for casting
Pouring the casting
Removing and finishing the casting
Color matching

Figure 1.

Figure 2.

Mold Preparation

The rosette on the right, as can be seen in Figure 3, was selected for use as the mold pattern, it being in the best condition of the two. S-111 type Por-a-Mold 2-part flexible mold material, a part of the Synair casting system, was used to create the mold. This mold compound provides good detail. It is flexible, hence it allows for easy removal of the casting without damaging the mold, thus allowing for reuse of the mold.

The procedure for making the mold was basically to pour the mold material onto the upward facing rosette, with a retainer surrounding the rosette that had adequate height so the mold material built up in it would provide sufficient body to the mold.

To create the retainer, a 1-3/4" hole was drilled through a 3/4" piece of wood, see Figure 4. The 1-3/4" hole was 3/8" larger in diameter than the rosette, to allow for a 3/16" lip surrounding the rosette design—this will be clarified later. The clock was placed on a bench, with the front surface on top. As shown in Figure 5, modeling clay was placed on the clock surface where necessary to provide a tight seal between the retainer and the clock case. The retainer hole was centered on the rosette and clamped in place with C-clamps. The mold to be generated by means of this set-

Figure 3.

Figure 4.   Figure 5.

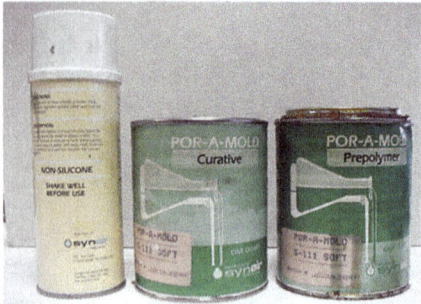

Figure 6.

up was to have on the bottom surface a reverse of the rosette design, a 3/4" thick backing to ensure adequate rigidity, and a 3/16" wide retaining lip surrounding the rosette.

The rosette and the retainer clamped over the rosette were sprayed with Synair Synlube 531 Release Agent. This served to prevent the mold material from adhering to the rosette and retainer surfaces. The two-part mold material was composed of Por-A-Mold S-111 Prepolymer and Por-A-Mold S-111 Curative (Figure 6), the two to be mixed together in equal volumes. The release agent is also shown in Figure 6. Each of two small paper cups was one-third filled with one of the two components. One of the components was then poured into the cup containing the other. The mixture was then stirred gently with a popsicle stick. Care was taken not to entrap air. After stirring for approximately five minutes the mixture was slowly poured into the retainer, again striving to prevent air entrapment. An air bubble trapped in the rosette surface would lead to a hole in the mold surface that could lead to rejection of the mold. The retainer was filled to slightly below the top retainer surface as shown in Figure 7.

Following overnight curing of the mold material, the retainer, with the mold in it, was lifted from the clock case. Figure 8 shows the reversed rosette configuration incorporated into the mold. As can be seen, detail was quite good. The flexible mold was carefully worked loose from the retainer. The mold following removal is shown in Figure 9. Note the 3/16" lip surrounding the rosette; this served later to retain casting material within the mold cavity.

Preparation for Casting

The Synair materials used for casting were Por-a-Kast Mark 1 Curative A, Por-a-Kast Mark 1 Prepolymer B, and Por-A-Kast Micro Bulb Filler. They are shown in Figure 10.

Parts A and B, in equal volumes, formed the basic two-part casting system, with the filler (glass beads) serving to reduce weight and provide a more rigid casting.

Prior to preparing the casting materials the mold was sprayed with Synair Synlube 531 Release Agents, using enough to cover all surfaces, but not enough to fill in corners causing loss of detail.

The equipment used to prepare the casting mixture is shown in Figure 11. Part A was poured into one cup, to one-third full, part B into the other to one-third full.

A third cup was one-third filled with Micro-Bulb Filler and was mixed into the Part A cup with a tongue depressor as shown in Figure 12. A like amount was then spooned into the third cup, poured into Part B, and mixed.

Figure 7.

Figure 8.

Figure 9.

Figure 10.

Figure 11.

Figure 12.

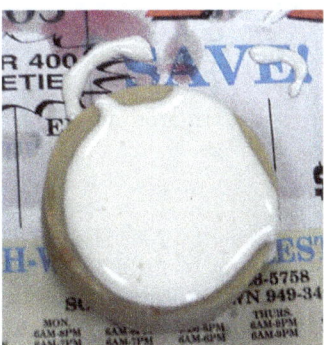

Figure 13.

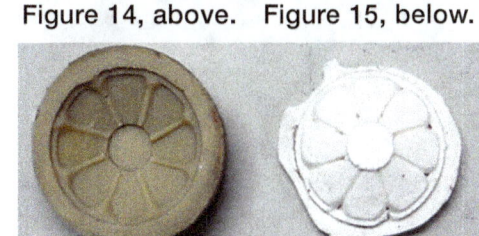

Figure 14, above.   Figure 15, below.

The mold was placed on a flat horizontal surface in preparation for filling with the casting compound.

Pouring the Casting

Both the Part A cup and the Part B cup were poured into the metal dish shown in Figure 11. The mixture was stirred rather quickly with a tongue depressor and poured into the mold, slightly overfilling the mold to a rounded upper surface, see Figure 13.

There is little more than one minute from pouring the two parts together until the mixture starts to set up, so mixing and pouring into the mold must be done quickly. Figure 14 shows what happens when the process is not concluded quickly enough. It should be noted that while curing, the casting material undergoes an exothermic reaction, causing it to heat up—this is normal and must be expected.

Removing and Finishing the Casting

Once the casting was cured and set for a few hours, the rounded overfill of Figure 13 was carefully sanded down to the top of the mold with a disk sander, being careful not to cut into the mold. The casting was then worked free from the mold and is shown beside the mold in Figure 15. The edges were cleaned up with a file.

Color Matching

The final step was matching the color of the cast rosette to that of the original. The coloring was accomplished through applications of Grumbacher[3] oil-based artist paints.

The casting was allowed to set for a day then sprayed lightly with Folk Art Clearcote Acrylic Sealer, Matte Finish Item 788, by Plaid,[4] to seal the surface. The two paints used were Grumbacher Burnt Sienna and Burnt Umber. Burnt Sienna was applied first with a brush, ensuring paint was worked down into all grooves and crevices. It was rubbed by hand into the surface, then brushed with a clean brush to remove excess from the recessed areas. The surface was lightly wiped with a paper towel. The paint was allowed to thoroughly dry for one to two days.

Figure 16.

Figure 17.

When dry, the surface was sprayed with the acrylic sealer. This sealed the initial coat, protecting it during the rubbing and wiping of the next application of paint. Mixtures of Burnt Sienna and Burnt Umber were applied a number of times, starting with a lighter color and gradually darkening until the color matched the original. In between each application of paint, the paint was allowed to dry, then protected with the acrylic sealer. This is not a fast process. When a satisfactory match was achieved, two coats of sealer were applied. Figure 16 shows the color matched casting on the right, adjacent to the original rosette. When dry, the surface was lightly buffed with 4/0 steel wool to deglaze the surface.

The cast rosette was glued into the original case location, Figure 17, with Elmer's Glue-All, after first roughing the case surface with coarse sandpaper.

Challenging Repairs to Interesting Clocks • 121

Figure 18.

Figure 19.

The three rosettes are shown in place in Figure 18. Figure 19 shows the completed case. It is concluded that the described procedure did indeed yield an attractive replacement for the missing rosette.

Notes

[1] Tran Duy Ly, *New Haven Clocks and Watches* (Fairfax, VA: Arlington Book Company, Inc., 1997): p. 330.
[2] Synair Corporation, P.O. Box 5269, Chattanooga, TN 37406; 423-697-0400.
[3] M. Grumbacher, Inc., New York, NY 10001; artist supply shops.
[4] Plaid Enterprise, Inc., 3225 Westech Dr., Norcross, GA 30092; hobby and art supply shops.

Acknowledgments

Attorney Pamella Weiss was pleased with the reproduced rosette, and agreed that a description of how it was accomplished would be of interest to others.

Clock Case Veneer Restoration

by Edwin U. Sowers III, CMC (PA)

This article describes the procedures I followed to repair a clock with seriously damaged veneer. The clock is shown in Figure 1; a fully original Ansonia Round Gothic 8-day mantel clock, in excellent condition except for the extensive veneer damage. There was loss of the original rosewood veneer on all sides of the base, with serious damage along the right hand vertical edge.

The repairs and procedures presented here document in detail the considerable work required to restore the case. The materials and tools used are described and then listed with sources in the Appendix. The specific topics addressed are:
- Securing loose and damaged veneer on a 3/4" convex case edge, with the veneer grain across the vertical edge.
- Fitting and securing a segment of missing veneer.
- Replacing veneer with a sharp bend across the grain.
- Plastic Wood application.
- Color matching and finishing.

Figure 1.

Securing Loose Veneer

Figure 2 shows a close-up of the worst damage to the veneer—the right hand edge of the case. It was apparent that someone had run a knife down the center of this edge, cutting through the veneer. This may have been done to relieve buckling of the veneer due to shrinkage of the soft wood beneath it as the case aged and dried out. In any event, the results, by the time I received the clock, were disastrous. This repair will be dealt with first.

The approach I used to repair the case edge was to work glue under the loose veneer, clamp the veneer with a block shaped to fit the edge radius, then fill in the small holes with Plastic Wood and color match the repairs.

The first step was to prepare a clamping block with the correct radius. This was done with a sanding drum in my drill press, as shown in Figure 3. The block was centered on the appropriately sized sanding drum and held in place with a 2" x 4" guide secured with a clamp.

Figure 2, left. Figure 3, below.

Figure 4.

Fortunately one of my sanding drums, 1-5/8" diameter, was of a radius that was very close to that of the edge. The block was held by hand, and the drum moved up and down with the drill press. It was necessary that the radius of the block be slightly larger than the edge radius so that the center of the edge would be contacted. If the radius was smaller, the outer edge would contact the case, with no pressure then applied to the center, where it was most required. Figure 4 shows the finished block. It was cut to approximately 4" in length, this being a good length to deal with in applying glue, ensuring good seating of the block on the case, and keeping the block in place while tightening the clamps.

The next step was to pry up the edges of the loose veneer to permit the insertion of glue beneath it. This

Figure 5.

Figure 6.

Figure 8.

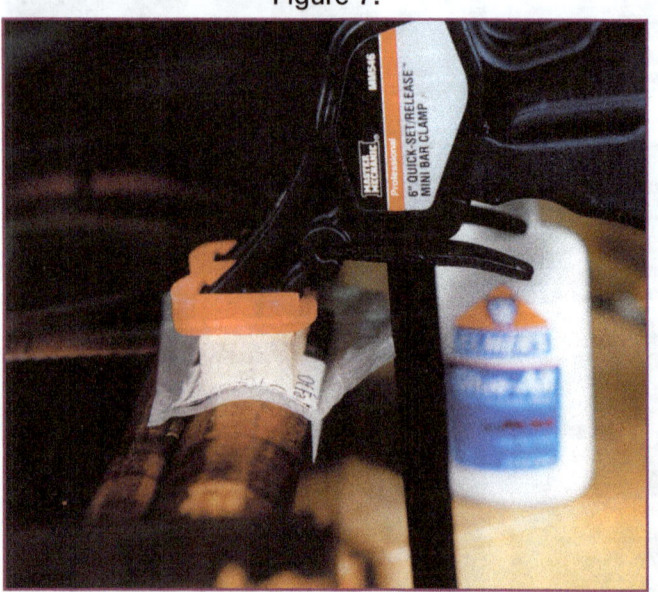

Figure 7.

was done *carefully* with an Exacto knife as shown in Figure 5. Elmers Glue-All was then applied with a 1/4" glue brush, with shortened bristles. It was worked under the loosened veneer, both sides, as much as possible with, as shown in Figure 6, a thin-ended punch. Excess glue was removed, wax paper was laid directly over the glue, and approximately six layers of newspaper were laid on top for improved load distribution. The block was then clamped with two Master Mechanic 6" clamps, as shown in Figure 7, the rear of the clamps contacting the back of the case. Care was exercised to ensure that there was good compression of the block in the area of the cut in the veneer. The glue was allowed to dry for six to eight hours before removing the clamps.

In some areas, as shown in Figure 8, the veneer had popped off when prying up the edge. In such cases, the veneer that remained in place was secured in a similar fashion to that described above. Glue was then applied

Figure 9.

Figure 10.

Figure 11.

to the surface where the loose pieces were to be placed; the pieces were put in place and clamped. The result is shown in Figure 9 (the location to the right at the top of the door shown by Figure 8). At this point the right edge curved veneer, between the larger missing patches, as seen in Figure 1, was secured. The relatively rough surface was smoothed with a file, as shown in Figure 10. Figure 11 shows the filed result. At this time small voids remained in the veneer. The filling of these will be described later.

Fitting and Securing a Veneer Segment

Next, the missing veneer at the bottom of the right side, as shown in Figure 1, with a close-up in Figure 12, was addressed. The loose veneer was trimmed away with an Exacto knife; Figure 13 shows the result. Holes were punched in the surface, Figure 14, with a scriber, to ensure good glue penetration (in some cases old surfaces are very dry and somewhat powdery—not an ideal surface for gluing).

The veneer used for all replacements was flexible Brazilian rosewood of 1/64" thickness, obtained from Bob Morgan Woodworking Supplies. It was thin enough to make the necessary bends across the grain, and was paper backed so it held together when cut or

Figure 12.

Figure 13.

bent. It was of light enough coloring to allow for darkening it to match the original. It should be noted that repair veneer darker than the original cannot be readily lightened to match the original, making color matching virtually impossible.

To create a piece of veneer shaped to match that which was missing, a piece of carbon paper was laid on the edge, carbon side up, and a piece of white paper laid on top. A tongue depressor was pressed down on the paper along the edge of the adjacent veneer. Figure 15

Challenging Repairs to Interesting Clocks · 125

Figure 14.

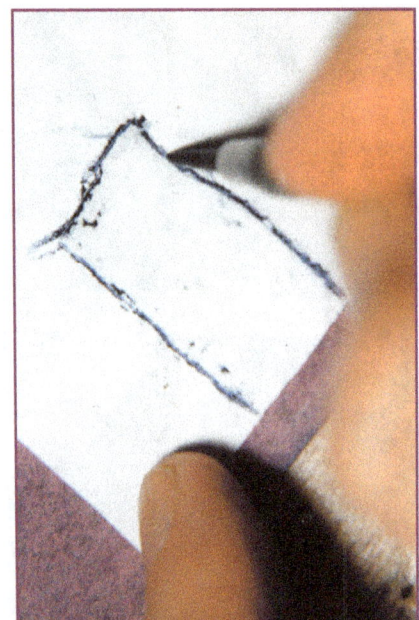

Figure 15.

Figure 16.

Figure 17.

Figure 18.

With the glue dried, the secured veneer is seen in Figure 17. While it is possible to obtain a good fit of the repair to the surrounding veneer, it is normally not good enough to be undetectable when finished. The approach I have taken to blending the surfaces is to apply Plastic Wood along the boundary of the repair piece. To satisfactorily accomplish this I cut a narrow slot around the boundary with a Dremel tool and small rotary cutter, as shown by Figure 18. The groove was at least as deep as the veneer and on the order of .040" - .050" wide. I found that this was adequate to achieve good fill with the Plastic Wood and to achieve adequate adhesion. (Without the groove cut around the edge, the Plastic Wood did not hold; it pulled out when filed.) The Plastic Wood was carefully filed and sanded to match the veneer adjacent to it. Application and finishing of the Plastic Wood will be addressed later.

shows the resultant tracing of the edge. As shown, the tracing was laid on a piece of veneer, with carbon paper beneath the tracing, carbon side down, and the shape traced onto the veneer. The tracing created was that of the *back* of the piece. Care was taken to ensure that the grain of the finished piece would essentially line up with that of the adjacent in-place veneer. The piece was cut out with scissors, then trimmed on the edge with a Dremel tool and sanding drum to ensure a good fit. Elmer's Glue-All was applied to the edge surface and to the veneer piece, and the piece was fitted into the proper space as shown in Figure 16, then clamped with the curved block, as described earlier.

Veneer Replacement with Sharp Bending Across the Grain

Replacing the veneer on the front left side of the base, shown in Figure 1, presented the problem of securing veneer around a sharp corner, with the bend occurring across the grain. Figure 19 shows the veneer trimmed and the base wood cleaned up and pricked with a scriber. A piece of veneer was cut to fit. The flat portion was glued and clamped in position, the result shown in Figure 20. The upper part, which had to be bent about the corner, was not then secured. Figure 21 shows a glue block cut to fit around the corner (shown here after gluing was completed). Of primary concern was the fit of the upper part. Prior to gluing, the veneer was massaged around the corner to minimize the chance of breaking. To ensure adequate bonding in this high stress area, the adhesive used was Devcon 5-Minute Epoxy. The block was clamped, as shown by Figure 22, pulling the block down and also against the base (wax paper had been placed beneath the block). Figure 23 shows the veneer secured in position, and the Plastic Wood applied, filed, and sanded. Loose veneer, which broke away while working on the corner, is shown replaced with Plastic Wood.

Application of Plastic Wood

As has been noted, Plastic Wood was used to fill in and repair small areas of missing veneer, and to fill in around replacement veneer. One could suggest that it would be more desirable to make all repairs with replacement veneer. However, doing so, and obtaining a perfect fit between the original and replacement veneer, is best accomplished by mating the new and original veneer *only* parallel to the grain of both, or nearly so. To be able to do this would require the removal of more of the original veneer, as fully across the right edge, or the full height of the base, in the present case. It was not obvious that this was justified, or preferable.

There are a variety of wood fillers available. I have used Plastic Wood since I have found it to adhere well, to file and sand suitably (if done carefully), and to satisfactorily accept artists' oil base paints for color matching the color of the replacement veneer to that of the original.

Figures 24 and 25 show an example of small repairs made with Plastic Wood, this occurring on the right edge adjacent to the top of the door. After ensuring that veneer adjacent to the repair location was secure, gluing and clamping to ensure this to be true, the original surface was pricked with a scriber. Plastic Wood was applied, thick enough to extend above the adjacent surfaces. After hardening overnight, the surface was carefully filed with a fine file. It is *essential* that the file

Figure 19.

Figure 20.

Figure 21.

Figure 22.

Figure 23.

Figure 24.

Figure 25.

Figure 26.

Figure 27.

Figure 28, above. Figure 29, below.

Figure 30.

Finish sanding was accomplished with emery paper backed up with a flat piece of wood. I typically started with 220 grit garnet finishing paper, followed by 400 then 600 grit 3M Wetordry paper. It is extremely important not to over-sand such that the Plastic Wood surface drops below the surrounding surfaces. If this happens, it will be remarkably obvious upon color matching and applying a finish. I continually changed to a new paper surface to preclude using a surface that had been loaded with residue. Sanding was done parallel to the grain. Figure 25 shows the repair ready for color matching.

As described earlier, pieces of replacement veneer were grooved around the edges with a Dremel tool and bit, as shown in Figure 18. (The new veneer had first been filed down to mate with the adjoining surfaces.) Plastic Wood was then applied, ensuring it was forced firmly down into the groove, see Figure 26. The Plastic Wood was allowed to thoroughly harden overnight. It be continually cleaned with a brush. If the file loads up it will gouge the surface. Filing was done parallel to the grain, to slightly above the adjacent surfaces.

128 • Challenging Repairs to Interesting Clocks

was filed and sanded as described earlier. This was done very carefully so that the surface did not fall below that of the adjacent veneer; this can happen very easily and is very noticeable after color matching and finishing. Figure 27 shows the result of filing and sanding. It may seem that the concern with over-sanding is over-stated. However, realizing that this has occurred, when progressing into color matching and finishing, and that the Plastic Wood must be removed and the whole subsequent process repeated, is not an encouraging event.

Color Matching and Finishing

The final steps were color matching and application of a protective finish. Figure 23 showed the repair of the left front portion of the base, ready for color matching. Color matching was accomplished by a number of applications of the Grumbacher artist paints; raw umber, burnt umber, and burnt sienna, mixed as needed to obtain the desired color. The surface was first lightly sprayed with Blair Spray, a clear acrylic sealer, to prevent undesired over-darkening of the color and to permit wiping off some of the paint if desired. Dabs of the desired paints were squeezed onto a piece of paper and mixed together with a shortened glue brush to obtain the desired color. This is a matter of trial and error, along with developed expertise. Care was taken to ensure the paint got down into recesses in the veneer surface. It was then worked into the wood by hand, partially wiped off, added to, and generally worked with, until the desired appearance was realized. The first application was a mix intentionally lighter than the final desired color, shown in Figure 28. After drying for a few days, a darker color was applied, see Figure 29. The original veneer to the right of the repair was then darkened somewhat. A light spray of the sealer was applied after each paint application had dried. This is not a fast process—each application must dry before the next is applied. Finally, a coat of the sealer was applied to all color-matched repairs and rubbed lightly with 4/0 steel wool.

There were additional repairs required which were accomplished using procedures that have been defined here. The end result was a very attractive clock, restored essentially to its original appearance, as shown by Figure 30.

Appendix—Materials and Tools

- Exacto knife, or equivalent, with pointed blade; hardware store.
- Elmer's Glue-All, Elmer's Products, Inc., Columbus, OH 43215-3797; hardware store.
- Master Mechanic 6" clamps, Quick-Set/Release Mini Bar, Part Number MM 546; True Value hardware store.
- Brazilian Rosewood Veneer, Bob Morgan Woodworking Supplies, Inc., 1121 Bardstown Road, Louisville, KY 40204.
- Dremel Tool, Dremel, 4915 21st St., Racine, WI 53406; hardware store.
- Plastic Wood, Bondex Indust-ries, Inc., St. Louis, MI 63122; hardware store.
- Devcon 5-Minute Epoxy, ITW Brands, Wood Dale, IL 60191; hardware store.
- 220 grit garnet paper; hardware store.
- 3M Wetordry paper, Minnesota Mining & Mfg. Co., St. Paul, MN 55101; hardware store.
- Blair Spray Clear, Gloss Finish, Order No. 200, Blair Art Products, Inc., Twinsburg, OH 44087, or equivalent (ensure a fine spray); hobby and art supply shops.
- 1/4" glue brush, round tin handle, brush cut to 3/8" length; hardware store.
- M. Grumbacher, Inc., 30 Engelhard Dr., Cranburry, NJ 08512.

Acknowledgment

I owe considerable thanks to Pastor Frederick S. Weiser, owner of the restored clock, for the opportunity to carry out the repair procedures I have described.

This article originally appeared in the February 2003 NAWCC Bulletin

Horological Helps

Note: The following pages have been found useful. Horological Hints *provides notes about caring for clocks in their homes.* The American Count Wheel Striking Clock Inspection and Repair Guide *presents an outline for working on clock mechanisms. The pages can be reproduced two to an 8 ½" x 11" sheet.*

HOROLOGICAL HINTS

1. Wind clocks regularly: Depending on clock – every 7 days, 1 day, or ½ day for most cuckoo clocks.
2. Wind fully, (without forcing) to ensure full run time.
3. Don't let the clock stop – if you plan to be gone for the normal run time, stop the pendulum before leaving and restart it when you return.
4. When you must move the minute hand to set it, move forward only, and pause to allow for chime and strike.
5. Do not hand lift weights while winding; it is possible to bump into and unhook the pendulum.
6. Clock must be in beat – tick & tock must be of same duration (this is more important than level). If not in beat, lift each side of clock and listen. Place shims under the side which improves the beat. With wall clocks, shift sideways to establish the best in-beat position. Make a small mark on the wall adjacent to the bottom edge of the case as a reference.
7. To adjust timekeeping:
   - Rating nut under pendulum bob:
     Turn right (clockwise) to raise pendulum bob and speed up, reverse to drop bob and slow down. When attempting to slow, be sure bob drops along with rating nut (bob can hang up on pendulum rod).
   - Square ended shaft in hole near top of dial:
     Turn right (clockwise) to speed up (usually). Reverse to slow. Use double ended key, with correctly sized small end. Adjust no more than ½ turn on first try check results in 3 – 4 days. Reduce turning as timekeeping becomes more accurate. You should be able to adjust a clock with a 7-day run time to within 2 – 3 minutes.
8. Some clock oils dry in 6 – 7 years. Recommend checking into possible need for cleaning, repairing, and re-oiling.
9. Never force anything on a clock.

Edwin U. Sowers III
Certified Master Clockmaker
(717) 273-3786

12/2003

HOROLOGICAL HINTS

1. Wind clocks regularly: Depending on clock – every 7 days, 1 day, or ½ day for most cuckoo clocks.
2. Wind fully, (without forcing) to ensure full run time.
3. Don't let the clock stop – if you plan to be gone for the normal run time, stop the pendulum before leaving and restart it when you return.
4. When you must move the minute hand to set it, move forward only, and pause to allow for chime and strike.
5. Do not hand lift weights while winding; it is possible to bump into and unhook the pendulum.
6. Clock must be in beat – tick & tock must be of same duration (this is more important than level). If not in beat, lift each side of clock and listen. Place shims under the side which improves the beat. With wall clocks, shift sideways to establish the best in-beat position. Make a small mark on the wall adjacent to the bottom edge of the case as a reference.
7. To adjust timekeeping:
   - Rating nut under pendulum bob:
     Turn right (clockwise) to raise pendulum bob and speed up, reverse to drop bob and slow down. When attempting to slow, be sure bob drops along with rating nut (bob can hang up on pendulum rod).
   - Square ended shaft in hole near top of dial:
     Turn right (clockwise) to speed up (usually). Reverse to slow. Use double ended key, with correctly sized small end. Adjust no more than ½ turn on first try check results in 3 – 4 days. Reduce turning as timekeeping becomes more accurate. You should be able to adjust a clock with a 7-day run time to within 2 – 3 minutes.
8. Some clock oils dry in 6 – 7 years. Recommend checking into possible need for cleaning, repairing, and re-oiling.
9. Never force anything on a clock.

Edwin U. Sowers III
Certified Master Clockmaker
(717) 273-3786

12/2003

Challenging Repairs to Interesting Clocks · 131

American Count-Wheel Striking Clock
Inspection and Repair Guide

Clock Information: Record the following upon receipt of clock:
- Customer name
- Clock description
- Date received
- Service requested

Prior to Disassembly: Record date defined by "**R**"
- Remove pendulum rod (to prevent damage to suspension spring)
- Do <u>not</u> remove pallet unit!
- **R** - Check hand clutch.
- **R** - Check that trains are operational.
- Apply clamps to mainsprings and let down.

After mainspring clamped and let-down:
- **R** - Check shake.
- **R** - Check pivot hole wear. Define and record where bushings required. Identify as TIR, SIF, T2F, etc.
- **R** - Check for pallet wear; define if recoil or half-deadbeat escapement.

Disassembly/Movement Service:
- Disassemble. Keep separate all components for each train.
- Identify time & strike mainspring arbors (scratch <u>small</u> T or S on wheels).
- Release mainsprings. <u>Use spring winder.</u> (Glove on left hand)
  Warning: Mainsprings are dangerous — be careful!
- **R** - Record mainspring data (width, thickness, length, free diameter, center set).
- **R** - Establish if new mainsprings required.
- **R** - Check clicks. Make <u>sure</u> they will hold!
- Clean, rinse & dry parts. Keep parts for each train separate. (Ultrasonic cleaning recommended).
- Inspect all wheels, pinions, and pivots for wear and straightness.
- **R** - Record problems, and corrective action.
- Hand clean any residue on wheels, pinions, or pivots.
- **R** - File, or stone, and polish worn pivots.
- Check pivot holes; peg to clean if necessary.
- **R** - Where bushing required, first reestablish original pivot hole center, then bush. (If hole is oblong, it is worn).
- Where bushings installed, locate between plates the arbor applicable to the bushed location, and the arbors prior to and following.
- Secure plates. <u>Check for arbor free drop and free spin.</u>

American Count-Wheel Striking Clock
Inspection and Repair Guide (Cont'd.)

- **R** - Resolve worn pallets; shift escape wheel or stone and polish pallets.
- Ensure correct friction of fly on arbor.
- **R** - Check all other components and correct as required; record problems and corrective action.
- Apply lubricant to mainspring. Rewind <u>on winder</u> and apply clamps.
- Make <u>sure</u> all between plate problems corrected <u>prior to reassembly.</u>

Assembly – Between plates: (Brief outline)
- Install assembly legs near 4 corners of plate to which pillars are attached.
- Install mainsprings and arbors into plate.
- Place remaining plate on top, loosely secure at bottom and work pivots into place from lower end (mainsprings) to top of movement. Maintain pressure on plate to prevent inserted pivots from popping out.
- Be careful not to bend or break pivots (do not allow arbors to tilt excessively from perpendicular to bottom plate).
- When all wheels, not fly, are in place, install pillar nuts or pins. (Fly is in the way when adjusting strike; better to install after adjustment.)

Post Assembly Check:
- Ensure free vertical drop of <u>each</u> arbor and <u>spin</u> each train to <u>ensure free sustained run.</u> Do not proceed until this is achieved!
- **R** - While spinning check for wobble of pivot ends, wobble suggests possibility of bent pivots, requiring correction.
- Ensure all strike levers properly positioned.

Repair Details, Strike & Pallet Adjustment and Lubrication:
- Recommend *Clock Repair Basics*, by Steven Conover, Clockmakers Newsletter, 203 John Glenn Ave., Reading, PA 19607. 1996.

Testing:
- Ensure clock is in beat in correct operating position. Adjust crutch to achieve.
- Test for <u>at least</u> the normal operating period. An 8-day clock with a good quality mainspring should keep time correctly within 2 – 3 minutes for 7 days, and continue operating for at least 8. Thirty-hour clocks should be similarly accurate for at least 24 hours.
- Continue test until satisfied that clock should <u>continue</u> to operate satisfactorily.

Edwin U. Sowers III
Certified Master Clockmaker
(717) 273-3786

12/2003

To Experience Adventures in TIME...
Join the NAWCC

It All Starts with Membership

The National Association of Watch and Clock Collectors, Inc. (NAWCC) is an international nonprofit association serving more than 17,000 members and 150 chapters and dedicated to preserving and stimulating interest in horology, the art and science of time. Our members are enthusiasts, students, educators, casual collectors, businesses, and professionals, who love learning about the clocks and watches they preserve, study, and collect. Members share their interests with other members and establish friendships around the world.

Membership Advantages

- Stay informed with the bimonthly *Watch & Clock Bulletin*, an educational journal, and the *Mart & Highlights*, a buy/sell/news publication.
- Go online for research tools and videos: NAWCC.org features all *Watch & Clock Bulletin* content back to 1943, NAWCC books and instructional videos, and much more for members.

- Buy, sell, and learn at regional buying and selling venues, and attend programs on all aspects of horology.
- Keep in touch with our bimonthly electronic newsletter—*eHappenings*
- Meet terrific people at local and special interest chapters
- Visit for free the National Watch & Clock Museum in Columbia, PA.
- Use your membership for free or discounted admission to over 250 museums and science centers.

Become a member today and begin your exploration of the fascinating world of horology.

Apply online at www.nawcc.org

Become a member today!
Mail this application, apply online at www.nawcc.org, or call 1-877-255-1849 or 1-717-684-8261.

*Required fields

*Print Name

Company Name (optional)

*Street

*City

*State/Province/Country   *Zip/Postal Code

( )   ( )
Ph.: Home   Work

( )   ( )
Cell   Fax

Email

☐ I agree to abide by the NAWCC Member Code of Ethical Conduct (see nawcc.org to review).

*Are you a former member of NAWCC? ☐ Yes ☐ No

If "yes," your membership no.

   /   /
Date of Birth Confidential for verification purposes. Required for Youth Membership.

Occupation

How did you learn about the NAWCC?
Interest: ☐ Clocks ☐ Wristwatches ☐ Pocket Watches ☐ Museum

From:

If this is a gift membership, print your name above and a gift card will be included with the membership card mailing.

Send this application with payment to:
NAWCC, Inc., 514 Poplar Street, Columbia, PA 17512-2130
Annual dues:
- ☐ **Individual $82** (mailed pubs.) ☐ **Individual $72** (electronic publications)
- ☐ **Business $150** (mailed pubs.) ☐ **Assoc./Youth $20** (electronic pubs.) (Spouse) / (Under 18)
- ☐ **Student $35** (electronic pubs.) Proof of enrollment required for student membership. Please call for information.

Payment:
☐ Check enclosed (U.S. bank only) ☐ Intl. Money Order
☐ Visa ☐ MasterCard ☐ Discover ☐ American Express

Credit Card No.

   /
Exp. Date   Security Code

Cardholder's Name   Amt. to be charged

Signature